Heart Strings

New York Times Bestselling Author
Melanie Moreland

Dear Reader,

Thank you for selecting **Heart Strings**. There are many choices available, and I am honored you choose mine to read today.

Heart Strings was a story original featured in the **What The Heart Wants** anthology in May 2017. A brief addition was created for bedtime stories in The Korner Facebook group. The readers loved Logan's alpha, possessiveness of Lottie. Here we are with their full-length story.

If you are interested in receiving up to date information on new releases, exclusive content and sales, please sign up for my newsletter here at https://bit.ly/MMorelandNewsletter.

Always fun book stuff - never spam!

xoxo,
Melanie

ALSO BY MELANIE MORELAND

Vested Interest Series

BAM - The Beginning (Prequel)

Bentley (Vested Interest #1)

Aiden (Vested Interest #2)

Maddox (Vested Interest #3)

Reid (Vested Interest #4)

Van (Vested Interest #5)

Halton (Vested Interest #6)

Sandy (Vested Interest #7)

Insta-Spark Collection

It Started with a Kiss

Christmas Sugar

An Instant Connection

An Unexpected Gift

The Contract Series

The Contract (The Contract #1)

The Baby Clause (The Contract #2)

The Amendment (The Contract #3)

Mission Cove

The Summer of Us Book 1

Standalones

Into the Storm

Beneath the Scars

Over the Fence

My Image of You (Random House/Loveswept)

Happily Ever After Collection

Revved to the Maxx

Heart Strings

The Boss

MORELAND
BOOKS INC.

Edited by
Lisa Hollett—Silently Correcting Your Grammar
Cover design by Karen Hulseman, Feed Your Dreams Designs
Cover Photography by Wander Aguiar
Cover Model Alex C of Zink Models
Cover content is for illustrative purposes only and any person depicted on the
cover is a model.

DEDICATION

To Matthew
Because of you, I don't walk
this world alone.
You are my very own heart strings.
Always.

CHAPTER 1

LOTTIE

Voices droned on about numbers throughout the boardroom. Projected budgets, debt ratio, timelines. All very important—all very dull. I stared out the window at the darkening late afternoon, losing myself in the sway of the tree branches as the wind lifted them, graceful and flowing. Snow swirled, light and diaphanous, the flakes caught in the streetlights beginning to flicker on. It was a dance of sorts—a beautiful, elegant display of the winter that was closing in all around us.

Much like these walls I felt closing in around me.

I shook my head to clear the cobwebs and tried to concentrate on the meeting. Casting my gaze around the table, I saw that everyone was now looking at the forecasted dates, so I hastily flipped the pages, knowing I had missed much of what they'd discussed.

"Charlotte, do you have any concerns in this area?"

I lifted my eyes, meeting the intense gaze of the CEO, Charles Prescott. His stare was calm and steady, yet I wondered if he knew I had been drifting.

I swallowed nervously. "Not at this time."

"Good. Ralph, what about your area?"

I huffed a small sigh of relief, grateful I had gone through all the notes on the project prior to the meeting. I knew the ins and outs, and at that point, barring some catastrophe, I had no concerns.

I made an effort to concentrate. I attempted to pay attention, jotting down notes and nodding as others around the table made comments. It lasted about fifteen minutes, until a gust of wind rattled the glass, and I looked over to see the snow getting thicker. A familiar thrill ran through me.

I loved winter. I loved the cold, the snow, and everything it brought with it. The sounds and sights of the upcoming holidays. Sledding, skiing, even walking in the newly fallen snow—especially at night when the flakes drifted down and the streets were empty. I would walk for hours, bundled up and protected against the frigid cold. I walked until my nose tingled and my fingers curled inside my mittens.

I loved mittens.

My favorite thing to do in the winter was to curl up on the sofa with a good book, a steaming cup of hot chocolate, and a cozy blanket. Alone and peaceful. It was a stolen pleasure most of the time.

"Charlotte?"

I blinked, bringing myself back to the present. My chest tightened when I realized I had drifted away again. My hand was slack, my pen rested on the open file, and my head was down. It probably looked as if I were asleep.

I raised my head, forcing a smile. "Sorry, I was lost in thought. Crunching some numbers in my head."

Charles lifted his eyebrows, leaving me no doubt he knew my mind had wandered from the meeting and my thoughts had nothing to do with numbers.

"I asked if you were available to be on the committee. I'd like you involved."

2

I stifled a groan. Another committee. More meetings to sit in on and boring discussions to have—to listen to other executives drone on about how important they were to the project. I hated those meetings.

"Of course. I'll make sure I clear my schedule."

"Excellent. Okay, everyone, that's it for today. The snowstorm is getting bad, so be safe out there."

I stood, grateful the meeting was finished.

Charles held up his hand. "A moment, Charlotte."

I sat down, keeping the neutral look on my face, knowing I was about to get a lecture. He waited until everyone was gone, stood and rounded the table, sitting beside me.

"Are you all right, Charlotte?"

"I'm fine."

"You don't seem like yourself. You've been off for the past while."

I traced the woodgrain with my finger, unable to meet his eyes. I knew I would see disappointment. "I'm a bit distracted," I admitted. "I have a lot on my plate."

"We all do. That's the nature of this business. I need your head in the game on this one. It's huge. I'm counting on you."

"I know." I cleared my throat. "It won't happen again."

He studied me for a moment, then tilted his head in acknowledgment. "I expect you to do better."

Shame tore through me. "I will."

"You look drained."

I was surprised at the unexpected, personal remark. "I'm fine. Honest, I am."

"All right. You're a grown woman, so I'll take your word for it. I suggest you limit your nights out to the weekends. I need you sharp. No more drifting during meetings."

"Yes, sir."

He stood, smoothing down his suit jacket, an action not required—Charles Prescott always looked impeccable. His silver hair gleamed under the lights, not a strand out of place. At sixty, he was still tall and broad, his posture stiff. His blue eyes were like ice—light and piercing. When I was little, I swore they saw everything, no matter how I tried to hide my mistakes. I was sure they still did.

He crossed the room, pausing at the door. "Your mother is expecting you for dinner this evening."

"I'll be there."

"Will you be riding with me?"

"No, I have a few things to do first. I'll take the subway."

He exhaled hard, the sound impatient. "You know how I feel about that, Lottie. I wish you would stop with that independent attitude and let me give you a car and driver."

It was rare to see a glimpse of my father in the office. There we were Charles and Charlotte. Lottie was never used. Personal things were never discussed. The lines were clearly drawn. It was business, plain and simple. It didn't matter that I was named after him or that I was his daughter. He was firm on his rules. I was used to it, and I made sure to follow them at all times. That was what was expected of a Prescott.

"I like to walk."

He snorted and rolled his eyes. "And take the subway."

I shrugged. "I like the people. I like watching them."

"You can do that from the comfort of a town car."

It was my turn to roll my eyes. "That smacks of being elitist."

He smiled at me—a cold smile that didn't reach his eyes. "Heaven forbid I sound elitist when it comes to the safety of my daughter."

"I'm fine. I'm careful."

"I still don't like it."

My stomach clenched at the thought of him insisting on the car. If that happened, the one thing that made my life bearable these days, the one bright spot, would be taken away. I couldn't let that happen.

"Please drop it," I begged, my throat tight with emotion. "Let me have this bit of freedom."

He pulled open the door. "Fine. For now. But the subject isn't closed."

I picked up my files, following him out the door. "I never expected it to be."

CHAPTER 2
LOTTIE

Time dragged. I watched the clock, its hands slowly counting down the seconds until I could leave. Everyone laughed at the old-fashioned battery-operated timepiece I kept on my desk. I liked the soothing sound of the soft movement of the hands as it ticked away the minutes. The quiet chimes it made every hour helped me through the days.

Finally, it was six. I slammed down the lid on my laptop, jamming it into my messenger bag. I made sure I had my pass, and I headed for the elevator. Before the doors closed, my father stepped in.

"Changed your mind? Are you coming with me?"

"Um, no. I'm heading home."

A look of displeasure crossed his face. "Your mother…"

I interrupted the start of his lecture. "I'm coming for dinner. I have to go home first."

His brow furrowed. "You live on the east side. We're on the west. What is so important you have to go all the way across town?"

My heart started to hammer in my chest. I felt the back of

my neck grow damp with anxiety. "I want to change, and ah, Brianna is calling."

"What nonsense."

"She needs to talk to me, Dad. I promised."

"Fine. I'll get the driver to take you."

"No!" I almost shouted the word at him.

He stepped forward. "Charlotte, what is going on with you?"

"Nothing. I just... I need to do a few things. Dinner is never until 8:30. I have lots of time."

He narrowed his eyes at me. "And you insist on taking the subway?"

"I like the subway. I listen to music, and it gives me some downtime."

"I don't understand you. You're distracted. I don't like it."

"I'm *fine*." The doors opened, and I hastened ahead of him. "I'll see you soon!"

He didn't chase after me. I knew he wouldn't. Charles Prescott would never make a scene in public. Still, I didn't stop until I was around the corner. I stood against the wall, breathing heavily, forcing myself to calm down.

He was right, of course. It was stupid to travel across town to my own condo, then head to their place for dinner.

But if I didn't, I would miss *him*.

I couldn't let that happen.

He was the only thing I lived for these days.

Even if he didn't know.

♫

I exited the train, my eyes scanning the area. I felt frantic tonight. The anxiety I'd been experiencing grew daily, and I was always tense until I saw him. Then my body would relax, my heartbeat slowed, and I felt better.

It happened every time.

I heard him first. The strains of his guitar met my ears, his music settling into my head, blanketing me with peace. I followed the sounds, finding him close to the benches as usual, playing. His head was lowered, shaggy brown hair falling into his face as he looked down at his hands. Streaks of white-blond mixed with the dark at the front, and I often wondered if it was bleached from time spent out in the sun. It gave him a bohemian look that suited him well. Casually propped against the wall, he was tall and broad, his chest tautly muscled under his well-worn leather jacket and tight T-shirt. His fingers were long and strong as he coaxed notes from a guitar so old, I was sure it was an antique. A battered case lay on the ground in front of him, coins thrown in by commuters glinting in the light. There were only a couple of paper bills among the collection, and I wondered, as I did every time I saw him, if he had collected enough to eat tonight. If he had somewhere to sleep.

My fingers curled around the bills I had in my pocket. Tonight, I would somehow distract him long enough to drop the money into the case. Every time I tried, he frowned at me. He let me know, silently, with his whiskey-colored eyes, he didn't want my money. He had accepted it once—and never again. The last time I edged closer, intent on dropping in some cash, he used his foot to snap closed the lid, giving me a glare and a firm shake of his head. When I retreated and sat back down on the bench, he flipped open the lid, letting others drop in money.

Why he wouldn't allow me to do the same, I had no idea.

As I stood, watching and listening, he lifted his head. Our gazes met, locking across the busy platform. The ghost of a smile curled the corner of his mouth. Tonight, his chin was dusted with a five-o'clock shadow, darkening the sharp edges of his jaw. Sometimes, he was clean-shaven. Other times, a beard appeared. I never knew what to expect.

His ever-present dimple deepened when he grinned. My

chest loosened as I moved closer, sitting down on one of the benches with a long sigh of relief.

I never spoke to him. He never approached me. But every evening, I was there, hoping he would be somewhere in the station, playing. And every evening, he was. His music soothed and calmed me. His presence did the same.

And tonight was no different. I was ready to let the day melt away.

♫

The first time I heard him, I was rushing through the terminal, stressed and upset. The latest project I was working on wasn't going well. It was behind schedule, and investors were balking, threatening to pull their support. My father had been on a tear, and it didn't matter that I was his daughter. I was included in the rant, which was long and loud. After he finally let us leave, I headed home, feeling exhausted and deeply distressed.

I hated my job with a passion. I hated every aspect of it. I did it because of obligation and duty. I was good enough at it but found no joy in the routine. Others around me lived for it, and I often wished for their drive.

My legs felt too weary to hold me up any longer, and I stumbled to a bench to sit and find enough energy to walk the short distance home. I shut my eyes, letting my head fall forward. A few minutes later, I heard it. The strains of a strumming guitar and the timbre of a low tenor singing. The notes and music filled me. As I listened, I felt a wave of calm flow through me, and my strength returned. I lifted my head, and I was met with a gaze that shook me to my very soul.

Eyes the color of the darkest, richest whiskey regarded me. His hair was long and shaggy, yet it suited him. Dressed in torn jeans and a worn leather jacket, he stood tall and confident, meeting my eyes. His brow furrowed as he observed me, still singing and playing. He tilted his head, as if silently asking me if I was okay. I found myself nodding in his direction, and it happened.

He smiled.

His dimple popped, his lips curled, and it felt to me as if the sun had suddenly burst forth in the station. I felt the warmth of his soul in that smile. Then, as suddenly as it appeared, it faded, leaving me feeling cold. Still, his eyes remained on me as he played, moving from one song to another.

I sat for as long as I could, listening. When I knew I couldn't put it off any longer, I stood. I loathed to leave. Leave him. I dug in my pocket, knowing I had a couple twenties in there. He watched me close the distance between us, pausing in front of him. For the first time since I opened my eyes, he faltered in his movements, no longer playing. Our connected gazes, however, never broke.

I tossed the money into his case. "Thank you," I whispered.

He resumed playing, another grin appearing on his face.

His music followed me all the way up the stairs and echoed in my head all evening.

He had been at the station every night since. His presence lingered in my mind long after I left.

Time went too fast. I knew I had to get to my parents' place. All I wanted to do was sit and listen to him for a while longer, but I knew I couldn't. I stood, brushing off my skirt, sliding my hand in my pocket. I glanced around, realizing how to get the money into his case. He expected me to go past him on the left and head toward the stairs. Instead, I would be heading back to the tracks, which meant I would pass him on the right where the case rested on the ground. I wouldn't stop; I wouldn't make eye contact. I would simply breeze past and drop it in. It was a large enough target; I couldn't miss. To be extra sure, I balled up the bills tight in my fist.

I inhaled and slung my messenger bag over my shoulder, walking toward him. Luck was with me as a few people stood in front of him, listening. He often drew a small crowd, which always pleased me, especially if they dropped money in his case. I felt his eyes on me as I approached. At the last minute, I veered to the right and went past him with hurried steps. I dropped the wad of bills into the case and watched them settle next to some coins. His guitar playing faltered, but I kept going, feeling satisfied. He accepted it from everyone else. I was his most appreciative customer, and it was important to me.

I waited on the platform to head back to my parents' side of town. I stepped on the train and sat down. Glancing up, I was met with those intense eyes through the glass. With his guitar in its case and slung over his shoulder, he had his hands on his hips, looking at me in disapproval from the short distance. Unable to help myself, I gave him a thumbs-up.

His smile appeared—the one that lit up my world, the dimple in his cheek deep and prominent. As the train pulled away, he stepped back, then, in an old-world gesture I didn't expect, laid his hand over his heart.

Mine sped up at the sight.

♫

"I thought you went home to change."

I lifted my wine to my lips, stalling for time. "Brianna talked longer than I expected."

"You could have called her from here."

"She wanted to Skype."

"You—"

"Enough questioning Charlotte, Charles," my mother interrupted. "Is Brianna all right?"

"Yeah, she's fine. Man trouble," I offered lamely.

My mother huffed through her nose, her impatience clear. She only approved of Brianna because of her parentage, not because she liked her as a person. I wasn't sure my mother truly liked anyone. "There usually is with Brianna."

My father made a strange noise. "At least she *has* a man in her life."

My head fell back with a sigh. "Really, Dad? You can't let up on that?"

He handed me the potatoes, frowning when I passed them on to my mother. "A woman your age should be married."

"I'm only twenty-six—hardly in my dotage. When I meet the right person, I'll get married."

My father made a noise in the back of his throat, but otherwise changed the subject.

"Is that all you're going to eat? I noticed you barely ate your sandwich at lunch during the meeting. You're far too thin these days."

"Okay… Can we stop the picking on Charlotte today?"

Mom laid down her fork. "Enough. Both of you. You're ruining my appetite with this bickering. Charles, let the girl live her life." She turned to me. "Show your father some respect. He deserves it." She cleared her throat. "We are your parents, and given what we have experienced, we have every right to watch over your health. Are you unwell?"

"No," I assured her. "I am perfectly healthy. I saw the doctor last month. Everything is normal," I stressed.

"Then your father is right. You are too thin. Eat your dinner."

"I'm fine. I wasn't hungry at lunch."

My father lifted the bowl of potatoes again in my direction. "And now?"

With a sigh, I accepted the potatoes, adding them to my plate. I wasn't overly hungry, but if it got him off my back, I would eat the damn potatoes.

After dinner, I helped clear the table. It was June's night off. I missed our housekeeper's sunny disposition, but I would see her next time. I was loading the dishwasher when my mother spoke.

"You know your father is concerned, Lottie. He has told me how distracted you are in the office."

"I'm fine."

She frowned. "You aren't yourself."

I wanted to ask her if she knew who I was anymore. But I refrained.

I shut the door, straightened up, and met her serious, dark-brown eyes. Like my father, I had blue eyes, but I was built like my mother with the same chestnut-brown hair. Although hers might receive a little help these days from her favorite salon. I was small, with delicate features, the same way she was, and inside, we were both fighters. We simply fought things differently.

Except lately, the fight had gone out of me.

"It's…work."

"What about it?"

I shrugged, unsure how to say the words aloud.

"Are you not happy with the project? Perhaps your father could put you on a different one."

I dragged in some much-needed oxygen. "I'm not sure I want any project, Mom."

Understanding widened her eyes. "Lottie. Have you talked to your father about this?"

"I can't. I don't know how to. You know his expectations."

"You need to speak with him. He would listen to you. He is your father, first."

I wanted to ask her if she honestly believed that. It felt as if he were Charles first and my father a distant second. It had been that way for years.

Since the day we lost Josh.

She reached over the counter, clasping my hand, her voice low and sad. "You can't bring him back by giving up your life, you know. He'd hate it if he knew you were trying."

"I know," I mumbled, shocked by her words. She never spoke of Josh. In fact, she rarely spoke of anything personal with me. She lived a life she'd once laughed at. Lunches, spa days, after-noons with "the ladies." My parents lived in an expensive high-rise, had a housekeeper who cleaned, cooked, and did the shopping. The woman in front of me was coiffed and perfect, totally unlike the memories I still carried of my mom, pushing a grocery cart, me trailing beside her as we snacked on an open bag of crackers and she instructed Josh what brand of cereal he was allowed. Those days ended years ago. My mom, or Jo-Jo, as my dad called her, disappeared the day Josh died, and Josephine replaced her.

Our gazes locked, and for a moment, I saw her pain. For a moment, I thought she was going to say something else, but she straightened her shoulders, and the cool mask I was used to seeing reappeared.

"If you need to do this, please approach your father carefully. He has already lost enough."

I heard the subtle warning behind her words, and I shook my head wildly. I thought of the look that would cross his face if I told him. The crushing disappointment. I couldn't face it. I couldn't be the one to do that to him. I already owed him so much.

"It'll pass, Mom. The latest project is very stressful. As soon as this next project completes, I'll take a little time off. Maybe Brianna and I will go on a vacation. I'll be fine."

She sighed, folding a dish towel and laying it on the counter. "I'll be watching, Lottie."

I stood, reaching for my coat. "I had better get going."

Mom stared at me knowingly. "Escaping while your father is on the phone so he won't insist on a car for you?"

I bent over and kissed her cheek. "You know as well as I do that Rodney will watch me walk down the street to the subway. I am perfectly safe. I have a five-minute walk on the other end."

She shook her head. "So independent."

"It's all I have."

She regarded me, frowning. "You have a great job. Remember how important your father's company is to him, Lottie. Many people would love to have your opportunities."

I tamped down my retort and smiled at my mother. No one knew how important the company was to him more than I did. It had replaced everything else in his life after Josh was gone.

I also knew the fleeting moment that passed between my mother and me earlier was gone. Any hope she would speak to my father on my behalf disappeared. She always sided with him. "Of course."

She patted my cheek. "Like you said, you can take a break when this next project is done."

"Right. I'll consider it later."

"Good."

"Goodnight, Mom."

I hurried away, worried my father would appear from the den and stop me.

My feet dragged coming off the subway; weariness made my body feel older than my twenty-six years. I climbed the steps, welcoming the cold air as I exited the station, and I tucked my scarf tight around my neck. I walked sluggishly, not in any hurry. I doubted I would sleep much with everything on my mind.

I felt trapped. I truly despised my job, yet I had no idea how to get out of it. My father owned the firm, and I was the heir apparent. It was expected of me. My heart ached when I thought of the reason why. It should have been Josh. Like my father, he'd loved all elements of business. He soaked it all up like a sponge. He had been the golden child, groomed to take over and carry on the Prescott name. Even at his young age, he understood the nature of my father's business and loved it. I was just the little girl, loved for being the baby of the family, with no expectations placed on me, until Josh got sick.

It happened fast. One day, he was fine. And it seemed, at least to the child I was then, the next, he was dangerously ill. Life revolved around the hospital and Josh. All I heard were discussions and plans for treatment options. Nothing else mattered. As options were tried, and failed, my parents began to shut down. When the doctors discussed stem cell treatments, my parents were tested, but they came back as not a good match. He was put on the OneMatch Network, but time was running out. All I knew was I missed my big brother, and I wanted him home. I wanted life to go back to the way it was. When the doctors suggested, despite my age, I be tested, that there was a good chance I could be a match, I saw the hope in my parents' eyes. I'd known how important it was that it work. I had been the last hope to save Josh.

And despite being a perfect match and going ahead with the efforts, it was in vain.

I would never forget the disappointed look on my father's face as he turned away from me when he realized it wasn't going to work. I had failed.

The day Josh died, my entire family did. It was as if they forgot about me. I tried so hard to get their attention. To bring back the people I once knew as my parents. I excelled at school. I put aside my silly dreams of being a pastry chef and concentrated on business. I went to work for my father since I was certain that was what he wanted.

I tried to step into Josh's shoes. To make up for his loss to my parents by giving them my life.

I failed at that as well.

CHAPTER 3
LOTTIE

I t was late when I switched off my desk lamp. My clock chimed out eight bells as I slipped on my coat, stretching my sore muscles. I didn't bother packing my laptop tonight. By the time I got home and had something to eat, it would be time to sleep, and I'd be back to work early.

I sat, unseeing, on the subway, my brain still processing the day. The meetings melted into one another, the emails and to-do lists constant. I could barely keep up. I wasn't sleeping well, and my appetite was almost nonexistent. I wasn't sure how much longer I could keep going that way.

My stop approached, and I stood, feeling the sadness of knowing I wouldn't see him tonight. I had missed him one night last week as well. The next day, when our eyes met across the platform, I was certain I had seen relief flash across his face, but that was probably wishful thinking. I had sat for a few minutes, listening to him, letting his music soak into my soul, then headed home to another evening of more work.

I wouldn't even have those few minutes tonight.

However, as I rounded the corner, I halted in shock when I

saw him, leaning against the wall, lazily strumming his guitar, an abstract tune I hadn't heard. He lifted his head, our gazes locked, and happiness welled in my chest. I didn't know why he was there so late, and I didn't care. He was there. That was all that mattered.

The station wasn't busy, and I sat close to listen. He began another song—one of my favorites—and I relaxed back, letting my eyes shut as the notes drifted over me, low and sweet. When he began to sing, a tear slipped down my cheek at the richness of his voice. It felt as though he were singing only to me. Another wistful thought, but it was how I felt.

His voice wrapped around me like a lover's embrace. I felt warm, soothed, and my body eased for the first time since I had left his presence last night. As the song faded away, another began, and I let myself remain. I needed that, him, so much tonight. With a sigh, I let my head fall forward, immersing myself in the song. His fingers coaxed the notes from the guitar; his voice weaved a spell around him and me.

And my miserable world disappeared.

Something was different. The music still played, but it sounded close. I blinked open my eyes, realizing in horror that I had fallen asleep in the subway station. I sat up straight, panicked.

"It's okay. You're okay," a voice soothed.

I knew that voice, but not from hearing it spoken. It was always raised in song. I turned my head, shocked to find him beside me. He sat, his guitar on his lap as he strummed, never missing a note.

"I've been watching over you."

"Wh—what?"

"You fell asleep. I made sure you were okay."

I didn't know what to say. "Thank you."

He tilted his head and studied me. "You're working too hard. You're exhausted."

I shifted, uncomfortable with his accurate observation.

"You don't know me. I'm not sure you should be making a statement like that."

His fingers stopped their strumming, and he rested his hands on the guitar. "I've overstepped. I apologize."

"Um, okay."

He held out his hand. "As for not knowing you, let's change that. I'm Montgomery Logan."

I stared at his hand. His fingers were long, the nails neatly trimmed. He waited patiently until I slipped my hand into his. He closed his fingers around mine, pressing lightly. And again, he waited, lifting one eyebrow.

"Charlotte Prescott."

He squeezed my hand. "It's great to meet you, Charlotte."

"Lottie. My friends call me Lottie."

He smiled, his dimple deepening. "My friends call me Logan. Montgomery is a mouthful."

"Logan," I repeated.

He nodded. "Now that we're on a first-name basis, I assume we're friends?"

"Okay?"

He hunched forward and winked. "You look tired, Lottie. You need to take better care of yourself."

That made me chuckle. "Okay."

He lifted the guitar off his lap, placing it inside the case, shutting the lid. He bent over, rested his arms on his thighs, and studied me. "You're late tonight."

"I was busy at work." I paused then looked around. "Are you always here at this time?"

He grinned, his face transforming into one of mischief. "Nope. I was waiting for you."

"Me?" I squeaked.

"I waited last week, too. You know, the night you pulled your little stunt."

"I didn't see you when I got back."

He shrugged. "I got hungry, so I went across the street and got something to eat. I saw you come out of the station, and I made sure you got home."

"You-you what?"

"I followed you."

I stared at him. He said it as if it meant nothing. As if following someone were normal. I swallowed, a frisson of fear running down my spine.

He chuckled, the sound low and rich. "You should see the look on your face right now. I bet you're trying to decide if you should run now or call the cops, aren't you?"

I licked my dry lips. "Um…"

He held up his hand. "That came out wrong. I saw you come out of the station. I stepped outside the coffee shop and watched you walk to your building."

"How do you know it was my building?"

"I've seen you come out of it as I'm passing by," he explained. "I wasn't *'following you,'* following you." He held up his hands. "Honest, Lottie. I only made sure you got there safely. Then I went back inside and finished my burger."

I mulled over his words.

"You shouldn't be walking alone at that time of night."

I snorted. "You sound like my father. It's a short walk."

He lifted one shoulder. "Just saying."

"It's a safe neighborhood."

He shifted a little closer. "Still, the thought of something happening to you…" He closed his eyes, and a shudder went through him. "I don't like it."

"I'll be careful," I promised, wondering why his words caused a warmth to spread in my chest. He sounded as though he cared. For some reason, I liked thinking that he did.

"Why were you waiting for me?"

He pulled in his bottom lip, worrying it, then lifted his hand, tucking a lock of hair behind my ear. His unexpected touch sent a shiver down my spine.

"You've looked exhausted the past few nights. More than usual. I wanted to ask..." He trailed off, clearing his throat.

"Ask?" I prompted.

"Ask if you would let me take you for coffee? Get something to eat with me?"

"Oh," I breathed out.

I wanted to. I wanted to go with him anywhere he wanted to go, listen to him talk. Spend some time with him. Get to know him. Still, I hesitated.

"It's a public place. You'll be perfectly safe."

"I'm not worried about that, Logan."

He ran a hand through his hair, impatiently pushing the strands off his forehead. It was a useless gesture since they fell right back into his eyes. He glanced away, then met my eyes, his gaze sad, voice pained. "You don't want to be seen with me? Is that it? A street musician?"

"No!" I insisted. "That isn't it at all!"

He stood, extending his hand. "Then come with me."

I didn't want to ask him if he could afford it, if he'd made enough money today to eat out again. I decided I would simply grab the check when it came. I let him take my hand and tug me from my seat. I had to lean back to see his face.

"You're really tall."

"And you're not."

"I'm average."

He bent low, a smile ghosting his lips as he chuckled, his voice a low hum in my ear. "I would never call you average."

"I meant height-wise."

"Well, I'm not. I've always been in the top percentile for that statistic."

"I think you're probably in the top percentile in many areas."

He grinned, tugging me beside him, keeping me close. His towering stature made me feel safe.

"I guess you'll find out, now, won't you, Lottie?"

I could only nod.

CHAPTER 4
LOTTIE

He led me across the street to the coffee shop where I assumed he had watched me the other night. He was obviously a regular, smiling familiarly at the waitress.

"Hey, Macy."

"Hi, Logan. Coffee?"

He glanced at me for confirmation and nodded at her. "Two, please."

"Coming right up."

We sat down, Logan setting his guitar case on one of the empty chairs. I looked around, curious. I had passed the place many times but never come in. It was a throwback to another time, when people congregated to share their day. Formica counters and tables, chairs with torn vinyl, and an aging linoleum floor made up the space. Despite its age, it was meticulous—counters polished, the floor spotless. There were some older men at the counter, drinking coffee, eating pie from cases that displayed the slices. Domed glass covers showed cakes piled high with frosting. The smell of coffee and the grease from the hot grill at the back permeated the air, making my stomach grumble.

"Best cheeseburgers in the city," Logan informed me, not even looking at the menu. "As long as you eat meat." His lips twisted into a frown. "Are you one of those girls who only eats salads? Is that why you're so thin?"

"I eat meat. And I'm not thin," I added, defensive.

"You are. You've gotten thinner lately."

I crossed my arms. "Exactly how closely have you been watching me?"

Macy appeared, setting down our steaming cups of coffee. "You eating or just coffee?"

"Two specials, Macy. Extra cheese on both."

She walked away before I could speak.

"Maybe I'm lactose intolerant."

"Are you?"

"No."

"Moot point, then. Besides, I saw you have coffee a couple times. You always add cream."

"Logan…"

"Lottie," he teased.

"You haven't answered my question."

He took a long drink of coffee, his eyes never leaving mine. The steam from his cup swirled around his head, his long fingers wrapping all the way around the large mug.

He set it down, resting on his arms. "How closely have I been watching you?"

I was almost afraid to hear the answer. "Yes."

He traced the handle of his mug a couple of times. "Close."

"Why?"

His reply was slow. "Because I think you need someone to watch out for you." He lifted his soulful eyes, the light shimmering in his whiskey-colored irises. "And you came to me first."

"I did?"

"That day in the subway. I saw you walking—your shoulders

were hunched, and you looked so sad. When you sat down, I felt this need to do something to make you feel better. So I started playing for you."

"For me? I thought it was, ah…" I stumbled, unsure how to say the words.

"For money?" he guessed accurately.

"Yes."

"It's always a bonus, but it wasn't the reason. I wanted to do something for you. You looked so lost, almost broken." He slid his hand along the table and hooked my pinkie with his finger, squeezing it. "I wanted—*I needed*—to help you."

I didn't know what to say. I stared down at our hands. Mine looked so small compared to his. The way his palm rested against mine, almost encompassing it with its size. His grip was strong, the ends of his fingers calloused from playing guitar, and what I assumed were many years of hard work. His rough skin didn't bother me at all. In fact, his touch brought comfort. I raised my eyes, meeting his gaze, finally plucking up the courage to say what I had been thinking for so long.

"Your music brings me such peace, Logan. It's the one thing I look forward to every day. I can't begin to express how much it means to me."

"I play it only for you."

I had no time to respond.

Macy arrived, setting down plates loaded with massive burgers and French fries piled so high, they tumbled over the edge of the plate. We broke apart, and for the first time, I realized how close we'd been leaning into each other. It didn't seem to embarrass Logan. He winked and picked up the ketchup bottle, adding a generous amount on his plate, offering it to me. I took it, putting a small squirt to the side of my plate.

I studied the burger, unsure how to eat it without it ending up all over me. I glanced up to Logan, who was attacking his burger with gusto. Cheese and ketchup dripped from the corner of his mouth, and with a smirk, he wiped it away with a napkin. He tapped my plate closer.

"Tuck in, Lottie. I want to see you eat it." He took another huge bite, chewing it leisurely. His Adam's apple bobbed as he swallowed. A handful of fries were dragged through the ketchup, shoved into his mouth, chewed, and swallowed, as I watched, fascinated by his actions.

He shook his head and leaned across the table. "Do I have to feed you?"

I snapped out of my trance. "No." I picked up the burger and bit down. Hot cheese, greasy meat, and fried onions hit my taste buds. I chewed and swallowed, my eyes closing on their own in pleasure. He was right. It was the best burger I had ever eaten.

His chuckle made me open my eyes. He winked at me, offering me a napkin. I wiped away the ketchup on my chin.

"It's good."

"I told you it was."

"You're awfully sure of yourself."

He bit and masticated, shrugging one shoulder. "I suppose I am. You have to be in this life."

"In this life? You mean in general or in, ah, your line of work?"

He pushed the hair off his forehead, shaking his head. "You mean as a young, single guy in a big city? Or as a struggling street musician?"

"Um…"

"That's what you see, right? When you look at me? Poor, struggling, in need of handouts, like the other night?"

His eyes never left my face, and I felt heat rush up my neck, blooming on my cheeks. "It wasn't a handout."

"What would you call it?"

"A thank-you."

"Do you toss a hundred bucks into every open guitar case?"

"No. But…"

"But, what?"

It felt as if the conversation had suddenly drifted into dark waters. Carefully, I set my burger back on my plate, wiping my fingers.

"Your music, it means something to me. More than I can tell you. It brings me peace. It–it's the only thing I have to look forward to every day." My voice rose. "And you never let me put money in. You let everyone else!"

"They're different."

"I don't understand."

He finished his burger, pushing his plate away roughly. He drained his mug and signaled for a refill, waiting until Macy brought him more coffee and left, taking his empty plate.

"You've barely touched your food."

I looked down at my half-eaten burger and the large pile of fries that still sat on the plate. "Not that hungry. You want it?"

"No. I want *you* to eat it."

"Tell me what you meant by that statement."

He scrubbed his face roughly. "I play for you. If other people listen and get some enjoyment, that's great. They want to drop in money, fine. But my music is my gift for you. You don't have to pay to hear it. Ever."

His words astounded me.

"What makes me different?"

"*You* make you different." He bent low, extending his hand across the table, running his finger over my wrist. "Ever since I saw you that night, I felt this draw…this need to watch for you. I was heading home when I caught sight of you. You looked as if the weight of the world were on your shoulders. It reminded me…" He frowned, falling silent.

"Reminded you?" I prompted.

"It reminded me of how my father used to look. Worn-down, beaten. Stretched to his limit." His eyes blazed as he stared across the table. "The corporate world killed him. He was dead at forty-two. He had a heart attack sitting at his desk. Just dropped dead."

I covered my mouth. "Logan," I breathed out.

"I was fourteen. I used to watch him, see how hard he worked. And it was never enough. If he gave ten hours, they wanted twelve. If he worked six days, they wanted seven. He struggled to be enough every fucking day—and he never was. He gave everything he had to a demanding corporation, and all he got in return was an early grave." He flung his napkin on the table. "And all I got was one foster home after another, until I ran away."

"What about your mother?"

"She left when I was a kid. She hated the mediocre life she led. She kept telling my father she wanted more. She packed up one day and left without a word to either of us." Logan closed his eyes for a moment. "My dad was stuck with me and a job he hated." He huffed out a loud breath. "Some life."

I didn't know what to say. Silence descended around us. Logan's fingers drummed on the table in a restless beat, his leg swinging like a pendulum in short, rapid movements. He reached across the table, dragging my plate closer, and started eating the French fries. His movements were jerky and tense, and he didn't meet my eyes.

Finally, he spoke. "Sorry, I shouldn't have dumped all that on you. I rarely talk about my past, but somehow with you, it just sort of came out."

"No, I'm glad you told me. What was your father's name?"

"William. William Logan."

"I'm sure he'd be very proud of you."

Logan brushed off my words. "Tell me about you."

"Not much to tell, really. I work at Prescott Inc."

"The investment company?"

"Yes."

"Prescott, as in your family?"

"Yes, my father owns and runs it."

"No nepotism there, I see."

A shot of anger went through me. "Actually, no. I went to school and *earned* my degree. I had to work my way up, just like everyone else. I'm only a manager of one small group. If anything, I have to work harder, prove myself more than anyone else there *because* of who I am." I lifted my chin, meeting his steady regard. "My father believes you have to earn your place, family or not."

He held up his hands in supplication. "Sorry, I was only teasing. I'm sure you're great at what you do."

I shrugged, picking up my mug. "I try to be."

"Do you like your job?"

My gaze drifted around the diner and settled back on Logan's face. He lifted an eyebrow, studying me. "If you have to think that hard about it, I would say the answer is a resounding no."

"I'm not sure anyone actually likes their job."

He pursed his lips with a fast shrug of his shoulders. "I do."

"Not all of us can wander the streets and play music for fun."

He indicated my plate. "Are you really not going to eat that?"

"No."

He pulled it closer and picked up the burger, demolishing it in moments.

I worried about how often he was able to eat. He was lean, but he didn't look undernourished. He was well muscled and in shape.

He caught me staring and chuckled, waving Macy over. "More coffee, please. And a piece of the spice cake. Two forks."

She filled both our cups and took away my now-empty plate.

He wiped his fingers and mouth and balled up his napkin. "I

can see what you're thinking. I assure you, I'm quite capable of taking care of myself."

"Oh, ah…"

Macy set down a large piece of cake and the two forks.

"Enjoy."

Logan speared a piece and bent over the table, holding his fork. "You have to try this cake—it's amazing."

I let him slide the fork into my mouth and sat back, enjoying the richness of the cake. It was dense, moist, and the flavors of the cinnamon and nutmeg burst on my tongue.

"Delicious."

"My favorite." He hummed, taking a large bite. "I have it every time."

"Do you come here a lot?"

"Enough. I'm not a very good cook—unless it's brunch. I rock scrambled eggs."

"And, ah, you have a place to cook?"

He laid down his fork and bent closer. "I'm not destitute. Just because I don't have an office to go to or wear a fancy suit doesn't mean I'm homeless. But no, I don't live alone. I have a place I share with some other friends. I, in fact, have a job. I even have a bank account and a credit card." He smirked. "Not everyone measures their success by what they do for a living."

Embarrassment colored my cheeks. "I'm sorry. I didn't mean to insult you."

"You didn't. I simply want to correct your thinking when it comes to me. I understand we're opposites in our views on success, and about how we live our lives. But you know what they say about opposites."

I frowned in confusion. "I don't know what you mean."

"You're part of the corporate world. You work endlessly, trying to please an unpleasable master. I choose not to be a slave to anyone. I come and go as I please. I don't answer to anyone."

"We all answer to someone. You have to be accountable."

"I'm accountable to myself. I live a simple existence, and I like it. I don't need all the trappings of what is considered a normal life."

"But what if you get sick...or hurt?" I asked, thinking how often I heard of muggings in the subway. "What if someone stole your guitar—how would you live?"

Macy laid the bill on the table, and I grabbed it. Logan frowned and reached for it from me.

"Don't even think about it. I asked you for coffee."

I held it to my chest. "No. I want to."

"Don't insult me, Lottie."

"I'm not insulting you. Please let me. I can afford it."

His eyes darkened. "And you, once again, assume I cannot."

"I..."

"Give me the damn bill."

Stubbornly, I shook my head.

"You're making me angry."

"I want to pay."

He stood, digging in his pocket. He flung a couple bills on the table and grabbed his guitar case. "There. You already did."

He strode away, and I looked at the table, recognizing the bills. They had been smoothed and straightened, but were badly wrinkled, as if they had, at one point, been balled up tightly. I was certain they were the bills I had tossed into his guitar case the other night.

Macy came over, frowning. She picked up the bills with a sigh. "He always leaves too much."

"He comes here a lot?"

"He has for years. Three or four times a week—and even when he was going to school to get his degree. First time he has ever brought anyone with him, though." She studied me. "He must like you."

"School?"

She pocketed the money. "He's a teacher. Didn't you know that?"

I shook my head, my mind reeling. A teacher? Why was he playing for money in the streets if he was a teacher?

I stood, pulling on my coat, feeling sad. I had upset and insulted him, so now I would never have the answer to that question. I doubted I would see him again. My heart grew heavier and my eyes stung as I realized I would probably never hear him play either. His music, his *presence* would no longer be there at the end of a long, grueling day. I gripped the top of the chair as emotions swelled.

He was right. I had made assumptions about him based on what I saw. Because he played music in the subway, I assumed he was homeless, jobless, and broke. That he needed my help.

The truth was, I needed his help.

Wearily, I made my way home, my footsteps slow and dragging. Once in my condo, I brushed my teeth, changed, and slid into bed, completely drained and feeling ancient.

Logan's words kept echoing in my head. I knew he was right. I made assumptions about him without actually knowing him or his story. He did the same to me when I told him where I worked. Most people did when they heard my name in connection with my father's business.

We had both wrongly judged the book by its cover.

I rolled over, clutching my pillow. I hated my job. I hated everything to do with it—the meetings, the business executives, dealing with egos, strict timelines and schedules. It consumed my life, and I detested it.

I never had time to do anything I enjoyed. I gave it all to my father and the company he loved so much. Hoping one day, he would, in turn, love *me* that much. That both my parents would wake up and see me. Not the sibling who couldn't help her brother. Not the girl who let them down. *Me.*

Except it would never happen.

I buried my face in the pillow and wept.

♬

The next morning, I was listless, still exhausted and discon-nected. I was grateful it was Friday. If I worked late again, I could take the weekend off. I only had to make it through one more day.

I paused as I stepped outside, the welcome cold hitting me. I inhaled slowly, smelling the snow in the air. Everywhere, it was fresh and white, thanks to the flurries that blanketed the city overnight. I pulled on my mittens, startling when a throat cleared in front of me.

I met Logan's eyes. He looked as tired as I felt.

"What are you doing here?"

"Waiting for you."

"I didn't think I'd see you again."

"I'm sorry about last night." He stepped forward. "I'm sensi-tive when it comes to money. I don't want you thinking I'm some impoverished street person you have to help."

"I don't."

He arched his eyebrow, and I had the grace to look ashamed. "I'm sorry."

"I think we need to get to know each other better."

I smiled at him, relief tearing through my body. "I'd like that."

"You look so tired."

"I didn't sleep well last night."

"Me either. You looked so upset when you left the coffee shop that I almost buzzed up to your place."

"What?"

"When you walked home."

"You saw me? You stormed away. You left."

"I did, but I was outside around the corner. Did you really

think I would let you walk home alone? I stayed back and made sure you arrived safely."

"Why didn't you come talk to me?"

"I needed to cool off, and I thought you would be too angry with me to talk."

"I would have. I was sorry I upset you."

He studied me for a moment. "Lottie, I know we're different. I know our goals and the way we achieve them are polar opposites. But I think we suit each other on so many levels. I want to explore this further—whatever we have—with you."

I hesitated.

He held out his hand. "Come with me. Spend the day with me. Come see my world for a few hours. You can show me yours. Maybe we can figure out a way to mesh them."

"I have to go to work."

He wrapped his hand around mine, his warmth seeping through the wool that covered my hand. "One day. All I'm asking for is one day. Work will be there tomorrow."

I was tempted. "Why?" I breathed out.

He hunched down, meeting my gaze. "I lost my father to the rat race of the corporate world. I'll be damned if I don't fight to save you from it."

"Logan…"

His lips touched mine. Featherlight, gentle, and sweet. His touch filled me with yearning. Warmth. Desire. He drew back, and I followed, wanting to feel his touch again. He gathered me into his arms, holding me close. He kissed me harder, passion simmering with his caress.

"Please, Lottie. Come with me. All I want is a chance."

I rested my head on his chest, feeling the way his arms encircled me so naturally. I felt cherished, and for the first time in many years, safe.

I glanced up into his warm eyes, seeing his care and worry.

His rich, whiskey gaze was intense, soulful, and *real*. Logan looked at *me*. He saw *me*.

I wanted to see that gaze every day. I wanted to hear his voice murmur my name. I didn't want to feel alone anymore.

I wanted to feel alive.

Logan made me feel that way.

I met his golden, anxious gaze.

"Yes."

CHAPTER 5
LOTTIE

Logan released me from his embrace and wrapped his hand around mine, tugging me down the steps. I faltered, and he stopped with a frown.

"No, don't change your mind, Lottie. Please."

"I'm not." I indicated my business clothes. "I thought I would change into something a little less formal. And I have to call the office and tell them I'm not coming in. My father will worry, and I can't simply abandon my responsibilities."

He shook his head. "Of course not. I wouldn't expect you to." He rested back against the wrought-iron railing. "I'll wait."

I smiled, feeling shy. "Why don't you come up? It's warmer inside."

He frowned. "You shouldn't be inviting strange men into your home, Lottie. For all you know, I'm as psycho as you thought I was last night."

I arched an eyebrow at him. "Are you?"

His grin flashed, lighting his face. "No. But still…"

"Maybe *you* should be afraid of *me*."

He threw back his head in amusement. His laugh was loud

and boisterous, cutting through the cold air and uplifting me with its infectious sound. "I think I can take my chances," he stated once he stopped chortling.

"Okay, then." I held out my hand, and he took it in his much larger one.

"Show me your place."

I was nervous as I opened my door. My condo wasn't big or fancy, but it was mine. It took all my savings to get the down payment, but it belonged to me. It overlooked the street, and I liked to sit and watch the snow fall in the streetlights from the big chair I had placed by the window. The building was older and still had the charm of gumtree moldings and chair rails, and the floors were all hardwood and creaked everywhere you walked. There were two decent-sized bedrooms, one I currently used for an office. It had a day bed for the occasional night that Brianna would stay over. There was a small dining area, and the kitchen had been done before I bought it, so it was in good shape. I had decorated it slowly, buying pieces as they went on sale or that I found in secondhand shops or antique markets. My mother had been aghast at my decisions, but it was all mine, and I loved every piece.

Logan looked around the room with a smile on his face. "Exactly how I pictured it."

"Yeah?"

He nodded and ran a finger over my cheek. "I knew you weren't a big-box kind of girl, and I couldn't see you surrounded by stuffy furniture. You have an old soul, Lottie, and this place suits you."

My breath caught. His words described how I felt to perfection. My parents never saw that about me. My father pushed for me to be a modern businesswoman, and my mother wanted my place to be a showcase like their condo. But Logan saw underneath all of it and into the person inside.

"How?" I asked. "How do you know me so well already?"

"It's just my observations. Your clothes, your handbag, even your briefcase. Nothing showy, no labels screaming 'Look at me!' You carry a book, not an e-reader. You're not glued to your phone. You're always elegant and classy. You're kind to people." He smiled ruefully. "You were certainly kind to me when you thought I was a street musician and needed to eat. I saw you give sandwiches to homeless people several times. I saw the trays of coffee you would leave." He paused, meeting my gaze. "I saw the softness in your eyes, the caring gestures you made when you thought no one was looking. That is what tells me the type of person you are—the person I thought you to be."

The air around us hummed. Logan stepped back with a sigh. "I think you'd better go get changed and make your call, or I might not live up to your expectations."

"Do, ah, you need to call anyone?" I asked. Macy had told me he was a teacher. Was she wrong?

He frowned. "I do work, Lottie. I'm a teacher. Well, at the moment, a substitute teacher. Full time is hard to get now. I wasn't needed today."

I studied him. His gaze was intelligent, and he was articulate and smart. I had already figured that out. "I bet you're a great teacher."

He shrugged off my compliment.

"I'm waiting," was all he said.

I hurried away, shutting my bedroom door behind me. I leaned against it, my hand on my chest.

What was I doing? I had never once taken a sick day, and now, because Logan asked, I was going to pretend to be ill and spend the day with him. And I wanted to do it. I wanted to spend today with him. For the first time since I could remember, I was choosing myself and what I wanted over what I felt I *should* do.

I pushed off the door and called the office. Audrey, the HR woman, sounded shocked when I explained I wouldn't be in, and she put me on hold for a moment. I wasn't surprised when my father came on the line.

"Charlotte? What's going on?"

"I'm not well, so I'm not coming in today. As I told Audrey, I left all the files needed for the meeting this afternoon on my desk."

"What do you mean *not well?*"

I had no idea what to say. I hadn't planned on having to defend myself to my father.

"I, ah…" I dropped my voice. "It's a woman's issue, Dad. I have cramps and—"

"I get the picture," he interrupted, as I knew he would. "Not great timing, Charlotte."

I rolled my eyes. "A little out of my control," I pointed out, feeling the guilt of fibbing to him.

"Do what you have to and try to make it in this afternoon."

I made a noncommittal response and hung up. I threw off my business suit and dressed in jeans and a warm cherry-red sweater. I rushed back down the hall. Logan was sitting on the sofa, thumbing through one of my dog-eared books. He glanced up and grinned. "You look beautiful."

He stood and came close. "You need one more thing, though."

"Oh?"

Reaching up, he delved his hands into my hair and pulled away the clips, letting it fall down my back in long waves. He ran his fingers through the thick locks. "Now, you're perfect."

Once again, the air began to thicken around us. His fingers tightened in my hair, curling into fists. Slowly, giving me a chance to refuse, he lowered his head. I slid my hands around his shoulders, and with a groan, he crashed his lips to mine. His grip was firm but gentle as he held me close. His mouth moved, his tongue sliding sensuously along with mine. I whimpered as he deepened the kiss, warmth spreading through my body, running down my spine. I curled my toes as he dropped one hand to my hip, pulling me tight to his chest as he kissed me, my senses reeling from his passion.

He broke away, leaning his forehead to mine. Our chests pressed together, his hard, toned body fitting to my softer curves so well.

"God, I've wanted to do that for so long," he murmured. "I want to do it again. And then again."

I shivered at his low tone. The underlying promise it held. I bent back, meeting his gaze. It was dark and hooded, filled with desire.

"Anytime," I breathed out.

I was rewarded with another hard, fast kiss. "God, you are amazing."

He stepped back, leaving me feeling cold without his warmth. "If I do, we won't be leaving this condo, and I have the day planned." He grabbed his coat. "Are you ready?"

I took my parka from the coat hook and tucked my wallet and phone into the large pocket. I grabbed my favorite mittens and paused.

"Wait."

I turned to the closet and pulled down a basket, digging through it. I found what I was looking for and held out a pair of large gray mittens.

"For you."

Logan took them, frowning.

"I made them," I explained. "Look, they can be worn like mittens, or fingerless." I demonstrated how the small flap opened and they became fingerless gloves. "They were my first attempt, so they aren't perfect, but they'll keep your hands warm."

He eyed the basket. "Should I ask about your mitten fetish?"

I giggled. "I like to knit. I make them and drop them off at homeless shelters. I also knit baby booties and blankets for the hospital." I waggled my fingers. "And I love mittens, but I lose them frequently, so I make them for me too."

He slid them on, pulling back the flap so his fingers were exposed and bending his knuckles. "I like them." He met my eyes, his gaze warm. "Thank you."

I was thrilled he accepted them in the spirit they were given. No hidden agenda, no worry about his financial capability of affording some mittens, just me giving them to him since I noticed his hands were bare and we were going to be outside.

"You're welcome."

He held out his hand again. "Shall we?"

I tucked mine into his, grinning. They matched. I saw he noticed too, and his eyes crinkled with amusement.

"Yes."

♫

We walked a short distance, neither of us talking at first, but enjoying the quiet. It felt strangely right to be walking beside him, holding his hand. Logan steered us in the opposite direction of the main road and into a neighborhood I wasn't familiar with. The streets were a little wider and quiet. Tall trees lined the road, and I gazed up in wonder at the snow-covered branches and how pretty they looked glistening in the sun.

"Is winter your favorite season?" he asked.

"Yes. It always has been. Josh and I…" I trailed off and swallowed. "Josh and I loved to play in the snow. He always helped me make the best snowmen."

"Josh?"

I had to blink at the sudden moisture in my eyes. "My brother."

"Do you still make snowmen together?"

"No," I said through tight lips.

"Does he work with you at your father's company?"

I swallowed. "He's dead."

Logan stopped walking, pivoted, and stared down at me. "Lottie, I'm sorry."

"He died when I was much younger."

"And you still miss him." It wasn't a question, simply a statement as if he understood.

"Every day."

Suddenly, his arms enveloped me, pulling me close. Despite my parka and his jacket, I felt his heat, the warmth of his embrace seeping into me, relaxing me. I accepted his comfort, clinging to his waist, holding him close.

"I'm sure he misses you too, baby," he mumbled into my hair.

His words unlocked something inside me. I was never allowed to talk about Josh. Every time I tried, my parents shut down. Right after his death, that was all I wanted to talk about, to share with someone how much I missed him. How badly I felt I failed him. But I couldn't. It was forbidden.

"He was a great big brother," I whispered.

He held me harder, then eased back. "You'll have to tell me all about him."

"Really?"

"You can talk to me about anything, Lottie. Obviously, you loved him—you still do—so of course I want to know about him."

"I'd like that. But not today. I want today to be about us."

He traced a finger down my cheek. "Okay. Whenever you want."

He clasped my hand in his. "Now, I'm ready for breakfast."

"Sounds good."

Logan led me to another small restaurant, where he was obviously well-known. He was greeted warmly, and he led me to a booth in the corner. I sat down, unzipping my coat and inhaling the scent of coffee and sugar hanging in the air.

"Do they know you in every diner in the city?" I teased.

He chuckled. "Only about four. I sub at the school a few blocks over. I usually stop for breakfast on the days I work there. I love their waffles. Great coffee too."

My mouth began to water. Waffles. I couldn't recall the last time I'd had waffles. My mom used to make them when we were kids—they were Josh's favorite. After he died, she never made them again.

"Lottie?" Logan's worried voice interrupted my thoughts.

I shook my head to clear it. "Waffles sound perfect."

He ordered each of us waffles and added a plate of bacon to share. I sipped the hot coffee, enjoying the strong brew.

Logan drank his faster, emptying his mug. The waitress reappeared and set a carafe on our table, then walked away looking amused.

"They know you well."

"I sometimes mark papers while I'm here. They know how much coffee I drink." He winked and filled his cup and sat back. "You don't do too bad yourself."

"Caffeine is the only thing that gets me through some days," I admitted.

"What do you do, exactly?"

I looked past him through the window. It was still snowing lightly, the white glittering in the sun as it drifted down to the ground. I disliked talking about my job, but I forced myself to give a quick explanation.

"I'm part of a group that works with investors on a project. We present and bring them into a new investment opportunity, and basically hold their hand until it is done. We meet with them, keep them up-to-date, calm their fears, ask them for more money at times. It varies. Sometimes it's short—a few weeks or months, other times longer, depending on the size of the project. I spend most of my time doing research and supplying the team with the information. It's my job to know each project inside and out. I have to be ready to answer any question the client, the investor, a team member, or my father asks."

"Sounds like a lot of stress."

"It is."

"And you do it because…?" He trailed off.

"Because I have to."

He lifted an eyebrow. "You have to?"

"It's expected of me."

"That's a huge responsibility to have on your shoulders."

I hated discussing my job. Simply thinking about it these days made me feel ill. I was grateful to see the waitress approaching, and I forced a smile to my face. "Oh, here's breakfast."

Logan took the hint. "Good. I'm starving."

The waffles were amazing. Light and fluffy, yet crispy. Logan watched, bemused, as I drowned the waffle in butter and syrup and took my first bite, groaning at the delicious explosion of sweetness.

"Oh my god," I mumbled. "I'd forgotten how good waffles were."

He cut into his, devouring his plate of food. I ate slower, but I did manage to eat almost three-quarters of the large waffle on my plate plus two pieces of bacon. Logan finished off what I couldn't eat.

"Are you a bottomless pit?"

"Most of the time." He met my gaze, his eyes serious. "I know hunger, Lottie. I never want to experience it again."

My heart stuttered at the pained look in his soulful eyes. I covered his hand with mine. "I'm sorry."

He frowned. "Don't feel sorry for me."

"I'm not," I insisted. "I feel empathy." I looked down at the table, tracing the scarred wood with one finger. "I know a hunger of a different kind. It's called loneliness."

He flipped his hand over, squeezing mine. "I know."

I met his eyes. "You do?"

"I saw it in your eyes the first time I played for you."

For a moment, our gazes locked, sharing a quiet, intimate moment of pain. Warm, understanding whiskey stared into my troubled blue. I was certain Logan looked right through me into my soul, seeing all the pain and worry, the abandonment and fear I had experienced. And somehow, with that gentle look, eased a small part of it away.

I blinked, and the moment was gone. The noise of the diner surrounded me again, but the warmth of Logan's hand never left mine.

He hunched over the table. "We have a lot to learn about each other, Lottie. Today is just the start. How about we make it a rule that today—this gloriously sunny, snowy day we have together—is only about now. Only today. It'll be the day we look back on years from now as our start. I want it to be a good one."

I tried not to gape at his words. He seemed so certain. As if our future together was a guarantee. I felt as if I should say something, remind him that the future was never secure. It could change in a heartbeat. Except, somehow, I knew he would simply smile and tell me that was what had already happened.

So instead, I agreed. "Okay."

We walked for hours, talking about nothing and everything. I discovered he was my age and his birthday was a month after mine. Logan informed me today was favorite day, so we shared all our favorites. Colors. Ice cream. Movies. Songs. He peppered me with questions, and I volleyed right back. We stopped in a park and got hot chocolate with extra marshmallows and whipped cream, because Logan insisted that was the only way to drink it.

We sat on a bench, sipping the warm treat, watching people, enjoying the cold and each other's company.

"What is your favorite day?" he asked, looking sideways as he sipped his hot chocolate.

Without thinking, I replied, "Today."

He turned on the bench and kissed me. He tasted like chocolate, snow, happiness, and Logan. He commanded my mouth effortlessly, his tongue sliding along mine in sensuous passes, his lips firm. He cupped my cheek with his large hand, his fingers stroking and warming my cheek as he caressed me. He broke away, his breathing fast. "Good answer."

"Good kiss."

He nudged the end of my nose. "Lots more of those for you if you want them, Lottie."

Then he pressed his forehead to mine. "Now, today aside, what is your favorite kind of day? Tell me what you would do if you woke up and had an entire day of nothing planned."

"Make a pot of coffee, curl up in my chair, and read until I didn't want to read anymore. Have a long, leisurely bath and read some more. Order noodles and dumplings and eat them with my fingers. Have a nap. Watch the snow. Keep my mind empty. No work, no clients, nothing but the music I would have playing, the scent of the candles I would burn, and my comfiest pj's and fuzzy socks on my feet. Bake something."

"You like to bake?"

"I love baking. It's my favorite thing to do. Always has been." I felt shy as I continued. "I wanted to be a pastry chef when I grew up."

He frowned but didn't react to that statement. Instead, he tapped his chin.

"What if it was the summer?"

"Hmm. I'm not big on the sun, but a shaded tree beside the water, my book, and lots of iced tea to drink, and I'd be happy."

"Would you swim?"

"Yes, to cool off. Maybe float a bit."

"No pj's, I assume." He grinned.

"No, shorts and a tank top I can let dry between my swims."

"Sounds good."

"What about you?" I asked. "What would your favorite day be?"

He lifted my hand and kissed the palm. "Being with you and enjoying your day. My head on your lap as you read. Scrubbing your back in the tub. Feeding you the noodles. Holding you in the water. Singing for you. Watching the candlelight flicker on your face. Any of it, as long as it was doing nothing—with you."

My breath caught.

It was too soon for him to say that. It was just too much.

And yet, I couldn't stop smiling.

CHAPTER 6
LOTTIE

My phone began to ring nonstop around two. I set it to silent, but even Logan felt the constant vibration.

"Why don't you answer it?"

I knew he was right. My father would keep calling until I answered, and the longer I stalled, the worse it would be.

I stopped and pulled out my phone. "Hello, Charles."

Logan raised his eyebrow, and I shrugged. My father liked it professional during business hours.

My father didn't bother with a greeting—his voice frosty and curt. "I told you to come in for the meeting. Not only did you not show up, you didn't have the courtesy to call. All because you had a few cramps? And I've been calling for over twenty minutes. You don't have enough respect to pick up the phone when your boss calls?"

I turned from Logan, not wanting him to see my embarrassment. I was sure he could hear my father's words and the tone he was using.

"I told you this morning I wouldn't be in. Everything I had for the meeting was on my desk."

"Luckily, Steve found it."

I rolled my eyes. My file wasn't hard to find and virtually empty. It was yet another meeting I was made to attend that really didn't impact me, but my father insisted. "I don't understand. I took a sick day—the first one in three years—and I still made sure my work was covered. Was there a problem at the meeting?"

"Not the point," my father stated. "Why weren't you answering the phone?"

"I went for a walk to get some fresh air and pick up a couple of things. I forgot my phone."

There was silence for a moment, then he spoke. "I am very disappointed, Charlotte."

The words were out before I could stop them. "Well, that's nothing new when it comes to me, is it, Charles? Feel free to dock my check. Or even better, take the day off my holiday time. I haven't had many of those since I started with the company either."

I hung up.

I sucked in some much-needed oxygen then met the concerned gaze of Logan.

"That's gonna cost me."

"Will he fire you?"

I snorted. "Worse. I'll get a lecture. Then my mother will make sure to let me know how much I upset my father and, therefore, her. She'll remind me how good I've had it and that I should be more appreciative of all they've given me."

He observed me in silence. "Your father never asked if you were unwell."

"No."

"Will your mother?"

I barked out a humorless laugh. "I hope not since I don't want to lie to her as well. But probably not."

"Given they lost your brother, I would have thought their first concern would be your well-being, not the fact that you've taken a day off."

My throat became tight, and I could only nod.

He wrapped an arm around me. "No wonder," he muttered.

"No wonder what?" I asked, staring at his chest.

"No wonder you need me."

I lifted my head in shock. "What?"

He ignored my question. "Do you skate?"

I blinked and repeated myself. "What?"

He pointed ahead. "There's an ice rink. I thought we'd skate a bit, then I'm taking you for noodles and dumplings."

"Um—"

He looked upset. "He isn't spoiling our day, Lottie. If we stop now, he wins. Don't let him."

He was right. It had been such a great day, and I didn't want it to end. My dad was making too much of this. The meeting was a general wrap-up of the week, and I had nothing major to contribute. He was simply angry that I wasn't toeing the Prescott line of perfection.

"I love to skate, but I haven't for a long time."

He tugged me forward. "I'll hold you up. Promise."

Somehow, I had a feeling he meant that on many different levels.

♫

I sat down, breathless and exhilarated. I had forgotten how much I loved to skate. Since it was early, the rink wasn't crowded, and Logan and I had skated for a long time. He chased me at times, twirling me often, then he let me speed skate around, enjoying the feel of the ice under my blades and the cold air on my face. They had the rink decorated with lights, and music was playing, making it inviting and fun.

Logan stopped in front of me with a flourish, sending shards of ice into the air, then sitting beside me. "You done?"

I had to laugh. "Out of shape. Sitting behind a desk isn't good for my stamina."

He moved close, waggling his eyebrows. "I get lots of exercise. Plenty of stamina. Maybe I'll show you if you ask nicely."

I tried not to giggle, but he was irresistible. His unique eyes sparkled under the lights, his smile was wide and bright, and he was sexy as hell with his taut frame and teasing.

He grinned, wrapping an arm around my waist and tugging me close. He bent low and brushed his mouth to mine, and I didn't try to resist. I didn't want to. I felt more alive than I had in a long time. His presence, his laughter, the light that seemed to spill from him intoxicated me. Nothing mattered in that moment. My father, my job, nothing. All that mattered was kissing this man. Being close to him.

I flung my arms around his neck, and he pulled me closer, burying his hands in my hair and slanting his mouth over mine, kissing me harder. Deeper. Our tongues tangled together, our breath mixing, heat replacing the cold air around us. He stroked my scalp gently, his caresses a direct contrast to the possessive edge of his kiss. He groaned low in his chest, pulled his mouth away, dragging his lips over my cheek, and burying his face in my neck.

"Jesus, you're addictive."

My heart was pounding, my head swimming from his mouth. The barely controlled passion. The desire I felt.

"Ditto," I whispered.

He eased back, slipping his fingers under my chin. He kissed my lips, then my nose, and finally rested his lips on my forehead, lingering and sweet.

"Thank you for today," he breathed. "For trusting me."

He stood and pulled me to my feet. "A few more turns on the ice. Then dinner."

"We've done nothing but eat today," I protested.

There'd been breakfast in the diner, midmorning coffee, lunch at one of the many trucks parked at the entrance to the park, hot chocolate, and he'd insisted on a snack before we went skating.

"Stamina." He winked. "The day isn't over, Lottie. You gotta keep up."

I let him pull me to my feet, and I followed him to the ice. With my hand tucked securely inside his, the flash of lights reflecting on the ice, and the warmth of his gaze, I didn't want the day to end.

Ever.

♫

I licked my fingers. "These are the best dumplings I've ever had."

He hummed in agreement, slathering hot sauce on his and popping one in his mouth. He ate the way he did everything—with gusto. "Stick with me, kid. I know all the best places."

The "best place" we were sitting in was a tiny hole-in-the-wall I would have walked past without a glance. But he had pulled me in, and although I was apprehensive at first, one sip of their jasmine tea and the hot and sour soup that appeared in front of me, and I no longer cared about the paper napkins or the mismatched tables and chairs. The food was delicious, and once again, Logan was well-known.

"Their son was in one of the classes I taught while his math teacher was off for a month. I could see he was struggling, so I did some one-on-one with him. His grades improved, and they insisted on meeting me. Kai's mom brought me food, and I was hooked," he elaborated.

That explained the hugs when we walked in and the effusive greetings from the kitchen.

"I'm hooked too," I agreed. "I love Chinese food."

A plate of noodles appeared along with a dish of spicy, crispy chicken. The aroma wafted up, and I groaned. "Oh my god."

Logan smirked. "I know. I eat here a lot."

I set down my chopsticks and took a sip of the fragrant tea. "Logan…"

He narrowed his eyes, warning me not to say it.

"Please. I want to treat you to dinner. You've paid all day."

"Nope. Today is my day, and I'm showing you my world. But I tell you what—next day we spend together is on you. I want to see your favorite haunts."

"And you'll let me pay?"

"I won't reach for my wallet once."

"Deal."

He lifted a piece of chicken off the platter, holding it over the table. "Now eat, my little Snow Queen."

I leaned forward and let him feed me. I closed my eyes at the burst of ginger, garlic, and chili. "So good."

He took one for himself. "I know."

I chewed in silence, wondering how I was going to top this day. We'd been so many places. Little spots I didn't know about. Small galleries where we looked at artwork. Parks I didn't know existed where we'd sat on benches, gazed at unknown statues, made a snowman, drank hot chocolate. We sat in the library, and Logan had quietly read his favorite passages from a book of poems. He showed me beautiful, ornate houses. Diners. Coffee shops. The Koi House where we were eating. Each place he knew intimately and shared with me—all pieces of his life.

What would I share besides my desk?

"Hey," he called, his low voice breaking the fog I was in. "Whatever we do, even if it's sitting in your place and you knit-ting, I'm good with it, Lottie. No pressure."

"Okay."

We ate in sporadic silence, but it wasn't uncomfortable. Logan fed me bites, insisted we needed more dumplings, and ordered iced lychee nuts and served them to me, dripping and sweet with that unmistakable tang that bit a little as you chewed. His student Kai dropped by the table and chatted to him, telling him about an advanced course he was taking next summer. He eyed me with curiosity and smirked widely as Logan introduced me.

"My girlfriend. Lottie."

Logan arched his eyebrow at me, daring me to contradict him.

Instead, I greeted Kai warmly and asked more about his studies. He was enthusiastic, filling me in on how bad he had been at math until Mr. Logan sat him down and unraveled the mystery no other teacher had been able to explain.

"Now, I'm in the advanced class. And I plan on being a teacher too."

"That's amazing."

We finished our dinner and headed back into the cold. Logan pulled a beanie out of his pocket and, before I could protest, tugged it over my hair, and then pulled out another one and yanked it over his shaggy hair. We walked a few blocks and I expected him to turn in the direction of my condo, but he veered to the right. I let him lead, secretly thrilled the day wasn't over.

We stopped in front of a small bar, and he scratched his head. "I sometimes play here on the weekends."

"Oh."

"My friend Mitch is playing tonight. He has a set at eight. Feel like listening to a bit of music?"

"I'd love that."

He huffed a long breath, the vapor hanging in the cold air. "Good, because I'm not ready to give you up yet."

He opened the door, bent low, and kissed my lips. "After you, my Snow Queen."

CHAPTER 7
LOTTIE

His friend Mitch was an amazing piano player and a crooner. His voice was clear and seductive, and he stroked the keys like a master. The bar was packed, and we were only able to say hello before his next set, but Logan promised him we would be back.

Snow swirled, the flakes settling on Logan's head and shoulders. The white flecks were bright on his hair, darkening the strands and glinting under the streetlamps.

I hugged his arm as we headed toward my condo, thinking about the past hours.

It had been a perfect day. The long walks, laughing over coffee, sharing plates in diners and cafes he liked to frequent. Learning about him and his life. Listening to his rich voice as he spoke, his hands expressive as they moved through the air, highlighting a statement or making a point. He was like the music he played, fluid and poignant.

He never ceased moving, even when sitting. His legs would move, his toes tapping out a silent rhythm. His fingers kept a beat to a song only he could hear.

And he touched me—constantly. Grazed my cheek with his knuckles, or mouth. Stroked my hand as we drank coffee. Entwined our fingers while we strolled, slipping both our hands into his large mitt. Tucked me into his side often. Touched my lips with his whenever he had a chance, leaving me wanting more.

I had never realized how much I missed physical contact until Logan.

Or maybe I had been missing *him* all my life.

He glanced down at me as we approached my building. "Did you have a good day, Lottie?"

I squeezed his arm in response. "Yes."

"Worth the trouble playing hooky today will cause? The extra work you have to catch up on?"

I had turned off my phone after the call from my father. A day with Logan was worth whatever I had to face when I returned on Monday.

"Yes."

He pressed a kiss to my head. "Good."

At the steps of my building, he faltered, looking unsure for the first time all day. He shoved his hands into his pockets, looking desolate.

"This is where I leave you."

The words were out before I could stop them. "Do you have to?"

His brow furrowed, and he looked past my shoulder, inhaling deeply. He let out the breath, the icy fog hanging around us. "I think I do."

"You don't want to come up and have coffee? Get warm before you go home?"

He pulled his hands from his pockets and stepped close. He cupped my cheeks, his hands a heated cradle against my cold skin. His thumbs rubbed soft circles on my face.

"I don't know if I can come upstairs with you. Coffee isn't what I want. I don't think it's what you want either."

He was right.

"If I come up...I don't know if I'll have the strength to leave you."

I covered his hands with mine. I could feel the gentle power in his hold, the slight tremor to his grip.

"Maybe you shouldn't, then."

He lowered his head, and I rose to meet him. Our lips melded. His were soft, cold, and pressing. I felt mine tremble. He wrapped one arm around my waist, pulling me closer. His tongue traced my bottom lip, and I opened for him. With a low groan, he shifted, yanking me tight. Our tongues met, sliding and skimming. Tasting and taking. His hold tightened, his leg sliding between mine, and I whimpered. He fisted my hair, holding my face close to his and devouring my mouth. Our breath mingled, our skin warming as he deepened the kiss. I had never felt possessed by another person, until Logan. He explored me, teased and licked. His taste exploded in my mouth, and I moaned, needing more of it. More of him. He dragged his lips over my cheek, sucking the lobe of my ear into his mouth.

"If I come upstairs, Lottie, I'll have you naked. I'll take you in so many ways, you'll never want another man again. I want to play you like my guitar. I want to pull the most beautiful notes from your body I've ever heard. My own private symphony. You'll sing just for me." He bit down on the skin below my ear, making me gasp. "I want to possess every inch of you. I have since the first time I saw you."

He crashed his mouth to mine again. I was lost in a vortex of feelings. Want, desire, and sheer need raged within me, need for this man overriding any common sense. I had never wanted anyone the way I wanted him.

"Come upstairs with me," I gasped, feeling his hand grip the back of my neck, holding me close.

His voice was so low, he was almost growling. "I need you to understand something. If I come upstairs, it changes everything. I don't do casual. I won't be the guy who sings to you in the subway. You won't be the girl I watch over anymore and leave alone. You'll be mine. Do you understand? *Mine.*"

"And you'll be mine."

He tugged me closer, his warm breath drifting over my cold skin. "I'm going to claim you. Every inch of you."

"Yes," I breathed out, my heart hammering in my chest at his words.

"I won't be able to walk away. I already know that. I'll fight to keep you."

"I need someone to fight for me."

His eyes softened, but his grip never lessened. "I know."

I slid my fingers over his face, tracing his lips. He pursed them, kissing the tips, capturing the end of one in his teeth and nipping at it playfully.

"I don't share," he stated emphatically.

"Neither do I."

"I won't be a fast fuck either. Someone you use to get back at Daddy and walk away. I'm not built that way." He dragged in a long breath. "I would rather walk away from you now than ever be that to you." He didn't move, waiting for my reaction.

"You're not," I assured him.

We stared at each other, need and desire wrapping us in our own bubble. His whiskey-colored eyes were passionate and fierce. They mesmerized me. His body was taut with tension, and I felt the evidence of his desire pressed between us. He was like a coiled cobra, ready to strike, yet I knew if I said no, he would back away and let me leave him. But that wasn't what I wanted.

"*You're not,*" I repeated. "I want you for me—just me. Because you're sexy, sweet, and because you're…*Logan.* No other reason."

"Ask me again, Lottie."

"Take me upstairs, Logan." I drew in a long breath. "Stay."

He wrapped his hand around mine.

"Yes."

♫

We didn't touch in the elevator. We stood on opposite sides as if we knew, once we touched, we wouldn't be able to stop. My breathing had picked up, and as the ancient elevator rose to the fourth floor, it became harder to fill my lungs. I lifted my eyes, meeting Logan's intense, passionate stare, the black of his pupils almost eclipsing the rich golden-brown I was used to seeing. He looked dangerous and sexy. I heard my gasp, and my breathing accelerated more, becoming short bursts of air.

Gripping the handrail as if he were holding himself back, Logan pushed his torso forward but still didn't touch me. "Breathe, Lottie. I promise I'll ease the ache soon. But I need you alone and the door locked."

I could only nod.

"Do you have your keys?"

"Yes." I managed to get out.

"Good." He exhaled hard. "I'm not going to be gentle. I'm not that kind of lover."

My breathing shuddered, and my body reacted to his words. My pussy clenched, aching like it never had before. I pressed my thighs together, needing relief.

Had I ever wanted anyone as much as I wanted this man?

The elevator door opened, and I went ahead of Logan. I could feel him behind me, hear his breathing. At my door, I fumbled, my shaking hand unable to insert the key into the lock. Logan edged closer, his large hand closing over mine.

"Let me."

Wordlessly, I allowed him to pull me back, his hard body crowding me against the door. The key turned, and Logan's arm wrapped around my waist, holding me close.

His hot breath drifted across my skin, his lips on my ear. "Last chance to change your mind. Once we go inside and shut the door, you're mine."

"I already am," I whispered, knowing deep inside it was true. I had been his since the night he had first sung to me.

He cursed low in his throat, picking me up and stepping into my condo as if I weighed nothing. Using his foot, he hooked the door fast, and it shut with a loud thud, the lock clicking into place. I heard my keys land somewhere on the floor, and he spun me in his arms, crashing his mouth to mine. He didn't hold back, his tongue plunging inside, licking and sucking. His long, talented fingers yanked on the buttons of my coat, pushing it off my shoulders, and jerked my scarf away from my throat, his mouth latching on to the tender skin and pulling it between his teeth. I fumbled with his zipper, shoving at his cold leather jacket. I wanted it off. When the coat hit the floor with a satisfying thud, it wasn't enough. I wanted his sweater gone. I needed to feel him. Gripping the bottom of his sweater, I tugged, cursing in frustration when he stepped back with a smirk.

"Tell me what you want, Lottie."

"You." I licked my lips. "I want you naked."

He laughed, the sound low and sexy in his chest. It was the laugh of a male satisfied with what he had just heard. It went along with the pleased smirk on his face.

"You want my sweater off?"

"Yes."

Reaching over his head, he tugged on the material, and slowly, his torso was revealed. Long, taut, with muscles in all the right places, he was gorgeous. His arms and abs were toned and hard. A musical score in black ink was etched into his skin, the start and finish curled around his biceps. I knew without seeing it was embedded across his back, waiting to be discovered, and I wanted to trace it with my tongue as he sang it for me. He trailed his hands down his chest, flicking at the nipple ring that glinted in the dim light from the small lamp I had left on. I wanted to take his nipple ring in my mouth and tug on it. Hear him groan my name. He stopped at the waistband of his jeans, slowly arching an eyebrow.

I knew I had spoken my thoughts out loud, but I didn't care. I wanted him to know what I was feeling. How much I wanted him.

"You'll get exactly what you want after I get what I want. Which, right now, is you naked."

I whimpered and, without a thought, tore my sweater over my head. It wasn't sexy and slow the way he removed his. It was desperate and fast. Needy. Exactly the way I was feeling.

He smirked, popping the button on his jeans and cupping his heavy erection in his hand. His boots were kicked off with a fast jerk of his feet, and he closed the small distance between us. Crouching down, he tugged off my boots, running his hands up my legs, over my thighs, and lingering on my ass. He straightened, pressing his nose to my skin, his lips trailing wet kisses up my body. His mouth covered my nipple through the lace of my bra, sucking on it, biting down, and teasing the hard nub. He spread his hand wide on my back, bending me slightly to repeat the action on my other nipple, then flicked the clasp open. My nipples were tight, hard peaks, wet from his mouth, aching for more. My clit throbbed with the need for his touch, my skin aching for more of his hands on it.

"So beautiful."

"Please, Logan."

In seconds, I was naked, lifted into his arms, with my legs wrapped around his waist and my back pressed against the wall. He plunged his tongue into my mouth, hard and twisting. He cupped my ass and slid his fingers between my legs, dragging them through the slickness. He circled my clit, pressing on the nub, and thrust two fingers inside. I cried out in pleasure at the sudden invasion, the sound muffled in his mouth. He began pumping his fingers and tongue in tandem, fucking my mouth and pussy at the same time. He strummed my clit, pressing, teasing, taking me to the edge and pulling away, ramping up my need, then leaving me aching for more, only to start all over again. I clawed at his back, yanked on his hair, desperate for him. I rubbed my aching breasts against the coarseness of his chest, the nipple ring cold and unyielding on my skin. I wanted to feel the bite of his metal on me. He ground his erection into me, the roughness of the denim an exquisite torture.

His movements picked up, becoming harder. Faster. Possessive and deeper. He played my body as if he knew it. As if he owned it. Every touch was sure, every strum of his fingers, perfect. Then he slid a finger into my ass, and I exploded. My body locked down, and I screamed, every nerve on fire. Waves of ecstasy crashed over me, and I rode his fingers until my body sagged in exhaustion.

He released my mouth, and I dropped my head to his shoulder with a quiet moan.

He moved, carrying me down the hall and tenderly laying me out on my bed. He leaned over, switching on the lamp, staring at me.

"That…" I whispered. "That was…"

He grinned and tossed some condoms onto the nightstand, then pushed his jeans and boxers over his hips, letting them fall to the floor. His erection sprang free, jutting out, thick and heavy, the head glossy and dripping with precome.

"The beginning," he promised. "Only the beginning."

He fisted his cock, pumping slowly, his eyes never leaving mine. "Is this what you want, Lottie? My cock?"

"Yes," I moaned, my voice pleading.

"I promised that you could have what you wanted, didn't I?" He smirked, wide and wicked. "I think you said you wanted my cock in that pretty mouth of yours." He ran his hand up his chest, tugging on his nipple ring. "You want to know how this feels on your tongue? How I'd react to your mouth on me, don't you?"

I whimpered, my fists clenching the sheets, desperate to touch. To feel. My mouth watered with the need to taste him.

"What else did I say?"

"That you got what you wanted first."

He crawled up the mattress, looming over me. He pushed me down into the bed as he lowered himself onto me. His mouth covered mine, and he kissed me hard. "It's a good thing we both want the same thing then, isn't it?"

He sat up, pulling me with him. "Use that pretty mouth, Lottie. Lick me. Touch me. Explore." He fell back, his erection hard and glistening. "I want to feel your mouth on me." He tugged my arm.

"Now."

I didn't need a second invitation. This time, it was me hovering over him, my legs straddling his hips. I kissed his full lips, driving my tongue between them, fucking his mouth the way he had done mine earlier. I dug my fingers into his silky hair, pulling hard on the long strands. He groaned as I kissed and licked my way down his neck, loving the slightly rough edge to his skin.

I explored the hard planes of his torso, feeling the way his muscles contracted under my fingers. He arched up with a hiss as I tongued his nipples, pulling his sexy nipple ring into my mouth and tugging. I lapped and teased my way down his stomach, discovering the ticklish spot by his bottom left rib, and smiling as he moaned in want when my mouth descended lower.

I eased down his body, crouching between his knees, his erection in my face. His eyes were wild with desire, his voice rough as he spoke.

"Do it, Lottie. Suck me. Suck my cock."

He shouted as I wrapped my lips around him, sucking the head deep into my mouth. I lapped and teased, engulfing him as much as I could. He was salty, musky, and delicious. I cupped his balls, stroked his shaft, paying extra attention to his sensitive spots with my tongue. He grunted and hummed his approval, murmuring my name, guiding my movements with his hands wrapped in my hair, and letting me know what he liked.

Which seemed to be everything.

Relaxing my throat, I took him in farther, sliding my hands under his ass, gripping him hard as I swallowed around him. He roared, thrusting up, cursing and pleading.

"*Jesus*, Lottie, I need...*fuck, baby*...I'm..."

He came. Hard. Long spurts of hot come jetted down my throat as he trembled and shouted. His body sagged, and I drew back slowly, letting his still hard erection slip from my lips.

He lay on my bed, an arm flung over his face, his chest moving rapidly as he gasped for breath. I kissed his thighs, crawled up his torso, and curled up on his chest. He wrapped his arm around me like a steel band, holding me tight.

For a moment, there was silence.

"Lottie?"

"Hmm?" I asked, tracing lazy circles on his chest.

"I don't want to know how you learned to do that, but just know you'll never do that to anyone but me—ever again."

"Is that a fact?"

In a second, I was under him, his eyes blazing down at me. "Yes."

"Okay."

He knelt back on his heels, running his hands up and down my legs, each time going higher. He nudged my knees apart. "It's my turn now. I get to taste you."

I shivered at the sound of his voice. He ran his lips over my thighs, swirling his tongue on my skin. I gasped as he bit down, marking the inside of one thigh, then the other, the sharp sting of his teeth turning me on even more. He sat back, admiring his handiwork, his fingers dancing over my skin.

His gaze met mine. "Everything between these two marks is mine now. I'm going to lick you. Eat you. Make you come all over my face. Then I'm going to fuck you."

I cried out as his mouth met my center. He teased my clit, flattening his tongue, licking me. He swirled and lapped. Long strokes of his tongue. Nuzzles of his full lips. Sucking. Biting. Kissing. Tasting. He added his fingers, touching a place so deep inside me I stiffened, coming in a rush so intense I screamed. He didn't stop, coming at me over and again, wringing another orgasm out of me before lifting his head, licking his lips, and smiling.

"So fucking sweet, baby. I'm going to feast on you every day."

He rose, grabbing a condom and rolling it on. Grasping my hips, he locked his eyes on mine, and he thrust forward, sinking inside, claiming me.

I cried out at the sheer mass of him. He began to move, my body adjusting to his size quickly. Long, firm strokes of his cock. Sharp thrusts that made me see stars. He kissed me passionately, the tang of me lingering on his tongue, mixing with the flavor that was all Logan. I was lost in the sensations he brought forth in me, my body a quivering mass of pleasure. Everything was magnified. The coarseness of his chest hair that rubbed my breasts. The touch of his metal on my skin. The feel of his back muscles under my fingers as he pushed and pulled. How he tasted. Smelled. Felt.

I was spinning out of control, every sense heightened, every nerve ending pulsating. Gripping his long, sexy hair with my hand, I flung my other arm out, my fingers seeking purchase. It was his hand sliding over mine, squeezing my fingers, that brought me back. The gentlest of touches amid the storm he created centered me, and with a cry, I came. Hard and wet, throbbing around him, his name echoing in the room. He stilled, his face buried in my neck, thrusting once, twice, three more times before he moaned my name, his cock swelling and pulsating as his orgasm tore through him.

There was no sound other than our breathing and the feel of his lips against my skin quietly uttering my name.

He rolled, tucking me close after discarding the condom.

Lifting my chin, he gazed into my eyes, the look on his face the tender expression I was used to seeing from him.

"You were amazing," he crooned, brushing the hair back from my face.

"We were amazing."

"Can I stay?"

"Yes."

"Tomorrow, I want to take you to my place."

"Why?"

He chuckled. "I want you in my bed. I want my sheets to smell like you. Like sex. Like us." He inhaled. "Just like this."

"Okay," I breathed out.

"Sleep now, Lottie. I've got you." He pressed a kiss to my head. "And when you wake up, we can start again."

His next words sent a thrill through my body.

"Because I'm not done with you. Not by a long shot."

CHAPTER 8
LOGAN

L ottie slept beside me, tight to my side. She had her arms wrapped around my waist, her head in my neck, her breaths soft puffs of warmth on my skin. If I shifted, she followed. I had the feeling she liked being held.

I liked holding her.

On occasion, simply for fun, I liked to play in the subway. I enjoyed watching people's reactions to hearing music. It changed the atmosphere, often lifting it and making the aura lighter in the station. I didn't play for money, but whatever cash was tossed in my case went right to the homeless shelter or the food bank. There had been a time when I'd needed that money and those places to survive, so I liked to give back.

Our meeting happened by chance. I was on my way home, a song stuck in my head, and I decided to stop and play it out. I only intended to play for a few moments, long enough to stop the swirl of notes in my head, but then it happened.

She appeared, and I looked at her, focusing all my attention in her direction. It wasn't the first time I had noticed her. The pretty girl with the rich chestnut hair who caught my eye. She always looked solemn and lost in her own world, and I was used to the almost blank expression on her face as she walked past me, never noticing anything around her, it seemed. She always intrigued me, and the urge to speak to her grew each time I would catch a glimpse of her.

But that night, she had looked as if the weight of the world were on her shoulders and the burden was too much for her to handle. She collapsed onto the bench, her legs seemingly unable to hold her upright for even one more step. Concerned, I turned in her direction, focusing my voice toward her. For a few moments, there was no reaction, then she lifted her gaze. I was close enough to see the unusual ice-blue of her irises, and the pain, sadness, and turmoil I saw in her eyes hit me like a punch in the gut.

I had never seen a gaze contain that much emotion. Pain I desperately wanted to ease. I watched as she listened, her body relaxing, her shoulders losing the tension that held them tight. The station faded as I sang to her—for her. I directed every word her way, strummed every note, and fed each line with my voice. She sat straighter, no longer broken, but slowly coming back to life.

I didn't stop. I sang and played for as long as she was there. When she stood and came closer, I was unable to take my eyes off her. She was beautiful. Small, delicate, and fragile. Yet stronger than an oak tree, standing tall and proud. The expression I thought was blank was nothing more than a mask. I saw the real woman tonight. She paused in front of me, meeting my eyes, her emotions hidden unless she allowed you to see.

And she showed me.

She tossed some money in the case, but it was her voice that made me falter.

"Thank you," she murmured and walked away.

I followed her with my eyes until she disappeared.

After that, because I had no choice, I returned every night to serenade her. Sometimes I waited, playing only when I saw her, but I was there. I couldn't explain the draw to this tiny woman. I couldn't possibly articulate to anyone the possessive need I had to surround her with my music. Somehow, I knew she needed it. *Needed me*. But I had no idea how to approach her, other than to offer her the gift of my music.

And she inspired me. I wrote daily, my once intermittent habit of jotting down phrases and notes now a seemingly endless stream since she had appeared in my life. I sang all the words and notes that would explode onto the pages to her.

Because they were all for her.

When she fell asleep on the subway bench, so exhausted and worn-down, I sat as close as I dared, watching over her. Desperate to touch and hold her, I held back and remained a silent sentinel for her. When she woke in a panic, I knew I could no longer simply be the voice and song in the background.

Her eyes told me she needed me to be more than that.

I needed to be more than that.

And now I was here, with her, in her home. She was in my arms, safe, content, and slumbering.

How, I wondered, would she feel in the morning when she woke? Would she regret the day? Regret giving herself to me?

I didn't know her whole story, nor did I know her parents. I did, however, know enough to recognize that they were blind when it came to her. That she needed to find a different path in life in order to be happy. It seemed to me, every decision Lottie had ever made was in some way to appease or please her parents. That way of life was slowly going to drain hers away—especially when they could not be appeased. It had something to do with her brother, that much I had surmised, but exactly what it was, I had yet to discover.

I looked down as she slept, her beautiful hair flowing down her back, her long eyelashes resting on the pale shadow of her skin. Even now, exhaustion was etched into her face. I thought of how beautiful she had been all day. How much she loved the cold and the snow. When flakes settled on her cheeks and hair, glistening in the light like small diamonds, she looked like a queen. A snow queen. My Snow Queen. The name suited her, and she smiled when I called her by it. I loved seeing her set aside the usual worries of a workday and simply be with me, enjoying the moment. The first time she had laughed, she looked startled, as if she weren't sure who had made that noise. As the day progressed, it slipped out more. She had eaten and enjoyed the food. Savoring it as if she were tasting for the first time. She was open and caring. Sweet and kind.

Lost and seeking.

I wanted to be what she was looking for. I wanted to show her she wasn't lost, and I was there for her. To show her there was more to life than a job that slowly killed you. Encourage her to do what she loved, not what she felt she had to do.

Whether she would listen or not, I wasn't sure. But I knew I had to try. I meant it when I told her I had lost my father to the rat race and I didn't want to lose her as well. She was already too important. She had been since the day I first played for her.

I only hoped I was important enough to have a chance to show her how different life could be.

Lottie was endearingly shy when she woke up later in the morning. I was awake long before her, relaxing with one arm tucked behind my head, the other holding her close as I watched her in the early morning light. She was wrapped around me, her head on my chest, her arm draped around my waist. As she woke, she stretched, her toes curling against my calf, her fingers tightening on my skin. I felt the flutter of her eyelashes as she blinked awake, slowly lifting her head, meeting my eyes. I smiled at her incredible beauty. Her hair was messy, her mouth still somewhat swollen from mine last night. There was a small mark at the base of her throat from my teeth. Faint traces of red from my beard along her collarbone. Her breasts pressed against my chest, her nipples little points on my skin.

And her lovely eyes. Luminous and soft. Peaceful. I had never seen them look so peaceful.

I cupped her cheek, drawing small circles on her skin. "Hey," I whispered. "Morning, my Snow Queen."

She yawned and turned her head to kiss my palm. "Hi."

For a moment, there was quiet, our eyes having a silent conversation. Mine beseeched her not to regret last night, not to regret me. Her gaze, already soft, became warmer, and she tightened her grip on me.

"I have never woken up with another person in my bed," she confessed.

"Ever?"

"No. My parents didn't allow the sleepover thing."

"Boyfriends?" I asked, even though I hated to think of her with anyone but me. "I wasn't your, ah, first."

"No." She looked away for a moment. "But there haven't been many. And the two relationships I had, neither were the 'stay with me' kind. I usually went to their place, and I never stayed over. I never felt that need to wake up with them."

I was surprised yet somehow pleased. "I'm honored."

She blushed slightly, making me grin. She lowered her eyes, then peeked up at me. "So, I assume since you're here, and um, naked, I have free access?"

I chuckled. She was already sliding her thigh along my leg, dragging herself against my erect cock. "I'm completely accessible to you, Lottie." I spread my arms wide. "Do with me what you will."

I groaned in pleasure as she sat up, throwing her leg over me and straddling me. The heat of her burned into my skin as she slid herself along my erection. "I want you like this," she murmured.

I cupped her full breasts, stroking the nipples with my thumbs. I reached for another condom and handed it to her. "Have me."

A long, slow groan left my lips as she slowly lowered herself on me. Inch by inch, I slipped into her heat, the sensation of being surrounded by her addictive and astonishing. When we were flush, she whimpered, fisting her hair with one hand as she braced herself on my chest with the other, her fingers spasming.

"Logan," she moaned. "You feel so good."

I flexed my hips, settling deeper, groaning with pleasure. "Ride me, Lottie."

She grasped my hands, guiding them to her hips. "Show me."

I set the pace, going slow, wanting to draw out her enjoyment. I loved watching as she lost herself in the motion and feel of our bodies moving together. Forgot about everything but us. How we felt together. The long buildup of ecstasy was so great, our bodies shook from the intensity. As her groans and pleas became louder, I sat up, encasing her fully. She buried her face in my neck, gasping at the intense connection. I gripped her hair, holding her close and speeding up, my thrusts hard and short. With a low cry, she convulsed, her fingernails digging into my skin as she orgasmed. I shouted as I spiraled, filling her until we both collapsed, our sweat-soaked skin pressed together.

I lifted her head, kissing her. She sighed, snuggling tight to my chest, and I held her close. She was starved for affection, and I wanted to give her as much as she needed. I felt an odd sense of pleasure knowing she hadn't stayed with anyone else, that she hadn't sought out this connection with anyone but me until now.

"Breakfast?" I asked.

She eased back, her eyes dancing. "Is that all you think about? Food?"

I winked. "I think I just proved I have something else on my mind a lot as well."

She laughed. "I suppose you did." She glanced down. "I think I need to shower."

"Good idea. Want me to come and wash your back?"

"Maybe I want to wash yours."

I waggled my eyebrows. "That, we can work with."

♫

LOTTIE

I eyed Logan over the rim of my coffee cup. He had insisted we go back to the diner he had taken me to the first night for breakfast.

"The Saturday morning breakfast special is awesome," he insisted.

"I can make breakfast."

He snorted. "Lottie, I looked in your fridge. It's barren."

"I do need to go grocery shopping," I admitted. "I've been busy."

He handed me my coat. "The diner it is."

We had walked hand in hand to the diner. It felt normal, as if I was supposed to hold his hand. He was affectionate and sweet this morning. Teasing and playful. I liked this side of Logan. I liked it very much.

He met my gaze as he drained his coffee and set down his cup to wait for a refill. He crooked his head to the side, studying me. "You, ah, have a little something on your neck."

I lifted my hand, brushing at my skin. "Did I get it?"

He leaned close over the table, touching my skin, then sat back, trying not to laugh. "Oh, I don't think it's gonna come off." He offered the waitress a wide grin as she filled his coffee, then looked back at me. "It should fade, though." He winked, looking mischievous.

I rolled my eyes. "How old are you? You gave me a hickey?"

His amusement grew. "Several, I think. Most of them are, ah, *private*."

I felt the heat build in my cheeks. I knew when most of those happened. When he'd followed me into the shower, he had insisted on washing me. I was, it seemed, *filthy*, given the inordinate amount of time he spent soaping up my body. Especially my breasts. Those were indecent. He had done a thorough inspection after rinsing me off—using his mouth.

Once he had me pressed against the tile, he had dropped to his knees, lifting one leg to his shoulder.

"I need to check this sweet little kitty," he growled. *"It needs a lot of attention."*

Now, sitting across from him, I was certain I had never been so clean. Or so thoroughly sexed-up. Logan was wicked with his tongue and his hands. Never mind what he did with his cock. I was quite surprised I was able to walk this morning.

Logan eyed me, his expression indulgent.

"I can't believe you can blush after what we did last night."

"I'm blushing because of what we did."

He reached across the table, linking our pinkies. "You liked it, Lottie?"

"Very much so." I cleared my throat, feeling nervous. Logan had way more experience than I did—that had become obvious last night.

"It was, without a doubt, the most erotic, passionate night of my life," he stated sincerely. "And just so you know, Lottie? I have never stayed the night with anyone else. Ever."

"Oh." I paused but had to ask. "Why not? Why me?"

He shrugged. "Sex has always been about release. It's never been emotional for me. Until yesterday. And why you, you ask? I have no idea, except you're different. What I feel about you is different." He rubbed his eyes. "I'm not particularly proud of my past. But before you jump to conclusions, I was always honest with my partners, and there haven't been as many as you're imagining in that pretty little head of yours. I'm not a manwhore."

"Oh," I repeated. "I didn't mean to make you think I thought you were."

"I'm simply being honest. I was monogamous with each of my partners—but they all ran their course."

"What happened?"

He frowned. "They moved on. Found relationships with a future."

"But I'm different?" I asked.

"Yes. You are my future."

Our breakfast arrived, and I looked at the overflowing plate, trying to take in his words.

"Eat," he encouraged. "We'll talk this through. We'll figure it out." He pushed my plate closer. "This is too heavy a discussion before I've had breakfast."

I picked up my fork, hesitating.

"Lottie," he murmured, waiting until I looked up to speak. "You are different. You're everything I've been waiting for and didn't know. I want you in my life. As long as you feel the same way, we're good."

"Okay."

"Eat your breakfast while it's hot." He scolded gently. "I need you strong." He winked lewdly. "I have lots of plans for you to burn it off."

His expression made me giggle, and I started to eat.

He tucked his shaggy hair behind his ear and picked up his fork.

"You need a trim."

He grimaced. "I know."

"Do you wear your hair down when you teach?"

"Usually not. I pull it back."

"The front of your hair is really blond."

He chewed and swallowed, then chuckled. "One of my

roommates has a girlfriend going through hairdressing school. She needed to practice, so I let her add what she called lowlights. But they bleached out in the sun over the summer. I'm trying to let them grow so I can cut them off. She wants to cut it now, but I've been waiting and haven't taken her up on the offer. I will eventually." He ate more off his plate, then eyed me warily. "You don't like it? The hair, I mean."

"Actually, I do. I think it's very sexy." I paused. "I think everything about you is very sexy."

He grinned so hard, his incredible eyes crinkled. "I like knowing that."

I patted my mouth with a napkin and took a sip of my coffee, unsure what else to say. He shook his head, still grinning. "You are adorable, Lottie Prescott. Totally adorable."

I rolled my eyes but didn't respond. I hadn't been adorable since I was six years old. But I kinda liked him thinking that way.

We stopped at a small grocer in the neighborhood. It was a rarity in Toronto. A family-run operation where you could still grab necessities, without having to go to a huge supermarket. They had a small produce and meat section as well, and I picked up a few things for my barren fridge. Logan carried the bag with one hand, his other holding mine. As we rounded the corner, I stopped, horrified at what I saw in front of my building down the block.

Logan frowned and followed my gaze. A large black town car was outside my building, running, the exhaust hanging in the air.

I stepped back, dragging Logan with me.

"Your parents?" he guessed.

"Oh my god," I groaned. "I had no idea they would show up this morning."

"I imagine your dad isn't happy about yesterday."

I grimaced in annoyance. "I took a day off. One day off. This is overboard, even for him."

"So, I assume this is where I leave you."

My gaze flew to him. He was regarding me sadly, but his eyes showed no hurt. Only understanding. "I, ah—"

He cut me off. "I'm not offended, Lottie. I'm not ready to meet your parents either. It would be better if I met them under different circumstances when I don't want to tell them what I think about how they treat their daughter."

I widened my eyes at his words. He traced a finger down my cheek. "I am sad to leave you, though. I wanted more time with you today."

"They won't stay long."

He huffed. "That seems even worse."

I remained silent. He bent low and kissed me. Gently, sweetly—his mouth tender, his lips ghosting over mine.

"My place is two blocks past yours. Number fifteen hundred. Unit twelve. Come find me when you're ready."

He hooked the grocery bag over my arm. "Now, go."

"What are you going to do?"

"Be a stranger." He paused. "I'll be waiting."

He kissed me again and rounded the corner, striding down the block alone. I waited a moment, then followed him, watching. He walked with his head up, his shoulders straight. His jeans hugged his ass, and his stride ate up the distance quickly. He didn't pause as he walked past the car, not sparing it a glance as he went by. My heart felt heavy as he moved farther away. My annoyance grew the closer I got to my building. I had checked my phone before we left for breakfast. There were no calls or messages. Not a word from my parents. Yet, here they were.

The back passenger door swung open, and my father stepped from the car, facing me as I drew close.

"Lottie," he said as I stopped in front of him.

"Dad. Or should I say, Charles? Is this business-related?"

He narrowed his eyes. "I don't really like your tone."

"I don't like you showing up unannounced."

He crossed his arms. "I wasn't aware it was illegal to come by your daughter's home to see her."

"Not illegal. But highly unusual on your part."

He had the grace to look uncomfortable. "Your mother wanted to check on you."

I lowered myself to peer into the car. "Hello, Mom."

"Lottie. You could be a little more welcoming."

"I'm surprised to see you here."

"That much is obvious." She paused, her foot swinging in agitation. "Are you going to invite us up for tea or not?"

I was suddenly grateful that Logan had tidied up this morning. I had teased him about being picky, but he had made sure the condo showed no signs of our frantic coupling when we first got in the door last night. He had straightened the pictures, picked up the buttons, and wiped the puddles from our boots and jackets. I had made the bed, although I doubted my parents would venture from the living room.

"Of course," I offered, knowing I had no choice. "Please come up."

My mother sat on the edge of the sofa, looking around my eclectic place with a barely concealed shudder. What I found homey and warm, she thought of as shabby and castoffs. I had to admit, many of my things came from thrift stores or were items I had bought on Facebook Marketplace, etc. I loved painting and fixing them to make them my own.

Her lips thinned as I handed her a cup of tea, in the only matched cup and saucer I had. I knew she preferred tea in a proper cup. I liked the mismatched ones better but didn't want to push it. I gave my dad a cup of coffee, knowing he disliked tea.

They were both uncomfortable in my space, aghast that I could choose to live here instead of one the sleek, modern places my father owed, or even better, in their building.

I would wither away and die under their scrutiny.

"Your father told me you didn't go into the office yesterday."

"No, I didn't."

"I don't recall you having womanly issues before," my mother stated primly.

I tried not to find her amusing. She was so stiff, if I poked her, she would explode. I recalled the mother I knew when I was much younger. She was warm and affectionate, always ready to talk or offer advice with a hug. Not this shell of a woman who barely made eye contact.

"It happens on occasion," I murmured. "I'm feeling better."

"You must be. You weren't here when we arrived."

"If you had called, I would have told you I was getting a few groceries. While I was out, I stopped and had breakfast."

"I hope you don't make a habit of disappearing."

My patience snapped. "It was one day, Dad. One day. Surely to god, even the great Charles Prescott has taken a day off?"

"I have never taken a sick day, no."

"What about when Josh died? You must have taken a day or two off to grieve? Or was the business more important than he was? I know it's more important than I am."

"Charlotte!" my father roared. "How dare you?"

"I dare because you showed up here this morning to check on me. Do you drop by every employee's home who calls in sick?"

He glared. "Only my daughter's."

"I had the flu last year on the weekend and stayed home. You never checked on me then. If I had known all it took for you to notice was me taking a day off, I would have done so sooner."

My father rose to his feet, the look on his face thunderous.

My mother cleared her throat. "I am shocked at your lack of respect, Charlotte."

I remained silent, my blood humming through my veins, and my heart beating fast.

"You are obviously still not feeling yourself, Charlotte. I am going to give you a pass this time."

"How magnanimous."

"We obviously aren't welcome here, so we will leave."

"My *parents* are always welcome. My boss is not. This is my private place."

His lips tightened again, and he held out his hand to my mother. "Josephine, we'll be leaving now."

"I will meet you in the car, Charles."

He walked to the door. "I hope you feel better, my *daughter*. If there is something you need, you have only to ask." He drew in a long breath. "I expect to see you, *Charlotte*, in the office on Monday. I also expect your fit of temper to be set aside by then." He walked out, closing the door firmly behind him.

"Was that necessary?" my mother asked, her voice frosty.

"Yes, actually, it was. It was Dad who drew the lines between daughter and employee, Mom. He crossed it by coming here to check on me—as Charles Prescott, not my dad."

"They're the same person."

"Not to me. They haven't been for years." My voice dropped. "Since Josh died, and you both became strangers."

She stood, her face pale. "You're being particularly spiteful today. Do you enjoy hurting us, Charlotte?"

"Why can't we talk about him? Talk about what happened?"

Tears glimmered in her eyes. "I cannot bear it," she stated. "You have no idea..." She trailed off.

My anger deflated. "I'm sorry, Mom. I didn't... I'm..." I was at a loss for words. I never challenged my parents. I toed the line because that was what I was supposed to do.

She tightened her lips. "I suggest you take the rest of the weekend and do some serious thinking. You've forgotten all you have to be grateful for. All we have done for you."

She swept past me, her shoulders back, her manner formal. "I will speak to you next week. I think we'll skip brunch tomorrow. Your attitude is tiresome and unbecoming."

Her words were meant to upset me. Except the thought of having the whole day, not to have to go to their place and pretend to be something I was not, filled me with relief.

The closing of the door brought me out of my thoughts. She hadn't said goodbye or waited for me to do so. I began to hurry toward the door but stopped. That was exactly what she wanted —for me to run after her and beg forgiveness. If I ever spoke back or flexed my so-called muscles, that was what happened— the game we played.

Only this time, I refused to participate. I wanted to talk about my brother. I needed to know why their love for me died when he did. Why nothing I did, no matter how hard I tried, made any difference. Why I wasn't worth the effort.

Why it still hurt me so much.

I sat down, letting my head fall into my hands.

I had a feeling I would never have my answers.

CHAPTER 9
LOGAN

I paced my apartment on a repetitive loop, unable to settle. I glanced at the heavy watch on my wrist for the hundredth time since leaving Lottie, the anxiety I was feeling bubbling and roiling in my stomach. I clawed my fingers through my hair, my nerves feeling as if they were on the outside of my body.

Why the hell hadn't Lottie shown up yet?

I had hung around the corner for about twenty minutes after she went inside with her parents. I had watched their exchange from a distance, noting the stiffness of their interaction. There were no hugs or even touching. Her father stood, his hands at his sides as he spoke, the only movement the shaking of his head. When Lottie's mother stepped from the car, I could see the resemblance to her daughter in her coloring and stature. But, like her husband, she was stiff, offering no kiss on the cheek or motherly hug. They followed Lottie upstairs, the car remaining parked outside.

Less than fifteen minutes later, Lottie's father stormed down the steps, almost wrenching the handle off as he flung himself inside the car, the loud slam of the door echoing on the quiet street. Her mother followed shortly after, waiting until the driver opened the door for her before joining her husband. Her movements were less strident, but her posture was rigid and angry. They had obviously exchanged words with Lottie. I waited a few moments to see if Lottie would appear, then decided she was probably collecting herself if they had, indeed, had an argument.

I was loath to leave. I had no idea why I was acting this way toward Lottie. The need to be close and protect her was paramount. I had never felt this way toward another person in my life. I wanted to go back to her place, sweep her into my arms and hold her, but I realized it would be too much. She had said she would come to me, and I had to let her do so in her own time.

Reluctantly, I headed home and waited for her to appear.

Now four hours later, I was still waiting. I cursed myself when I realized I had never taken her cell number, so I couldn't call her. I perched on the arm of the sofa, eyeing my guitar. Not even it held its usual draw. The thoughts in my mind were too chaotic and disjointed for music—unless it was an angry, violent tune. Doubts were piling up in my head.

What if Lottie realized yesterday was a mistake? What if she decided she didn't want to see me again? Could she have come to the realization we were different people, wanting different things from life and that I was too much to take on?

I tugged on my hair with a low, frustrated groan. Was she avoiding me? Had she purposely not given me her number? I tried to recall if I had asked for it, but nothing came to mind. We had both been caught up in the day and each other, and until she saw her parents' car, our parting hadn't been planned.

We had simply forgotten—I was certain of it.

So why wasn't she here?

Another thought niggled at my brain. Maybe her parents upset her so much she wanted to be alone. There were times I needed solitude, and I shut myself in my room with only my guitar for company. Since she didn't have my number either, she had no way of letting me know.

That had to be it.

Except, I couldn't settle until I knew. With a low curse, I grabbed my jacket and yanked it on, shoving my feet into my boots. I slid my phone into my pocket, and the last thing I picked up were the mitts Lottie had knit and given me yesterday.

I had to see her.

♫

I was lucky when I got to Lottie's building. Another resident was leaving, and I grabbed the door and headed inside. I hurried up the stairs to her floor, too impatient to wait for the old elevator. I had spied lights on in her place as I approached the building, so I assumed she was inside.

I hoped she wouldn't be angry with me for coming over, but I couldn't wait anymore.

I knocked on her door, stepping back in surprise when she flung it open. She was wearing a soiled apron, and there was a streak of flour on her flushed cheek. Her hair was gathered in a chaotic bun on the top of her head, tendrils escaping all around her face and neck. Her eyes widened in shock when she saw me, then in a move I hadn't expected, she launched herself at me, wrapping her arms around my waist and burrowing into my chest.

"Logan," she breathed out.

I embraced her, feeling the tension drain from my body at the way she relaxed into me. I had made the right decision coming over.

"Lottie," I murmured. "I was worried."

She looked up with a frown. "I did it again, didn't I?"

"Did what?"

"Lost track of time."

"I've been waiting four hours."

She pulled away and glanced behind her. "Well, that explains my productivity." She stepped back into her hall. "You had better come in."

I followed her inside, hanging up my coat and walking into the kitchen. It smelled like heaven, the air laden with the scent of sugar and spice, heavy with cinnamon and the richness of butter.

There were piles of cookies. All sorts on plates and cooling trays. Some filled, some iced, one large platter so beautifully decorated they needed to be displayed as art, not eaten. On a turntable was a cake Lottie was working on, beautifully iced with intricate details, roses and piping that she was in the middle of creating.

"What on earth?" I asked.

She sighed. "When I get upset, I bake."

"Your parents upset you this much?"

"Yes."

I picked up a cookie—one of the iced, beautiful creations and met her gaze. "These are stunning."

"Try it."

I frowned, and she shook her head. "I make them to be eaten, Logan. I enjoy the decoration part."

Not needing any other encouragement, I bit down. The buttery cookie was dense and rich, the icing sweet and smooth on my tongue. "Amazing," I mumbled.

"I always wanted to be a pastry chef. I love to bake."

"How do you eat all this and stay so tiny?" I asked.

Lottie picked up her icing bag, beginning more loops and swirls on the cake. "I give to my neighbors and take stuff to the office. If I have a bad day and make a huge batch of simple cookies like gingersnaps or chocolate chip ones, I take them to the homeless shelter." She wrinkled her nose. "They prefer those to the fancy ones—easier to hand out for people to enjoy."

I studied her work. "You should follow your dream."

Her sigh was low and long. "Maybe one day."

I watched her in silence for a while, simply relieved at being in the same room as her. She was confident and fast, the cake becoming more beautiful by the moment. She busied herself with another pastry bag, and a few moments later, she slipped small roses on top of the cake. I watched in awe at the ease with which she created the pretty cake.

"So, you do this often?" I asked quietly.

"I suppose so. At least once a week and most weekends," she admitted.

I hated knowing how unhappy her job made her. That she struggled that much.

"You forget to buy food for yourself..." I began, only for her to finish my sentence.

"...but my cupboards are always full of baking supplies. I know."

"You need to take better care of you," I surmised.

She met my concerned gaze with her lovely eyes and indicated the large amount of baking all around her. "This feeds my soul."

She slid another small group of flowers onto the top of the cake and nodded as if pleased. It looked like a garden—almost too pretty to eat. Yet, I wanted a piece of the cake she had baked. I wanted to sample her creation. To savor something that brought her joy and maintained her sanity. I wanted a piece of her soul.

"If this—" I indicated the various treats "—makes you happy, why don't you do it full time?"

"Because I have to fulfill my obligation."

"To your parents?" I guessed.

The happy light in her eyes died as she frowned. "Yes."

"Are you done here?"

"For now."

I extracted the icing bag from her hands. "We need to talk."

"I don't know if I can talk about this."

I slid my arms around her waist, pulling her close. The way she immediately relaxed into me made me happy. I liked knowing how much she needed to be held by me.

"I will listen to whatever you can say. But I need to understand, Lottie."

She was silent for a moment, then tilted back her head. "No one ever asks."

"I'm not no one. Don't you get that? Don't you feel this connection between us?"

"Yes." Her eyes held my gaze. "It's…intense."

I tightened my arms. "It is. It is also unbreakable. I'm here for you. So, today, tomorrow, next week, whenever you want to talk, I'm here."

"Okay."

I brushed my lips to hers. "Can I have another cookie?"

"You liked it?"

"Next to you, it was the most delicious thing I've ever eaten."

Her cheeks flushed and she glanced away. I slipped my finger under her chin and met her eyes. "You and your cookies are amazing. So, yes, I want another one, or six. And I want to talk. Then I want to spend the rest of the day with you. Naked."

"Oh," she breathed. "Naked together?"

I chuckled. "It would be a little awkward if I was the only one naked." I bent low and kissed the soft spot behind her ear as I stroked along her forearms with my thumbs. "Besides, what I want to do with you? You need to be naked too."

She shivered, goose bumps rising on her skin. Tugging on the apron, she stepped back and pulled it away, tossing it to the counter. "Okay, then."

♫

LOTTIE

We sat in the living room. I made coffee and brought in a plate of cookies. I wanted the cake to set up before I sliced into it. It was always tastier after it cooled completely and the flavors melded. Logan picked up another cookie, biting and chewing, his eyes drifting shut in appreciation. He hummed in pleasure.

"All of these are incredible."

"Good."

He held out the cookie he was eating, pressing it to my mouth. "Bite," he instructed. I hesitated and he frowned.

"Surely, you at least eat your own cookies, Lottie. You don't give them all away?"

I opened my mouth and let him feed me. The spicy ginger and cinnamon flavor enhanced with the vanilla and lemon glaze burst in my mouth. It was one of my favorites, and this was a particularly good batch.

"I do," I mumbled around my mouthful. "I eat a few of them."

He tossed the rest of the cookie into his mouth, chewing. "Not enough."

His concern touched me. He seemed to notice everything about me—and after the past many years of feeling invisible, it was an odd sensation. Yet, one I thought I quite liked.

He took my hand, stroking the skin. "When you didn't show up at my place after your parents left so quickly, I thought perhaps you had changed your mind about me," he confessed.

"How did you know they left quickly?"

Two streaks of crimson slashed over his high cheekbones. "I, ah, waited on the corner. In case…" He trailed off.

"In case?" I prompted.

"In case you were upset and needed me. If you came out right away, I wanted to be there for you. But you didn't, so I went home and waited." He met my eyes. "I don't have your number, so I couldn't call you. I got tired of waiting and worrying, so I came to find you."

I moved closer and cupped his cheek. He covered my hand with his, pressing my palm into his skin. His beard was heavier than this morning, soft and bristly all at the same time under my touch. "I'm sorry I worried you. I had words with my parents, and when they left, I had to do something, so I started to bake. I only meant to make one batch of cookies, but I got caught up… I lost track of time."

"I need your phone number," he rasped, his voice low and demanding.

"You can have it," I assured him.

"Why did you and your parents argue?"

"They didn't like my attitude."

He sat back, folding one leg under the other and facing me. "What attitude?"

"I was angry they came to check on me. Not as my father, but as my boss."

"Why do you work somewhere you hate, Lottie? Why do you do this?"

I looked down at our entwined fingers, marveling at the difference. Logan's hands were large. Dark from the sun, calloused from the guitar and hard work. He had a scar that went from side to side, the line slightly paler than the rest of his skin. His fingers were long and thick. Strong. But capable of such tenderness. My hand looked minuscule in his, pale and fragile. My fingers barely reached his knuckles, while his enclosed the back of my hand with ease. I took in a long breath and told him about Josh. How much I loved him and how he made me laugh. The way he took care of me.

"He was a great big brother. Protective and overbearing at times, but always caring. Funny too—he teased me all the time and called me Squirt. We would watch movies, and he would make me popcorn if our parents went out. He'd let me stay up past my bedtime. We'd take long walks in the woods behind our parents' house, and he'd teach me about birds and the different trees. He was four years older than me, but he never treated me like a kid."

Logan hummed but didn't interrupt.

"He knew how much I loved the winter. We'd make snowmen and forts and have snowball fights. Even though he was older than me, he was my best friend." I swallowed the lump in my throat. "Then he became ill."

"Leukemia?" he asked.

"Yes. A very aggressive type. They tried everything." I was quiet for a moment, remembering the dark days that followed Josh's diagnosis.

"He died just before his seventeenth birthday. I was their last hope, Logan," I whispered. "I was a match."

"But it didn't work," he stated.

"No."

"But you tried. You went through the procedure, and you tried to save your brother."

"Yes."

"So how on earth can you feel anything close to guilt? You didn't fail, Lottie. Your body didn't fail. Your brother was too sick, and it didn't work. It wasn't your fault." He stared at me, aghast. "Did your parents tell you it was your fault?"

"Not in so many words. But all their hopes were pinned on me."

"They were pinned on the results, Lottie. Not you. You didn't fail. You gave of yourself unselfishly, trying to help him."

"He died."

"Again, not your fault. Blame the disease, not yourself."

"Maybe if I'd been stronger, older…"

He looked furious. "Again, none of your doing. You were a kid. Just a kid. There is no blame here on your part." He ran a hand through his hair, looking vexed. "Is that why you work for your father? To make up for your brother's death?"

I blinked. He saw it right away. He knew exactly what I was trying to do. I cleared my throat. "I wanted to try to help my father. To be what he lost the day Josh died."

"You can't do that, Lottie. Trade your life for his." He wrapped his hands around my biceps, shaking me a little. "You are killing yourself for nothing. It won't bring him back." His voice softened. "It won't make them better."

"I just want them to love me."

The words hung in the air.

"Oh, baby," he murmured. "You can never make someone love you. Giving them your life on a platter isn't right." He frowned. "I think the day your brother died, your parents lost themselves to grief—and somehow never found their way out of it. But I don't think it means they don't love you—they've just forgotten how to show it."

"For the first while after he died, they smothered me, yet still ignored me. They hired people to look after me. Report every cough or scrape of my knee. Fussed too much, but still kept away. But as I got older, the caregivers went away, and they became even colder and more removed. It was as if they resented me yet feared losing me. I was lost and confused so much of the time. The closest I got to a real, honest exchange was the day I showed my father I was taking the same courses Josh planned to take before he got sick," I explained, feeling wistful. "He actually looked pleased and said he could hardly wait until I joined the firm. I was sure if I followed through and became everything he wanted for Josh, he would love me again."

"I'm sure he never stopped. Either of them. They just don't know how to get you back."

I met his empathetic gaze.

"They don't understand me."

"They don't know you," he replied. "They only know the

person you think they want to see. And by hiding, you're killing yourself, Lottie. Slowly but surely. The same way my dad did."

I had no response to that.

"You need to do something you love." He indicated the plate of cookies. "Bake. Create."

"I can't simply walk away."

"You can't, or you won't?"

I rubbed a weary hand over my face. "I don't want to argue with you, Logan. I've argued enough today."

His face softened. "I know. I'm sorry. And I'm repeating myself, but I will say this again. You don't owe your father your life, Lottie. You owe it to yourself to be happy. You only get one chance at this." He took my hand. "I only know what you told me about Josh, but I think he would want that for you too. I think he would hate that you're trapped in a job you dislike." He sucked in a long breath. "He would hate that you think you failed. Because you didn't. You were brave and strong. The disease won."

My breath caught.

He stroked my cheek. "It's awful and tragic, but it happens sometimes. The disease can be too big to fight. And that time, it won." He grimaced. "What I hate is that it robbed you of your parents too. Of a normal childhood."

"They refused to talk about him—they still do. I missed him so much, and I had no one to talk to about him." My voice cracked.

"You have me now, Lottie. I'll listen. You can tell me all about him. As much as you want."

And suddenly, I was in his arms. He held me tight as I cried, somehow pushing together the little fragmented bits of my heart and fusing them together. I felt safe in his embrace. As if I had found my home.

I knew that was ridiculous. I barely knew him.

And yet—it was true.

CHAPTER 10
LOTTIE

Logan lifted me into his arms and carried me down the hall to my bed. He tugged off my shirt and jeans, then tucked me under the blankets, his hands gentle, his touch soothing. He disrobed and slid in behind me, pulling me to his chest. His heat soaked into my skin, the warmth of him spreading deliciously along my body, easing the tension. He wrapped his arm around me, holding me tight.

"I'm right here, Lottie," he murmured.

I sighed, my body relaxing into his embrace, feeling emotionally exhausted. "Thank you."

"Sleep, baby."

"I don't want to."

"Tell me what you do want."

"I don't want to think." I ran my hand over his forearm, feeling shy. "Would you-would you sing to me?"

He pressed his lips to my head. "Anytime."

He began to hum, the sound rumbling in his chest. I shut my eyes as he started to sing, his deep, sexy tenor a low rasp in my ear. He sang a soft lullaby, the words soothing. He kept time with his fingers, a slow, steady rhythm he tapped out on my skin. My weariness hit me and I drifted, yet even in my light slumber, I could hear his voice. As always, it filled me with peace, his rich tone easing my tension and filling me up.

When he paused, I lifted my head, turning to meet his beautiful, unusual, whiskey-colored eyes. "Thank you," I said again.

"I will always sing for you, my Snow Queen." He slid his fingers under my chin and kissed me. His lips were gentle on mine, his tongue sliding sensuously along my bottom lip. I opened for him, and he deepened the kiss, still gentle and sweet, yet filled with passion.

I shifted, turning into him, and he gathered me close, his lips never ceasing their possession. He cupped my ass, bringing me tight to him, and I felt his erection growing between us. I slipped my hand down, cupping him, and he groaned low and rough. My nipples hardened against his chest, the coarse hair causing a delicious friction on my skin. His nipple ring was warm and stroked against me smoothly. He dragged his mouth across my cheek to my ear. "I want you."

"Yes," I replied. "I need you, Logan. Take it away. Take it all away."

His answer was to roll me onto my back and hover over me. He loomed above me, his expression intense yet tender. "Slowly this time, Lottie. I want you to feel how much you mean to me."

Then his lips were back on mine, tasting and caressing. He touched me everywhere, his hands stroking and light. He kissed his way up and down my body, not leaving any spot undiscovered by his mouth. My underwear disappeared in one fast flick of his wrist, the lace and silk torn from me easily. I had no idea how he took his off, but they were gone, and as he pinned me down with his body, the evidence of his desire was hot and heavy on my skin. I pleaded and begged as he dragged his lips across my collarbone, his tongue swirling around the mark he had left yesterday.

"I branded you as mine, Lottie," he whispered. "Are you?"

"Yes," I gasped. "Yours."

I felt his smile on my skin. "That's right. Mine."

He grabbed a condom and settled between my thighs. Our eyes locked as he sank into me, slowly easing inside, inch by inch, until we were flush. "You feel so good," he groaned. "I love how wet you are for me."

"Only you," I whimpered, feeling the fullness from his cock inside me.

He braced himself on one elbow and began to move. Slow, languid strokes that made me sigh in pleasure. He hooked one leg over his shoulder, changing the position, and withdrew to the tip, then sank back in, deeper than ever. My breath caught at the new angle. He was hitting me in a place I had never felt until now, and I began to quiver with the rush of sensation it caused. Tremors raced through me, and I grasped at his shoulders, my nails sinking into his skin. He gripped my leg, grunting as he moved.

"Yes, Lottie. *Like that.* Move with me. *Fuck…yes.*"

My body took on a mind of its own, matching his rhythm. The room was filled with the sounds we created. Our skin sliding together, the low moans and grunts that fell from Logan's lips. The pleas and whispers from mine. The bed creaked as we moved, the headboard a low, steady beat of our movements. My hand slipped off his neck, curling around his bulging bicep, as my other found purchase in my sheets, twisting and gripping the soft material. Logan kept one hand on my leg and anchored himself to the headboard. Our gazes remained locked, his hooded and dark, mine wide and wanting. My orgasm hit me suddenly, sharp and wild, and I cried out, arching and shuddering around him. He cursed and kept moving, shaking his head.

"You're going to give me another one," he growled, grabbing my other leg and flinging it over his shoulder as he thrust harder.

I thrashed my head side to side, the angle so intense, I clutched at him. "No, Logan, I can't... You need—"

He cut me off. "You can, Lottie. For me."

He rose up on his knees and began to plunge harder. His hair fell in his face, the sweat trickling down his cheek. The coil inside me tightened again, and I cried out, my body beginning to spasm and grip him. He closed his eyes, flung back his head, and came in a long, low growl of curses and muttered words. I lost myself to him and his demands, crashing into the pleasure as it gripped me, taking everything I had and giving it to him.

To Logan.

We stilled, the only sounds in the room our heavy breathing. Logan's head hung down, his chest pumping fast. His hair covered his face, the long strands hiding him from me. Playfully, I teased his ear with my toe, and he peeked up, a knowing smirk on his face.

"How was that for taking it away?"

"If I were a teacher, I'd give you a gold star."

He slipped my legs off his shoulder, rubbing them briskly. He slid from me, disposing of the condom and returning to gather me in his arms. He nuzzled my forehead.

"As a teacher, I'm giving you an A++, and trust me, that never happens."

I smiled and ran my hands through his hair. Quiet settled around us.

"Tell me about your life, Logan."

LOGAN

I knew what she wanted. She'd had enough heavy from her parents, and she didn't want to think about it anymore today. I had been pleased to sing to her, feeling her relax in my arms as my voice drifted over her. I had also been more than happy to make love to her, always ready for her in that sense. She had shared a lot of her life with me, and now she wanted to know about mine. But not the past. What my life contained now.

I tucked an arm behind my head, holding her close with the other one as she snuggled into my side.

"Do you like being a teacher?" she asked.

"Yeah, I do."

"But it's not full time." I heard the worry in her voice.

"No, but I get by fine for now. I'm in good with a couple of the secretaries, and they steer as much time my way as possible. In fact, starting next term, I have a mat leave I'll be covering. I'm hoping it leads to full time since it's the teacher's fourth kid and she's been talking about not coming back."

"Oh," she responded. "That would be good."

"It would be," I agreed. "It's a great school—it's one of the ones I showed you yesterday. I can walk to and from it easily, and the kids are pretty good. It's a decent area, and I like the other teachers."

"What grade do you teach?"

"Six and seven, mostly. I like that age. I still have a chance to make a difference before they're too old not to care anymore—especially the boys. Once they hit high school, it's often too late. But I love teaching. Even if I reach one kid, it makes a difference."

"Like Kai?"

"Exactly. He struggled so hard, and he is such a bright kid. Once I figured out where his block was and helped him get past it, he soared."

"So, ah, how do you make do when you don't get much teaching?" she asked, her fingers playing on my chest in nervous little circles.

Chuckling, I lifted her hand to my mouth and kissed it. "Relax, Lottie. We're just talking."

"I know. I don't want to upset you."

"Like the other night?" I asked with a frown. "I shouldn't have gotten so angry. I don't want you to see me as some sort of bum needing a handout."

"I don't."

I arched my eyebrow and gazed down at her. She lowered her eyes. "Not anymore."

I had to chuckle.

"I didn't think you were a bum, but I worried about you. If you had enough to eat, a place to stay, if you were safe at night… and you would never let me leave you money!" she grumped and smacked my chest for good measure.

I tried not to chuckle at her anger. It was endearing that she would worry about me so much.

"When I'm not teaching, I tutor, I give music lessons, I tend bar, and yes, I sing. But in a club, Lottie. Not on the street for money—at least, not anymore. I kept playing in the subway for you. All the money people threw in went to the food bank or the homeless shelter." I huffed out a long breath.

"You need to understand something." I waited until she looked up and met my eyes. "I am never going to climb the corporate ladder. I will never wear a suit and tie and carry a briefcase. There won't be a huge paycheck and fancy dinners. I live modestly. I like simple things. If that frightens you—" I swallowed "—I guess we need to stop now. I have no plans on changing my life. But I want you in it, if you want to be. If you can accept me for who I am."

"I don't want you to change, Logan. I want to know about your life." She frowned. "Can you accept *my* life? The fact that I am, as you say, part of a world you detest?"

"I don't like what your world is doing to you, Lottie."

She lifted one shoulder. "I know."

"I would like to help you discover another one, but I know you have to want that too." I tucked her closer. "I'll do whatever you need me to do to help you. Even if it's just to sing to you and calm you. But I won't ever stop hoping you find a different path —one that makes you happy."

She was quiet for a moment. "You have roommates?"

I let her drop the subject—for now.

"Yes, I have two. Rex, who is an IT guy at a bank. His girl-friend, Gretchen, is the one studying to become a hairdresser. And Trevor is our other roomie. He's a personal trainer and owns his own gym—he lets me use it for nothing, which is great. Our apartment is too small for any equipment except a set of dumbbells in my room."

"Does he have a girlfriend?" she asked.

I snorted. "Too many to count. Let's just say, Trev rarely sleeps at home."

"Oh."

I chuckled. "We've been roomies since university. We get along well and respect one another's boundaries. I think Rex will be gone soon enough—he's pretty smitten with Gretch. Trev, I have no idea."

"What about you?"

I slid my hand down her back, cupping her firm ass in my hand. "What about me, Lottie? You asking my future plans?"

She peered up at me. "If they left, would you stay there or move?"

"Probably move or find other roommates. The place would be too big for me."

She nodded, and I saw the concern in her eyes.

"Stop worrying about my finances, Lottie. I'm careful with my money, and I'm quite solvent. I certainly don't pull in the salary I expect you do, but I'm fine. I promise not to embarrass you."

She sat up, her eyes blazing. "I never said you embarrassed me. I never thought like that at all. Don't put words in my mouth, Montgomery Logan!"

I tried not to grin at her tone or the way she used my full name. She was beautiful in her indignation, her color high and her eyes flashing at me.

"I'm sorry," I said automatically. "I simply meant you don't have to worry. I'm fine." I studied her, waiting until I saw the fire disappear from her gaze. I tucked a strand of hair behind her ear. "I was homeless and broke once, Lottie. Alone. Not long after my father died, I had nothing, and I lived on the streets when foster care didn't work."

Her eyes widened. "How did you survive?"

I sighed, hating to discuss that period of my life. "I played the guitar for money. I begged. I took odd jobs for cash. I finally got into a program that helped me. I went to school and finished my education. Got a scholarship and went to university. Met Rex and Trev. I know what it's like to have nothing."

She stroked my hand with the scar, a question in her eyes. "Yes," I replied to her unspoken words. "I got that on the streets. A few other scars too. It's a dangerous place to be. I never plan on being there again."

"I hate that happened to you," she whispered, lifting my hand and kissing the scar.

"I hate what you went through," I replied, pressing my hand to her cheek. "Money doesn't guarantee happiness, Lottie. How you live your life, the people in it, that is what makes the world good."

"I think Josh would have liked you."

"I think I would have liked him." I tugged her back to my chest. "So relax, Snow Queen. I'm good. I'm a simple guy, but as long as you're okay with that, we'll figure things out."

"I like things simple too, Logan. It's one of the biggest problems between my parents and me. They live a different lifestyle than I do, and they want me to live it too. But I'm not comfortable in their world."

I stroked her hair, not speaking. I wasn't sure she'd be

comfortable in mine either. I wanted her to be, more than I thought possible, but only time would tell. Finally, I spoke.

"You need to find what makes you happy. Live for yourself. Not for Josh or your parents. Not even for me. For Lottie. Once you accomplish that, your own world comes into focus."

She looked up. "Will you be a part of that world, Logan?"

I slid down and pulled her up to my mouth. "I want to be the center of it, Lottie Prescott. I want to be your nucleus. I want to be the one who makes you happy."

There was no more talk. I kissed her until she was lost. Until I was lost.

Until the world outside these walls ceased to exist.

CHAPTER 11
LOTTIE

We spent the rest of the day in bed, eating cookies, and watching mindless TV. Logan lay on the sofa with me draped over his chest—my own living, breathing heating pad. I discovered he liked my hair down. He ran his hands through it constantly, often rubbing the ends between his fingers. He would slide his large hand under my hair and run it up and down my back in a soothing manner, then go back to playing with my hair. Every time I tried to move, he grunted low in his throat.

"Stay," he would order. "I like you there."

So I did. I liked it there too.

He made scrambled eggs and bacon as I toasted bagels, and we ate standing up in the kitchen, sharing the plate and feeding each other bites of the bagels. I was shocked to discover he'd made a dozen eggs and consumed most of them, but I realized I shouldn't be. He had a voracious appetite for food, coffee, sex—any and all of it. I had a feeling he felt the same way when it came to life. He grabbed it and lived it.

His words earlier gave me a lot to think about. I thought he would bring it up again, but he didn't. We fell asleep on the sofa, and I woke up to him carrying me to bed and sliding in beside me, a gentle kiss to my head and his low voice rumbling in my ear, the last thing I heard until I woke up in the morning.

Sunday, we got up and showered. Once again, he got me filthy, then scrubbed me clean, leaving me boneless with pleasure and barely able to return the favor. He kissed me and promised *I could make it up to him later.*

We went for breakfast, and he wolfed down a stack of pancakes as well as eggs and hash browns and his usual gallon of coffee.

"Doesn't the caffeine affect you?" I asked after he emptied the carafe on the table.

"Nope. I'm sure one day it will catch up with me. But for now, I'm good."

I pretended to go to the washroom, instead paying the bill. When I got back to the table, he glared at me, and I narrowed my eyes in return.

"Suck it up, buttercup. I watch my finances too, you know. I can afford to treat my boyfriend to breakfast."

He threw his head back in laughter and pulled me to his lap, kissing me.

"I'll let you get away with it this time," he teased. "Only because you called me your boyfriend."

"Aren't you?"

He kissed me again. "Damn right, I am. I liked hearing you say it."

We walked to his apartment building, hand in hand. He still wore the mitts I gave him, the flap folded back so his fingers were out and wrapped around mine. The sun was shining, glinting off the snow, and despite the cold, it was a glorious day. I couldn't recall the last time I had felt so content. Normally, since it was Sunday, I had brunch with my parents, then after heading home, I would already be worried about Monday and what it would bring. But right now, that felt very far away, and I was happy to be with Logan.

"This is it." He indicated the brick building with a wave of his hand. It was similar to mine. Older, with faded red brick and large windows that faced the street. "We're on the top floor."

"Same as me."

"Yep. But I don't have the luxury of an elevator," he teased.

We headed inside. Logan stopped and emptied his mailbox, muttering about the lazy SOBs he lived with as he pulled out a pile of mail and flyers. But he grinned the whole time, then took my hand again, and we climbed the steps.

"I gotta admit, I wish for an elevator when I have bags of groceries. But the apartment makes up for hoofing it most of the time." He winked.

Inside, I looked around. It was an open space with a large living room and a good kitchen tucked at the back. Three doors led off the living room, and Logan indicated them with a tilt of his head as he took my coat. "Trev's and Rex's rooms and the bathroom."

"Where is yours?"

He took my hand and pulled me past the kitchen and into a small hall I hadn't noticed. He pushed open a door and flicked on the light. His room was a decent size, with a queen bed against the wall and a tall dresser. The opposite wall had a keyboard, his guitar I recognized, plus a couple of other ones. Sheet music was piled on top of the keyboard, with more lying on the floor. I walked over, looking at the piles of music. His name was written across the top, with song titles underneath. There were pages of compositions, some completed songs, some half written, others with only titles. Hundreds of them. I picked up one, studying it. It was called "Your Eyes," and as I read the lyrics, I knew.

It was about me.

My gaze flew to his, and he nodded. "I wrote that the first

night I sang to you." He wrapped his arms around me, pulling me back to his chest. "I had never seen eyes that held such pain." He kissed the side of my neck. "I never wanted to erase something so much. I wanted to ease you."

"You did. You have no idea."

His arms tightened. "Good."

I indicated the piles of music. "You perform these songs?"

"Yes. I, ah, I hope one day to sell some. I just need to find the right person to hear them."

I turned in his arms. "You want to perform?"

"No. *Christ*, no. I like small stages and singing for an evening." He bent down and touched my nose with his. "I like singing for you. But I have no aspirations to be famous. I write what my heart tells me to. I would love to hear someone else perform my work."

"Then I hope you get it."

He smiled, but for the first time ever, it didn't reach his eyes. "We'll see."

I realized in that moment, we both harbored a dream we were certain would never come true. It was yet another thing that drew us together.

A noise startled me, and I glanced behind Logan. "What was that?"

He held out his hand. "Come meet the inmates. Trev probably just got back from the gym, and no doubt he's waking up Rex and Gretch. They're both serious gamers and stay up half the night playing video games. He likes to piss them off and roust them out of bed for roomie brunch. It's a Sunday tradition."

"Oh, but we ate."

He lifted an eyebrow. "That was a snack to tide me over, Lottie. Trev makes a wicked stir-fry every Sunday. It's epic." He grabbed my hand. "Come meet the guys. They think you're a figment of my imagination, so prepare yourself for the open mouths and disbelief."

I laughed as I followed him, certain he was teasing.

Except, he wasn't. The looks on their faces when Logan appeared, his arm wrapped around me, were priceless. The two men, Rex and Trev, I assumed, looked at each other, then at Logan.

"And who is this?" one asked.

Logan's arm tightened. "This is Lottie. My girlfriend."

"Your subway angel know about this?" the other one teased.

There was no mistaking the satisfaction in Logan's voice. "This is my subway angel."

They stared, blinked, and looked at each other.

"You shitting us, Logan?"

I tried not to laugh, instead stepping forward and holding out my hand to the taller of the two. "You must be Trevor."

He shook my hand. "I am."

I turned to Rex. "Hi, Rex. I'm Lottie."

He beamed. "You're real?"

"Last time I checked."

Trev whistled low. "Holy shit. You weren't kidding, Logan. She's stunning."

"And she's taken," Logan snapped.

"Now, boys." A beautiful woman stepped into our odd circle, a wide grin on her face. "Hi, I'm Gretchen. Aren't you pretty? Look at that hair! Logan, you were right. Amazing."

I looked up at him. What exactly had he been telling these people?

Ten minutes later, it didn't matter. They accepted me for me. Lottie. Logan's girl. I felt as if I had known them all my life.

Rex and Gretchen sat with me on the sofa, handing me a coffee cup that was well laced with Baileys. Gretch, as she insisted I call her, perched on Rex's knee, chatting away. She was tiny, with white-blond hair and huge blue eyes. Rex was average height, with sandy-colored hair, no doubt styled by Gretchen. He wore glasses that emphasized his dark-brown eyes and had full sleeves on both arms, the colorful ink a splash of brightness against his black jeans and T-shirt. They were a cute couple, affectionate and funny—finishing each other's sentences and joking constantly.

"The way Logan talked about you, we were sure he was exaggerating," Gretch admitted. "We never thought he'd get up the courage to talk to you."

"Or that you were even real," Rex added. "I was sure he was singing to some mystical being only he could see."

"Nope. I'm real."

"And he finally talked to you," Gretch breathed out.

I looked over to the kitchen, where Logan was helping Trev chop vegetables. He caught my eye and winked, making my cheeks flush.

"He did," I assured her. "I was so exhausted, I fell asleep in the subway, and he sat and watched over me until I woke up. Then we went for burgers and talked. We, ah, spent the weekend together."

Gretch clapped her hands. "How romantic! Isn't that romantic, babe?"

Rex grinned, his eyes crinkling behind his glasses. "Yep. Romantic. That's our Logan."

She slapped his chest. "Stop it."

He grabbed her, kissing her hard, and I averted my gaze to the kitchen. Trevor was saying something to make Logan laugh, and I liked seeing him in his own environment. He was relaxed and happy. Trevor was about Logan's height and a wall of muscle. He had a head of dark hair and hazel eyes. He was clean-shaven and wore a tight T-shirt that emphasized his chest and arms. Obviously at home in the kitchen, he chopped and stirred, talked and teased, all at the same time. Remembering the box I had brought, I went to Logan's room then returned to the kitchen, sliding it on the counter.

"I brought dessert." When Logan had said he was taking me

to meet his roommates, I had insisted on bringing the cake. I was glad I had something to contribute.

"Awesome." Trevor agreed. "Sundays are my lax days. I eat whatever I want." He elbowed Logan. "Not all of us can chow down like this big guy." He flipped the lid on the box. "Wow. That's an awfully pretty cake. Special occasion?"

"Um, no. I just made what I felt like."

"You made this?"

"Isn't she talented?" Logan asked.

Gretch hurried over and peeked in the box. "That is fabulous."

"And it tastes even better. Her cookies are to die for," Logan assured her.

"Then let's start eating and get to dessert!"

"Sounds like a plan. Stir-fry ready in ten." Trev winked at me. "Dessert after that."

♫

I curled up next to Logan, tracing lazy circles over his chest. I peeked at the clock, dreading the way the day was flying by. The brunch had been delicious, the stir-fry packed with veggies, shrimp, and chicken. The sauce was spicy, making me need lots of water. The cake had been devoured amidst groans of appreciation. I was fairly quiet, but the constant banter and teasing that flew around the table made me smile. I was thrilled to see my fears of Logan's living conditions were way off. The apartment was comfortable and warm, and his friends supportive and caring. They were obviously a little family unit, and it made me happy that he had that. It was so much better than the shelter I'd worried about him being in, or the street I was scared he walked every night.

We had spent time with his roomies, and I saw a different side to him. He was obviously the leader of the group. They all seemed to defer to him as they discussed shopping, meals, paying the rent. There was a lively discussion about a new TV Rex and Gretch both thought the place needed.

"You mean, you need," Logan snorted. "I am not bankrolling your obsession with a bigger TV so you can play even more games."

Trev agreed. "You two want one—you buy it."

That led to more arguments, but it was all done in good fun. Then Gretch broke out the Scrabble board, and I discovered Logan's competitive side. He was all snarls and glares, going for big-point words and triple-scores. I laughed so hard, my sides ached.

It was a great day. I hated thinking of leaving, but I knew I had to go.

"What are you thinking about that made you so tense?" he asked quietly, his arm tightening. "Don't say you have to go."

"I do have to go soon," I admitted. "I have laundry and work I never did this weekend. I have to be ready for tomorrow." I lifted my head, meeting his worried gaze. "Back to reality."

He rolled, pinning me under him. "Not totally, Lottie." He traced his fingers down my arms, making me shiver. "Your reality now contains me. I'm in your life and plan to be a part of your day-to-day."

I opened my mouth, and he stopped me from speaking. "I know you're busy. I'll be teaching every day as well. But we can text and call. Have dinner. Spend some time together. And we have the weekends, right?"

I nodded sadly. I didn't have the heart to tell him I usually worked from home most of the time on the weekends. He looked so happy; I didn't want to burst his bubble yet.

He lowered his head and kissed me. "If you play your cards right, you might entice me to sleep over during the week, my Snow Queen. I can wake you up early and send you off to work with a smile on your face." He ghosted his lips over mine. "And me all over you."

My core clenched at his words. I liked how that sounded.

"Hmm," I breathed. "That sounds naughty."

"Oh, it is. I promise you." He kissed me again, this time harder. "We're just starting, Lottie. We'll figure it out. Just promise you'll try. Find time to live, not only work."

"I will."

He glanced at the clock. "I'll walk you home in an hour, and you'll have all evening to do your work, okay?"

"An hour?"

He nudged my collar down with his nose and licked at my skin. "I told you I wanted to have you in my bed. I want my sheets to smell like you when I get in later. Smell like us. I need at least two rounds for that to happen."

I pulled him down to my mouth. "I could get up a little earlier in the morning. Give you two hours now."

He smiled against my lips. "Now you're talking."

CHAPTER 12
LOTTIE

Logan walked me home, leaving me at the front door of my building. He kissed me slowly, thoroughly, before he left, striding away, often turning to look behind him. I watched until he disappeared from my sight, a small ache forming in my chest when I could no longer see him.

I trudged upstairs, my condo feeling empty without his presence. I shook my head, made a cup of tea, and sat at my home computer. Fearfully, I opened my email, then purposely put Logan and everything else out of my mind and concentrated on the work waiting in front of me. I was a little surprised at the small number of emails needing my attention. Most of them were group-based, and the information they required had been provided. The few that were for me only, I responded to, leaving the ones that needed data from the files on my desk until the morning. Before I had sat down, I'd thrown in some laundry, and by eleven, I was in bed. My sheets smelled like Logan. Crisp snow and cedar—a woodsy fragrance that suited him. I tried not to smile when I realized he even smelled perfect. I glanced at my phone and sent him a text message. He had made sure we exchanged numbers before we left his place earlier.

Lottie: *Hi. Going to bed. Thank you for today.*

His response was fast.

Logan: *Got your work done, SQ?*

Lottie: *Yes.* I paused, then added, *My bed smells like you.*

I got back a smiley face and his reply.

Logan: *And mine like you. I would prefer if it were the real thing.*

Lottie: Me too. Have a good day tomorrow.

There were a few beats of silence until he replied.

Logan: Sleep well, Lottie. I'll see you soon. xx

I plugged in my phone and curled up, hugging the pillow he had slept on. I inhaled his fragrance, letting it wash over me. I yawned, my body tired, but my mind still awake. I wondered what would happen tomorrow at the office. If my father would punish me for my supposed transgressions of taking the day off and talking back to him. The words Logan had said went through my head on repeat—of doing something I loved rather than trying to make up for something I had no control over. I could only imagine the horror on Charles Prescott's face if I told him I was quitting to go and bake cakes. He would probably have me committed. As the minutes crawled by, I wondered what it would be like not to dread each day. To be eager to get to work because I was doing something I loved. I sat up, punching my pillow, and rearranging my blanket.

That was a pipe dream. I had spent years of schooling to earn my degree in business and investment. I still had the student loans to prove it. My father had paid for half my schooling, and I'd lived at home to keep expenses down and concentrate on my education. The rest, I paid for. I often had to tamp down the feeling that if it had been Josh, my father would have paid for all of it without question. He confessed once to thinking I would give up partway through and it was his way of making sure I had an incentive. I had to resist calling him on that when I graduated and pointing out I had completed it, so therefore, he could pay the rest of the debt. I knew that would get me nowhere. So I paid my loans monthly, which left me enough to pay my mortgage and live a modest life.

It certainly didn't give me the freedom to leave my job and bake cakes for a living.

I curled back up and shut my eyes. I needed to stop thinking about it. Life was hard enough without adding more what-ifs.

I simply had to accept it and keep moving forward.

♫

In the morning, I felt exhausted, the euphoria of the weekend gone and reality staring me in the face. I got into the office early, even beating my father, cleared my desk and emails, and was ready for the nine a.m. meeting. I was already at my place when my father walked in, and I met his frosty glance with a tight smile. He was obviously still angry with me. How angry became evident not long into the meeting.

"I've decided to make some changes," he announced, after the usual updates had been dealt with and noted. "I'm switching some people around on some projects. Todd, you take over the

Jetson dossier from Charlotte. Andrew, I want you on the merger with Alcore. Meet with Charlotte and get all the files."

I kept my gaze on the papers in front of me. The two biggest projects I had been working on had now been pulled from me. From the stunned silence in the room, it was obvious my father's announcement had caught everyone by surprise. I knew he was doing it to punish me, yet all I felt was relief. I should be upset, indignant, but the thought of all the hours needed to complete the files was daunting. It didn't even matter that the bonus I would have received would be gone. Relief still won out.

I lifted my gaze, meeting my father's eyes calmly. "I'll make sure they have everything as soon as possible."

He nodded, not giving away a thing. "I have three new mergers we've been asked to investigate. I'll have the files delivered to your desk."

It was another rebuke. Pulling me off the two big ones and no doubt giving me smaller files, which meant more work and less money. But in the long run, less stress since the demands would be less stringent.

"Of course," I said, my voice even and steady. I refused to let him, or anyone else, even suspect I was upset or that this was anything other than simply a business decision.

But I knew.

I bent my head, scratching out a few notes as my father reassigned some other tasks and files not related to me. The meeting was adjourned, and I headed to my office, shutting the door behind myself and leaning against the wood. I blew out a long breath and let my head fall to my chest, releasing some of the tension. I sat down at my desk, turning my chair to stare out the window. It was overcast today, the light a gray hue filtering through the clouds. It suited my mood—especially now.

It wasn't unusual for my father to change teams. To hand over various files to different people and groups. But these were two of the biggest, and I had been working on them for weeks.

Both were difficult and intricate, with lots of players involved. I had been against both of them, but he had overridden me at the time. His decision made it appear as if he'd lost confidence in me.

Which, I assumed, in many ways, he had.

I knew I could go into his office and argue with him—he probably expected it. But I was surprisingly calm about it. I would hand over the files and all the pertinent information. The fact was that it would free up a lot of my time. I would take my new assignments and figure out how best to proceed with them.

As I was sorting out all the files, there was a knock at my door, and Lorie, one of my father's assistants, came in, carrying some folders. She looked uncomfortable as she approached my desk, and I smiled at her, wanting to put her at ease. I wasn't upset with her.

"I have these for you."

"Great." I indicated the corner of the desk. "Put them there. I'm almost done with these."

"Mr. Prescott, ah, wants me to schedule a transfer meeting as soon as possible."

"Sure. An hour?"

"Okay. In here?"

"That works. Is he attending?"

"Yes."

"Okay. Set it up, and I'll have this all done."

"Can I—can I get anything for you?" she asked.

"No, I'm good."

"Lunch later?"

I realized she was trying to offer her support in the only way she could. "A tuna salad on rye would be great later, Lorie. Thanks."

"With an iced tea?"

"Perfect."

She nodded and left. I returned my attention to the files,

making sure everything was up-to-date on the server and all my notes were clear. By the time Todd, Andrew, and my father walked in, I was ready. I was brisk and efficient, going through everything with them, handing over the file boxes and the passwords to the documents on the server. I was responding to a question from Todd when the receptionist appeared in my doorway, a small arrangement of flowers in her hands. I was flummoxed when she knocked, came in, and slid them on my desk.

"They wouldn't leave without a signature," she explained. "The instructions said only you could sign."

I took the clipboard and signed the delivery slip, my gaze on the flowers. Tiny roses, little irises, button carnations, and baby's breath filled the vase. It was girlie, pretty, and the scent wonderful. There was a small card tucked into the middle of the flowers, but I already knew who sent them.

Logan was making sure I knew he was thinking of me.

I pulled open my drawer and slipped a five-dollar bill onto the clipboard. "Thanks, Marie."

She nodded. "Sorry for the interruption."

"No problem."

It was all I could do to return to the meeting. Luckily, we were almost finished. This was the easy part—handing it off. By tonight, I would have a list of questions to respond to, and I wondered how late I would be staying. I wrapped it up, and Todd and Andrew stood, taking the files and departing.

My father unfurled himself from the chair. I met his gaze, refusing to let him see anything but a composed expression.

"You have the new documents?"

"Yes. Lorie brought them by. I will dig into them."

He tugged his shirtsleeves into place, although there was no need. "This isn't punishment, Charlotte."

"I never said it was."

"I felt you had gone stale on those files. I needed fresh blood."

"I disagree, but your decision, of course."

"Yes," he said coldly. "My company, my choice."

I didn't acknowledge his words.

"Special occasion?"

"I beg your pardon?"

He indicated the flowers with a tilt of his head. "You received flowers."

I ran my finger over the soft petals of a pink carnation. "From a friend who wanted to brighten my day."

"I wasn't aware your days needed brightening."

"I suppose that isn't surprising."

He glared at me. "I appreciate my employees keeping their personal lives outside of the office, Charlotte. I would expect the same from you."

"Of course you would."

"I really don't like your attitude these days."

"I'm not doing anything, Charles. I've turned over the files, and I will start the new ones right away. I assure you some flowers on my desk are not going to distract me."

"Something is," he snarled.

I didn't reply. He turned and left my office, shutting the door behind him.

With a sigh, I plucked the card from the flowers. It was simple.

Think of me
Counting the moments
Logan xx

I sighed. I was counting the moments too. Once again, I stroked the velvety flowers. Such an old-fashioned, wonderful gesture. At times, Logan surprised me. The action in the subway. The way he insisted on opening doors, walking closest to the road, holding my hand, these flowers. His father must have instilled those traits in him. I loved the contradiction to the roughness of his appearance. Under the shaggy hair and beard beat the heart of a poet and a true gentleman.

Until it came to sex. There, he was as rough and demanding as his appearance suggested. Yet even that was tempered with tenderness. His dirty words, his demands, the way he handled me —nothing he did gave me cause for concern. He would never hurt me—or any other woman. Of that fact, I was certain.

And another fact that I was certain of was I didn't want him handling any other woman except me.

With a sigh, I sent him a text thanking him and got back to work. It was going to be a long day.

Hours later, I stretched my neck, glancing at the clock, shocked to see it was past seven. The hours had flown by as I'd studied the new projects I'd been assigned. All were fairly straightforward. The sort of ventures I would have handled when I first came to the company. But I refused to let that bother me. I would give them all the attention and due diligence other clients received. My father would have zero to complain about, and I would make sure the clients were happy. At least one was interesting. Two small indie recording companies wanting to combine and bring on investors. I had spoken with one of the parties involved, and Carmen had invited me to an event they were hosting on Wednesday evening. I was going to attend and then meet with them on Thursday to talk more. He extended the invite to others in the office, and I promised to pass it along. The other two were a hotel looking to expand and another start-up seeking investment. I had notes on both of them for investors and would follow up more this week.

My stomach grumbled, and I grimaced as I looked over at the half-eaten tuna sandwich on the corner of my desk. The edges of the bread were dry, the tuna soaked into the bottom piece. My iced tea had long since grown warm. I tossed both in the garbage and decided to head home.

I glanced at my phone and saw I had missed two texts from Logan. One stated he was pleased my flowers had arrived, and the last one asked when I was leaving work. I frowned when I saw it had come in over two hours ago. I decided to call him when I got home. As I turned off the light and headed out the door, I felt a wave of disappointment. There would be no serenade tonight. Even though I knew he would sing to me any time I asked, there was a small part of me that was sad I would no longer be treated to his voice at the end of every day. It always gave me the strength to head home and made the end of my day better. Maybe I would ask him to sing to me over the phone. With that comforting thought, I headed out into the cold, now anxious to get home and hear his voice.

But when I stepped off the subway and rounded the corner, he was there. Playing, smiling at people—and waiting. Our gazes met, and his smile grew wider, the dimple appearing like a small divot in his cheek. He lifted his eyebrows and tilted his head, indicating I should sit, so I did. He strummed his guitar and sang my favorite song, the notes and music swirling in my head. I shut my eyes, letting my stress dissolve, the terrible day fading away at the sound of his voice. As the notes softly finished, there was a lull, and I sighed, opening my eyes to find him beside me, watching, assessing as he always did. His guitar was slung over his shoulder, the case on the ground by his feet.

"Hello, my Snow Queen," he murmured, leaning forward and wiping under my eyes. "I don't like seeing you cry."

"You're here. Waiting."

He nuzzled my cheek, his breath warm on my skin. "I walked past your place, and the lights were still off. You hadn't returned my text, so I figured you were still at work. I came to wait." He winked. "The food bank is getting a good donation today."

"I'm sorry."

"Nope. No sorry is needed." He laced our fingers together. "It was a bad day?"

"Not anymore."

He smiled so wide, his beautiful eyes crinkled, and once again, I got a glimpse of his dimple. "Did you eat dinner?"

"No."

"Diner?" he asked hopefully.

"You can't eat burgers all the time," I argued halfheartedly.

"I was going to have a clubhouse sandwich and a salad."

I narrowed my eyes at him in disbelief.

"Or at least that was what I was going to order for you." He winked. "I haven't had a burger since Thursday."

"Such restraint."

"Please," he asked simply, and there was no way I could resist him.

"Yes."

♫

"Your father is a piece of work," Logan snarled after I told him about my day.

"He is very exacting. He runs a tight ship, and I'm treated the same way as everyone else."

I speared a piece of lettuce and chewed it slowly. "He wasn't always that way." I could still remember the man who picked me up, tossed me in the air, pushed me on the swing, and kissed my scraped knees. I could still recall his love.

"I shouldn't have asked you to spend the day with me."

I was quick to object to his words. "Don't say that. It was one of my favorite days ever. I wouldn't trade it for anything."

"Even losing those accounts?"

I traced the worn Formica on the tabletop. "He thinks I'll learn a lesson, but if I'm being honest?" I looked up and met Logan's eyes. "The lower stress is welcome for a while. None of this work is easy, but these are definitely less complex—not as many players or as much money at stake."

"Well, good. Maybe you can relax a little until he decides you've been punished enough. Maybe by then, you can go work elsewhere."

"Logan," I warned.

He held up his hands. "Okay, I'll shut up. I hate seeing you look so exhausted after one day."

I didn't have a response that would satisfy him, so I shrugged. "It happens."

He shook his head, and I changed the subject. "How was school?"

He entertained me with a few stories about some of the antics the kids got up to, all the while encouraging me to eat. What I didn't finish, he polished off, insisting on a piece of his favorite cake to share. That, he fed me, mouthful by mouthful, in between yawns.

We walked to my building, and he followed me upstairs, stopping in my doorway. "Go to bed," he murmured gently, stroking my cheek. "Promise me you won't do any more work tonight."

"You're not coming in?"

"That's not a good idea, Lottie. I don't think I can resist you, and you are far too tired."

"Do I at least get a kiss?"

He set down his guitar case, cupping my face. "You never have to ask."

He covered my mouth with his, his lips warm and pressing. We kissed easily, our mouths reacquainting themselves, then he slanted his head and deepened the kiss, his tongue sliding inside my mouth and stroking along mine in sensuous passes. Over and again, he explored me, pulling me tighter, holding me close, wrapped tight and safe in his embrace. He tasted like cake. Coffee. Logan. His scent—the winter-like fragrance that clung to him—filled my head, and I held on to him as hard as I could. He filled me up with desire, with light. The day faded far into the background as he claimed me with his mouth, making me want more.

"Stay," I pleaded.

"I don't have anything," he groaned. "I didn't plan…"

"I'm on the pill. I'm safe. I haven't been with anyone for over a year."

He met my beseeching gaze.

"I haven't been with anyone in a long time, Lottie. Since before I started singing to you. A long time before that. I was tested, and I'm negative too. If you trust me, and you want this, I am not going to tell you no. I will never tell you no."

"Please," I whispered.

He hooked the door shut behind him and flipped the lock. I yanked off my coat and boots and waited as he did the same. I gasped as he swooped me into his arms and carried me down the hall.

"Your day is going to end a lot better than it started, baby."

I buried my face in his neck and bit down on the skin, teasing it with my tongue. "I'm counting on it."

Quickly, I discovered another side to Logan—his tender, love-making side. There was no dirty-talking, no rough tearing off of our clothes. Instead, he surrounded me with him. His body, his warmth, his gentleness.

He slowly removed my outfit, brushing kisses onto every inch of my skin as he bared it. He rubbed my shoulders, working magic with his strong fingers as he loosened the muscles, all the while humming low and soft into my ear. He discarded his jeans and shirt, tugging me down on the mattress with him. We kissed endlessly—long, languid swipes of his tongue on mine, all the while touching me.

I shivered as he stroked along my collarbone, his lips light and teasing. He kissed the tender skin on my inner elbow, teased my pulse at my wrist, found the sensitive spot behind my ear. He murmured reassurances, sweet promises, quiet thoughts.

How beautiful I was. How much he wanted me. The way he had missed me all day. He promised to never stop touching me like this.

I was lost to his words, his touch—and to him.

I gripped him hard, needing to feel him. To know he was there. He soothed me with his body, covering mine like a warm, protective blanket, his heat soaking into my skin. He was a welcome weight pinning me to the mattress. He never stopped in his explorations until I begged him.

"Please, Logan. I need you."

He settled between my legs, hovering over me like a dark angel. He slid inside, both of us groaning at the raw, intimate connection. He was silk over steel, my body welcoming him inside as if it had been waiting for this.

For him.

He stilled, hanging his head. When he lifted his chin, his eyes were intense, the whiskey almost black.

"You feel better than any fantasy or any dream could ever be," he rasped. "You were made for me, Lottie."

There was nothing rushed tonight. Long, slow thrusts of his hips, whispered words of adoration, gentle, lingering kisses. The overwhelming intensity of the moment, his piercing gaze, his low words hit me, and I orgasmed without warning, the rolling waves crashing over me as I climaxed and clung to Logan. He buried his face in my neck and groaned out my name as he came, holding me tight as he shuddered, then stilled, his body pushing me down into the mattress as he exhaled and collapsed to my chest. I clutched my arms around his neck, breathing him in, feeling the relaxation rolling over us.

He rolled to his side, his grip never loosening. He tugged me to his chest, running his fingers through my hair, pressing kisses to my forehead. "Amazing."

I moved to get comfortable and let out a low laugh. "Amazing but messy as hell. You're all over me."

"I like being all over you."

I groaned and relaxed back to his chest. He wasn't letting me up—at least not yet. He tilted up my chin and kissed me. It was one of his soul-shattering, deep, intense kisses that made my toes curl. The man could kiss like there was no tomorrow. It was highly addictive. When he pulled back, our eyes locked, the silence filled with unspoken words.

I shook my head.

"Stop."

"What?"

"Looking at me like that."

"How am I looking at you?" he asked, a smile curling his lips.

"As if I'm your entire world."

"You're quickly becoming exactly that."

My heart fluttered. "Logan," I whispered. "It's too fast."

"I'm just putting it out there. I'm not a player. I'm a one-woman guy. And you are my one woman." He paused, a small vee forming between his eyes. "If you want to be."

There was no hesitation. The way he treated me, how he made me feel—as if I mattered. It was the first time in years I felt as if I mattered to someone. I felt safe, protected, and cherished.

"Yes, I want to be your 'one-woman.'"

"Good. Then we're on the same page." He tucked me closer. "Go to sleep. I'm right here."

I snuggled close and, without another word or thought, drifted to sleep, his words comforting and perfect.

He was here.

CHAPTER 13
LOTTIE

I woke to Logan's lips on my forehead, his voice low in my ear. "I have to go, baby. I can't be late, and I need to shower and change." He dropped another kiss to my forehead. "I hope today is better for you."

He started to back up toward the door, and I sat up, the blankets falling off my chest. He groaned. "Don't tempt me, Lottie."

I rolled my eyes and tucked the blanket under my arms. "I forgot, I have a business event tomorrow that Carmen is hosting. He extended the invitation to the team and told me to feel free to bring a plus-one. Would you like to go with me?"

"That won't cause you a problem?"

"It's a casual event. Drinks, music, schmoozing is what Carmen told me. A chance to see what they're about and meet them. I think you'd enjoy it."

"Your father?" The words hung in the air.

I knew what he was saying, but I refused to be worried. I wasn't ashamed of Logan, and I wanted him to know that.

"I can't see him even thinking about going to something like that. He likes the formal dinners, not a plate of finger food and loud music. I only have two members on this team, and I'm not even sure they'll go. I would love to have you with me."

"And it's casual?"

My lips quirked. "Maybe clean jeans and an un-holey shirt, but yes."

He winked. "I can do that. I would love to go with you."

"I'll probably work late tonight. Don't wait, Logan. Please. Be here tomorrow at seven."

He lifted a shoulder and walked out the door.

"Can't promise that," he called. "We'll see."

Somehow, I knew I would be seeing him later.

He was there, a smile on his face, his guitar in hand. But this time, he sat beside me on the bench and crooned just for me. We shared a piece of cake at the diner, and he walked me home, refusing to come upstairs.

"I have no self-control when it comes to you," he confessed. "If I come upstairs, I can't leave you." He kissed my forehead, his warm lips lingering. "Don't ask, baby. I can't say no."

"But you'll be here tomorrow?"

"Seven on the dot. Clean, un-holey shirt on. Promise."

I rolled to the tip of my toes and kissed him. "Okay."

He watched me walk in and waited until he saw my light go on. I waved from my window, and he strode away, his long legs eating up the distance quickly. He texted when he got home and sent a voice mail. It was of him singing a lullaby, and I listened to it when I went to bed, the sound of his rich voice soothing me into sleep.

The next night, he buzzed at seven promptly, and I let him up, opening the door and waiting impatiently for him to arrive. My breath caught in my throat as he pulled off his jacket.

"Will this do?"

His shaggy hair was around his collar, pushed back from his face. He wore a dark blue Henley stretched tight across his chest and arms and a black leather vest overtop. He had on thick khaki pants and heavy Doc Martens on his feet. His beard was trimmed, and his eyes danced with mischief. With the various leather and braided silver cuffs on his wrist and knotted Celtic rings on his hands, he looked every inch the bad boy. A seriously sexy bad boy.

I tried not to whimper. I think I failed.

"You're coming home with me tonight," I informed him.

He grinned and indicated my outfit. "Damn right, I am."

I glanced down. I wore tight black pants tucked into ankle boots and a long glittery, silver tunic. It was pretty, yet not over the top. I wore my hair up in a long ponytail and had slipped in some delicate, dangling silver earrings that brushed my shoulders. I had added eyeliner and red lipstick.

"You are smoking hot," Logan growled. "I love the lips." He stepped closer. "I want those lips."

"They're yours," I murmured, feeling a long shiver of desire run through me.

"I don't want to mess you up."

"It's smear-proof," I assured him. "And I want you to mess—"

That was all I got out before his mouth was on mine. Hard. Demanding. So satisfying, yet not enough. I wanted closer. I wanted more. I had never felt this way about a man, but Logan was different. He brought out feelings in me I had never known until now.

He eased back with a smile. Affectionately, he rubbed his nose along mine. "We need to go before I throw you over the back of that sofa and have you in those sexy little boots, Snow Queen."

"Rain check?" I breathed out, hardly recognizing my own voice.

He grinned. Wide and wicked. "Absolutely."

"Let's go, then."

♪

The venue was packed. It was a converted warehouse, the top floor decked out for the party. There were lights strung from the open beams, various bars and food stations set up, and a rhythmic beat thumping in the background. They had numerous bands and individual performers playing as well as a DJ spinning during breaks. I was greeted at the door by a tall woman with a wide smile and a fashion flair I wished I dared to have. Her dress plunged, ending just below her ass, and her makeup was intense. Her blond hair was short, slicked back, and she was simply stunning. She was also incredibly warm and friendly.

"Carmen asked me to point him out to you if he wasn't at the door," she said, indicating a tall bald man with a beard talking to another gentleman. "He's looking forward to meeting you. I'm Roxanne."

We shook hands. I knew from my notes she was the marketing executive at the record company. "Great to meet you. This is Logan."

He held out his hand. "Hey."

She eyed him up and down, her gaze frank. I felt a frisson of jealousy at her appraisal but shook it off when Logan snaked his hand around my waist. "My girl made my day including me in the invite. Roadside is an awesome label. Your artists are top-notch."

She laughed. "We think so. And we look forward to working with, ah, *your girl*."

He nodded.

"Go introduce yourself to Carmen and help yourself to food and drink. If you need anything, don't hesitate to ask." She handed us VIP badges. "Enjoy!"

We stopped to slip on the lanyards. "You didn't tell me your client was Roadside Records, Lottie."

I shrugged. "I had no idea you knew them."

"They're a well-known indie label. Rumor is they treat their artists well."

"Well, they and Ravaged Records want to team up and bring in investors—expand."

He whistled. "Another familiar name. Some of the guys I play with in bars would kill to be here tonight." He bent low and kissed me. "And not just for the party. Have I mentioned how incredibly sexy you are?"

I cupped his chin, running my fingers through his beard. "Not as sexy as you are."

He winked. "Let's go be sexy together."

We made our way toward Carmen. I introduced myself and was given a hug. He was charming and gregarious. He informed me he was thrilled that Mr. Prescott had given the account to me.

"I've heard many good things about you, Lottie."

"I hope I live up to your expectations."

He winked. "I have no doubt. Now go, enjoy yourselves. Tonight is about fun. We'll work on business tomorrow."

Logan and I headed to the bar, each getting a drink and filling our plates with food. We wandered the room, looking at various posters, album covers, and short write-ups on the history of the companies. Logan read them all, often making comments about the artists or something he knew about the labels. I was impressed with his knowledge but realized I shouldn't be. He loved music and played around town. Of course he would know more than I did about the indie music scene. I had a feeling he would be invaluable to me during this process.

A steady beat filled the air, and Logan glanced toward the center of the room. He held out his hand. "Dance with me."

I let him lead me to the dance floor and watched in awe as he lost himself to the music. He was lethal, moving sensuously, completely comfortable. He wrapped an arm around my waist, pulling me close.

"Relax, Snow Queen. Feel it. Just feel it. Move with me." He nipped my ear. "Like you do when my cock is deep inside you."

My eyes flew open in shock at his words, but I let him move me, and soon I was lost with him. Our eyes held, the desire blatant in his. The beat slowed, morphing into a love song. He pulled me close, and I wrapped my arms around his neck. His gaze never left my face, his mouth forming around the lyrics as he sang them to me. I felt his stare to my core. I wanted him.

Except, right now, I couldn't. I had to concentrate on my job. I shook my head to clear the fog of lust.

"Stop."

"What?"

"Looking at me like that."

"How am I looking at you?" he asked, a smile curling his lips, a repeat of the last time he'd asked me that question.

"As if you don't know."

"I have no idea what you're talking about, Lottie. I'm simply looking at you. I *like* looking at you."

"You're all smoldery."

"Smoldery? As a teacher, I gotta tell you—there isn't such a word."

"There is. It's my word. And you are. All smoldery and sexy, with that wicked look on your face."

His smile became a smirk, and he bent lower, his breath washing over my face. "Wicked look?"

I decided to shock him. "The one that says 'You're gonna let me fuck your ass one day, baby.'"

His eyebrows shot up. "My face says that?"

I smacked his chest. "Sometimes it does."

He placed his lips against my ear. "And *will* you let me, Lottie?"

"Maybe," I breathed out.

"I'll take that as another rain check."

"Whatever."

He kissed my neck, nibbling on the skin. "Trust me, Lottie. When I claim your ass, *whatever* isn't the word you're going to be screaming out."

I felt a thrill run through me as he ran his hand over my ass, cupping it and squeezing.

"I do plan on having this spectacular ass one day." He chuckled and slid his hands back to my waist. "But somewhere far more private and without an audience."

"Good plan."

He nudged my nose with his. "I have lots of good plans when it comes to you."

The song stopped, and Logan pulled me over to the bar where we got another drink. Both of us ordered tonic water with lime, and I sipped the icy beverage in appreciation.

Carmen approached us, smiling.

"Enjoying yourself?"

"Immensely," Logan assured him. "Great music."

Carmen nodded. "Some of our artists. Our studios are down-stairs, as well as our offices."

"I bet the acoustics are awesome in this building."

"They are." Carmen studied him. "You look familiar, Logan. I thought so as soon as Lottie introduced us. Have we met before today?"

I couldn't stop myself. "Logan plays at different clubs around town. Maybe you've seen him? He's very talented," I added.

Logan shot me an irritated look, but Carmen simply laughed. "Your lady is proud."

I glanced over Carmen's shoulder and froze. My father was standing by the wall, observing us, his arms folded over his chest, looking displeased.

I left them talking. "Excuse me," I murmured, and I approached my father.

"Charles." I frowned. "I didn't expect you to see you tonight."

"Given your display, obviously."

"I beg your pardon?"

He lifted one eyebrow. "Do you make a habit of allowing a stranger to grope you on the dance floor on a regular basis, Charlotte, or are you simply trying to fit in with the crowd?"

I was shocked he would think I would use someone as a prop.

"He is *not* a stranger," I spat. "And he wasn't groping me—we were dancing."

He stepped forward, his voice low and furious. "Is he the reason you're distracted these days, Charlotte? That...that *degenerate* is the reason you're falling down on the job?"

"He is *not* a degenerate. I am doing my job, Charles," I shot back. "I'm handling everything you're allowing me to. You chose to switch my projects. Not me."

"Who is he to you?" he demanded. "Someone you're using to get back at me?"

I stared at him in horror.

That was what he thought of me. He assumed I was dancing and spending time with Logan to get back at him. He wrote him off as not being good enough because he wasn't wearing a suit and tie. I shook my head sadly.

"You don't even know him, and you're casting aspersions on his character. Why? Because he has long hair? A beard?"

"I don't like the way he touched you."

"At least he does touch me, Charles. He holds me and kisses me. Comforts me when I need it. When was the last time you did that?"

"You will stop seeing him."

I crossed my arms. "No, I will not." I held my head high. "He is a teacher. A sweet, caring man who looks after me. I will not give that up because you have some sort of preconceived idea in your head about him. That's your problem, not mine."

Our gazes clashed, his anger battling with my indignation.

"Take away every account, Charles. Fire me. But I'm not giving up Logan."

He narrowed his eyes. "This conversation is not over."

"It is. Otherwise, I will have to talk to HR about my boss overstepping into my personal life."

He spun on his heel and disappeared into the crowd. Seconds later, Logan's strong arm wrapped around my waist, pulling me tight to his chest.

"You shouldn't have done that," he murmured in my ear.

I settled back into him, his warmth welcome. "Done what?"

"Provoked him."

I turned and met his eyes. "He was insulting you. Us. Making assumptions about you."

"He was being, ah, protective?" he asked, sounding dubious.

"He was being an ass," I snarled.

"You stuck up for me. For us."

"Yes."

He slid his hand around the back of my neck, his long fingers stroking the skin. He bent close to my ear, his breath hot against my neck. "Do you know how that makes me feel? Hearing what you said, watching the way you went toe-to-toe with your father over me? No one has stood up for me in a long time, my Snow Queen." He flicked his tongue against my lobe. "You amaze me."

He claimed my mouth in an ardent kiss. "Thank you."

"I'm sorry," I replied, then met his eyes. Dark, intense, and steady. Focused solely on me. It didn't surprise me that my father would have a negative reaction to Logan, but it was still embarrassing.

"It's not your fault."

"Do you think they noticed?" I asked, worried about our hosts.

"No. Carmen's back was to you, and he went to speak to someone else. I don't think he even noticed your father here."

"Good." I sighed, suddenly weary. Logan held out his hand.

"Dance with me. Forget what just happened and let me hold you."

I let him lead me onto the dance floor, and I slid into his embrace. It was a soothing sensation as his arms closed around me. It felt like coming home. As if I was meant to be there.

Perhaps I was.

CHAPTER 14

LOTTIE

I was decidedly nervous the next morning. But nothing happened at the staff meeting. My father spoke as usual, getting his updates. I thought his voice was extra cool when he spoke to me, and he didn't meet my gaze. But otherwise, nothing seemed out of the ordinary. I prepared for the meeting with Carmen, making sure I had everything I required. My phone buzzed with a text, and I glanced at my screen as I headed to the meeting.

Logan: *Go get 'em, my Snow Queen.*

Logan's simple words made me smile.

We had stayed only a short while after my father left. I spoke with Carmen and Roxanne and met Alfred, the owner of Ravaged Records. I found them all articulate and passionate, and I was looking forward to our meeting the next day. I confessed to Logan I was getting a headache from the loud music and no doubt the lingering stress of the confrontation with my father

Logan and I took a cab back to my place. Then, the degenerate man my father thought he was had poured me a bath and rubbed my shoulders and aching head. He tucked me into bed, holding me close until I fell asleep. He left me a note on my pillow telling me to have a good day and he would see me tonight at the subway.

I had to blink away the tears in the early morning light. He was filled with so much goodness. It upset me terribly my father only saw what he chose to see. The shaggy hair, the beard, the rougher-looking side to Logan. If he sat down and spoke with him, he would discover Logan's intelligence and warmth. He would see how he cared for me. Sadly, though, I wondered if he ever would.

We arrived at the restaurant, and I shook my head to clear it. I needed my game face on for this meeting. I planned to nail it.

♫

Carmen sat back, sipping his coffee. "I like your ideas."

Alfred hummed in agreement. "Out of the box. I like people who think out of the box."

I smiled as I shuffled some papers back in order. "I think if I approach these investors with a plan like this, we won't have any trouble getting you the capital you want. You can proceed with your merger, add to the building, and sign more talent. They'll make back their money, and you'll still have controlling interest." I paused. "And a very successful business."

They looked pleased. Roxanne beamed at them, her expression enthusiastic. "I firmly believe Ravaged Roadside is going to be the force behind indie artists."

"Admittedly, I don't know much about the music business, but I agree. Your plan is sound, you have great people, amazing talent from what I heard last night, and with the right backing, you'll have a solid company."

Phones rang out, ringtones filling the air, and both Roxanne and Alfred muttered apologies and answered their phones. I chuckled and met Carmen's gaze.

"I'm excited by the future," he said. "When I started Roadside, I had a vision that one day I could help artists find their voice. You're going to help make that come true."

"I will certainly try. I have a small group of investors I think will be a good fit." Younger, more open-minded investors I had cultivated during my time with my father's company—but I didn't voice that out loud.

"I enjoyed talking to Logan last night. I thought about what you said, and you're right. I have seen him at a few places." Carmen lifted an eyebrow. "Although when I tried to pin him down, he informed me he only sings for you these days."

I chuckled. "Me and whoever else is in the subway when I get home at night."

At Carmen's quizzical gaze, I explained, giving him the briefest details. "He serenades me. That's how we met."

"I recall his work was original."

"It is. His talent is amazing, but he prefers to write rather than be in the spotlight."

"That's rare these days." He rubbed his chin. "This is unusual, but would you be willing to give me his contact information?"

I paused. Carmen waved his hand. "Get his okay, of course. But I would like to talk to him." Then he flashed me a grin. "And this won't affect our working relationship at all. No conflict of interest or whatever else you're thinking. This is me talking to someone I met at an event. Who caught my professional interest."

I thought about it for a moment, then nodded. "Okay. I'll ask him."

♫

Logan frowned. "Why does he want to talk to me?"

I sipped my wine and pulled a hand through my hair. "I

assume to ask you about your music. Or maybe where you get your hair done. I don't know," I teased.

He set down his bowl, wiping his mouth. "Smartass," he shot back, squeezing my leg.

I grinned, settling into the sofa cushion. Logan had met me at the subway, and we came to my condo. I had been awake early enough, I'd thrown together a stew in the crockpot, and it was ready when we arrived. I refused to let him take me to the diner yet again. He polished off two bowls plus most of a loaf of bread, thoroughly enjoying the simple dinner I had made.

He drained his water, took the bowls to the kitchen, and returned. "Okay, give him my number."

"Why do you look so torn? This could be the start of an opportunity for you—you told me you dreamed of doing something with your music one day."

"I always thought I'd do it on my own, I suppose. Not have my girlfriend hook me up."

I rolled my eyes. "You're an idiot. Carmen remembered seeing you. He remembered your music. I'm simply the connection. You did do it. Now stop being so stubborn and shortsighted."

In seconds, I was under him on the sofa, his large frame pinning me down. "Stubborn?" he growled. "Shortsighted?" He nipped at my neck. "An idiot?" He slid his hand along my arms. "You're awfully lippy for someone the size of a hobbit."

I giggled as his hands wandered, his fingers ghosting over my skin, finding the sensitive areas to tickle and tease. "Listen, Hagrid," I gasped, trying to get away from his tickling fingers. "I'm just saying…" I trailed off, panting as his mouth followed his fingers, his lips hot and wet on my skin.

He lifted his head. "You're mixing up your movies, Lottie. *Harry Potter* and *The Lord of the Rings* are not the same. I guess I'll have to kidnap you and make you binge-watch them with me on the weekend. Teach you."

I moaned as he slid his mouth lower. "Yes," I pleaded. "Teach me everything, Logan."

"Oh, I intend to," he promised, hooking his fingers into my waistband. "It's going to be an intensive lesson, Lottie. Very hands-on." He paused. "Very lengthy."

I bucked against his hand. "I plan on getting a gold star."

He winked. "I bet you will. I'll make sure of it."

Then I lost myself to him.

♫

I was on a high the next day, setting up meetings, creating the prospectus to give potential investors. I also set up consultations with the other two projects I was assigned, although they were far more cut-and-dried. A few calls to my usual investors would take care of them easily, I expected.

I also contacted Carmen with Logan's number. He replied quickly, thanking me.

No doubt he was loath to give it, his text read.

How did you know? I replied.

I know artists and their pride.

I had to chuckle. I recalled Logan's anger over the money that first night. His insistence on paying for everything the day we spent together. His hesitance in granting me permission to give Carmen his number. Carmen had Logan pegged perfectly, although I thought it was more than the artist in him that made Logan that way.

Good luck, was my response.

My phone rang, and I was thrilled to see the name on the screen.

"Brianna!" I exclaimed as I lifted the receiver. "You're home!"

"I am," she replied, sounding amused.

"How was the trip?"

"Boring."

I laughed, leaning back in my chair. "Only you can go to the Mediterranean and call it boring."

"It got better when I broke up with Dan."

I groaned. "Another one, Brianna? Really?" I hadn't fibbed to my mother when I told her that Brianna always had man trouble.

"He was a jerk. I caught him with one of the hotel staff. I dumped him and left. I didn't pay the bill either. I decided he could handle that."

I chuckled. Brianna was wealthy. Exceedingly so, which made her a target at times. She had the worst luck with men. I always thought she was so desperate to be loved that she gravitated to the wrong type. She was looking to belong—and most of the time, they were looking for her bank account.

"How about you?" she asked. "Life as riveting as always?" Brianna knew I hated my job. She also knew why I did it. She admitted she didn't understand it, but she supported me as best she could.

We had met at university when we'd both tried to grab the same sandwich at the café. It was the last one, and we glared at each other for a moment, neither of us wanting to relinquish the only decent sandwich they made.

Then she had grinned, her green eyes dancing. "Share?"

"I'll get some chips and pop," I agreed.

We'd been friends ever since.

She was wild and bohemian. She ran her own boutique and traveled constantly, finding treasures to fill the shelves. It wasn't a huge moneymaker, but she loved it and didn't really need the money. I missed her when she was away, but I understood her inability to stay in one place very long.

"Ah…I met someone," I admitted, thinking of Logan.

"Please tell me he isn't one of the parent-approved stiff suits?"

I shuddered, thinking of the few men my parents had tried

setting me up with. Dull, uninspired men my father knew. Successful, well-off, and all with the personality of a wet dishrag. But every one in keeping with the lifestyle they wanted for me, which, in their eyes, made them perfect.

"No," I assured her. "Definitely not approved. I met him on my own."

"All right. We need dinner. I need details. I'll meet you at your place at seven."

"Oh, ah, Logan was coming over."

"Awesome, even better. I'll get to meet him and give you my approval. I'll pick up Chinese on the way over."

"Sounds good."

I hung up and glanced out the window. Snowflakes were falling, light and gentle, drifting on the wind. It wasn't a storm, more like a light dusting. Enough to cover the gray mounds on the sides of the roads and make everything fresh and beautiful again. I would convince Logan to go for another walk tonight once Brianna left. He loved walking as much as I did.

I sent him a quick text, explaining the added guest, and he replied with a smiley face and the words, *"Can't wait."*

I glanced at my phone, idly wondering if I should call my mother. It was Thursday, which normally meant it was dinner with my parents. But I hadn't heard from her, and my father hadn't said a word. I knew better than to simply show up at their place—my mother had to stop being angry with me first. Which meant she was waiting for me to apologize. I reached to pick up the phone, then changed my mind. Maybe it would be better to wait and let her cool down. Hopefully if I gave her a little more time, she would be ready to listen, and we would mend fences. I wondered if my father had said anything to her about last night.

I picked up the phone and called Lorie. She answered quickly, always efficient.

"Hello, Charlotte."

"Hey, Lorie, the party next month—can I change my attendance to add a plus-one?"

"Of course. Is Brianna coming with you?"

I chuckled. Brianna loved the holiday party. Mostly because she loved to rile up my parents and flirt shamelessly with the single men. With her golden-blond hair, green eyes, and the lithesome figure she liked to show off, she caused quite a stir. If her parents weren't such an important investor to my father, he would no doubt tell me she wasn't welcome, but because of the status of her family, he allowed it. Unhappily. He always held the party mid-December so as to not interfere with all the other events that happened closer to the holidays. I personally thought he did it early simply to get it over with. It was not his favorite night of the year, but I looked forward to it.

"No, um, I'm bringing my boyfriend."

"Oh," she breathed. "I didn't know."

"We're pretty new, but I thought he'd enjoy it."

"I'll mark you down for two."

"Thanks, Lorie."

I hung up and got back to work. I needed to be out by six tonight.

I heard him as I stepped off the train. The notes of his guitar and the timbre of his voice. My shoulders relaxed, and I rounded the corner, stopping to look at him. He was in his usual spot, his gaze locked where he knew I would appear. He smiled, his dimple showing, and he directed his voice my way. I approached the bench, knowing he expected me to sit and listen to him before we left. It was his gift to me. I spied Brianna sitting, staring at him in awe, and I crossed to where she was seated.

"Hey," I greeted her.

She looked up and yanked on my sleeve. "Oh my god, sit down. Listen to this guy. He is amazing!"

I tried not to laugh. "Yes, he is."

"I haven't been able to move. He's mesmerizing. Is he here a lot?" she asked, not taking her eyes off him.

"Yes."

"I'm moving. I need to be at this station every day, then." She glanced over at me. "I mean, seriously. He is hot."

I sighed, meeting his gaze. "He is. He makes every day better." He winked and smiled, and I couldn't help my returning grin.

She glanced at Logan, then back at me. "*Holy shit.*"

"What?"

"That's him?" she breathed out. "That's the unapproved man?"

I hummed in reply, not wanting to miss a moment of Logan's song.

Logan stopped playing and, in seconds, strode toward us. He set down his guitar case and bent, brushing his mouth over mine. "Hello, my Snow Queen."

"Hi," I whispered.

"Oh my god," Brianna groaned.

I chuckled and introduced them. Logan shook her hand, and she gazed up at him. "What are you doing playing in a subway station?"

He responded by cupping my cheek and stroking my face with his thumb. "I play for her."

Brianna sighed. "I'm going to get dinner, and I'll meet you at your place." She stood and wagged her finger at me. "You have a lot to tell me, and you don't get to leave a word out."

Logan tugged on my hand. "We'll walk with you. It's dark, and you shouldn't be out alone."

She stared at him as if he were a figment of her imagination.

"Sexy, talented, and a gentleman? My god, you've hit the jackpot, Lottie."

I stood, and we walked behind her. I squeezed Logan's hand. "Yes, I have."

Over spicy beef and sticky, delicious noodles, Brianna grilled Logan. What he did. Where he grew up. How we met. What grade he taught. Where he lived. I was currently laughing at her last question. Asked with her chin propped up in one hand, the other clutching an egg roll.

"Do you happen to have a twin brother? Even an older one. I'd take him."

Logan chuckled as he chewed a dripping wonton, wiping the sweet-and-sour sauce off his lips. He swallowed and picked up his water glass, shaking his head. "Just me."

"Damn. Any spare DNA around? Maybe we could make one."

He choked as he laughed, meeting my eyes with a wink. "Bit young for you, then, Brianna."

"Damn it, you're right. Okay, friends who like to follow your example?"

He grinned. "Maybe."

"I'm rich," she stated. "Happy to be a sugar momma."

He studied her, then spoke, his voice serious. "I think perhaps you're selling yourself short, Brianna. I believe you have way more to offer than your money."

Brianna gaped at him for a moment and did something I had never seen until that very moment.

She blushed.

Her cheeks flushed, her mouth opened, but no words came out. Instead, she shoved in a piece of beef and chewed, the incredulous look on her face priceless.

I squeezed Logan's knee. I always told her that, but I had never heard anyone else say that to her.

The rest of the dinner was quiet, although Logan teased me about my ineptitude with chopsticks, often leaning close to feed me a bite. I knew he was using it as an excuse, and I was fine with that.

After dinner, Logan reached for his coat.

"Where are you going?" I asked, confused.

He bent over and kissed my forehead. "You need some girl time."

Brianna shook her head. "I'm the one who crashed your night, Logan. I'll go."

"Nope. I know Lottie has missed you. I've got some papers to mark, so I'll go get that done." He slipped his hand under my chin, tilting up my face and pressing his mouth to mine. His lips lingered, warm and firm, then he drew back. "By the way, I have a gig at The Tavern tomorrow." He tapped my nose. "Want to come see your man play?"

"I didn't know that."

He winked. "Last minute. I got a call this afternoon."

"Absolutely. I would love it."

He smiled at Brianna. "You're welcome to join. I have a table reserved."

"Awesome."

He ran his finger over my cheek. "Call me later, Snow Queen."

"I will."

My eyes followed him until the door clicked closed. I sighed and met Brianna's gaze.

"He looks as good going as he did coming." She smirked, leaning close. "And you have to tell me how fucking spectacular is *that* vision?" Dramatically, she opened her eyes wide. "He's an animal in bed, isn't he, you lucky bitch?"

"You have no idea," I whispered.

"Well, I'm about to find out, because you're going to tell me. Don't leave out a single detail." She cocked her head to the side.

"And I want all the details on how you met, not the PG version. Now, spill."

An hour later, we had consumed a bottle of wine, and I had told her everything. It felt good to be able to talk about Logan. To say out loud the things I'd been thinking. To share what a wonderful person had come into my life. She had listened, hardly interrupting, although she laughed at the part about my father seeing us on the dance floor.

"Charles probably shit himself."

"He wasn't happy."

She looked at me wryly. "He never is."

It was something we had in common. Parents who ignored us. Hers were too busy jet-setting and enjoying life to let something as insignificant as a child slow them down. Brianna had been raised by a succession of nannies and sent off to school. Although she portrayed a carefree face to the world, deep inside, I knew her most intimate dream—a home and family of her own. To be loved and cared for and know she was the top priority to someone. I hoped she would find it—she deserved it. We both did.

"I can't believe you never told me about him," she stated, then threw a pillow at me. "And I can't believe you went to dinner with him—a perfect stranger! He could have been a psycho."

I caught the pillow and set in on my lap. I shook my head slowly. "But I knew he wasn't. He watched over me. He made me feel safe." I sighed. "He still does. When I'm with him, it's as if the world revolves around him. And he surrounds me."

"My god." She stared at me. "You're in love with him."

I scoffed. "It's only been a little while. I'm not in love with him. We have great chemistry and I like him a lot, but it's a little early for the L-word."

Yet even as I denied it, I felt it.

I was falling in love with Logan. In the time I had known

him, he had become more important to me than anything. Anyone.

How was that possible?

I had no idea, but I knew it was the truth.

Brianna pulled her legs to her chest, wrapping her arms around them. "What are you going to do?"

I copied her position and shrugged. "What can I do? Logan's important to me. My parents will have to learn to deal."

"What if your father keeps making an example out of you? Giving you lower-profile projects?"

I blew out a long puff of air. "That's the rub here. Aside from the embarrassment I felt at first, I've actually enjoyed working on these ventures. Less stress. Less time needed." I rested my chin on my knees. "I've spent more time with Logan than at the office. I like it."

She studied me for a moment. "Have you thought that maybe this is the time to make a change, Lottie? Do what you really want to do rather than paying back a debt you don't owe? Maybe putting yourself first for a change?"

I worried the seam on my sweater, pulling at the fraying hem. "Logan hates what I do. Not my job per se, but the stress it causes me." I explained about his father and how he lost him. "He's worried the same thing will happen to me."

"I agree with him. I always told you that job wasn't for you."

"I'm good at it."

"At what cost? This is the first time in years I've seen you this relaxed. Logan is right—stress does terrible things to a person."

"So what am I supposed to do? Quit my job and find a place that will take me on and bake cookies and cakes?" I stated dryly. "I don't think I could even afford to keep my condo."

"Then move in with me. I'm hardly ever there. Or even better, let me loan you the money, and open your own place."

"I can't do that. It's risky at best. I have no experience, and chances are you'd lose your investment." I smiled grimly. "Trust me, I know what I'm talking about."

She rolled her eyes. "I could afford it."

I reached over and squeezed her hand. "Thank you."

"Think about it. Promise me."

"I will."

She grinned. "Now, tomorrow, how slutty should I dress?"

I smirked. "Your usual."

"Oh, I have some planning to do, then. What about you?"

"Haven't really thought about it."

She groaned. "Girl, your man is gonna be onstage singing the way he does and looking all sorts of hot. The women will be flocking. You need to arm yourself. I'm talking about looking so hot he won't be able to take his eyes off you."

I feel a small ripple of pride. "He never does."

She winked. "He certainly won't once I'm done with you."

It was useless trying to argue with her. I lifted my hands in supplication.

"Okay, then. I'm yours."

CHAPTER 15
LOGAN

"I'm surprised to see you home," Trevor stated dryly, flinging himself on the chair across from me. "Haven't seen much of you these days."

"It's only been a week," I muttered. I had to admit, it felt like longer. I couldn't recall what my life had been like before Lottie. Even the weeks leading up to when we finally spoke, she had been in the center of my thoughts and I had been at the subway station every night waiting for her, so I hadn't been around much.

He laughed, popping the top off a beer and taking a sip. "How goes the teaching?"

"Good. I like this school. Kids are great, the staff is nice. It'll be good to have a steady place for a while."

"Great."

"How's the gym?" I asked.

"Swamped. I can't keep up with new clients. I had to hire two more instructors."

"That's awesome, Trev." I grinned and took a sip of the water I had poured earlier. "Try not to screw them, and maybe you'll keep them a little longer."

A strange look passed over his face. "I haven't screwed anyone in a while, Logan. It's been over a month. Longer, even."

"That's a record for you."

He focused on something over my shoulder, not meeting my eyes. "It suddenly seemed so empty. Useless." He shrugged. "I decided I needed to step back and focus on the business instead of my dick."

"Sounds as if it's paying off for you."

He nodded, taking another sip of his beer.

"I have a gig tomorrow, if you're interested. The Tavern. Nine o'clock. I have a table reserved."

"Your lady coming?"

"Yes. I think she's bringing her friend Brianna. I met her tonight."

"Hot?" he asked with a salacious grin.

I frowned. "Yes. But lost."

"What do you mean?"

"Obviously, I don't know her very well, but I think she's trying to find herself."

"Aren't we all?"

"I suppose." I shrugged and went back to the papers I was grading. Trev stood and stretched.

"I'll see you tomorrow."

"Great," I replied. "Night."

He left, and I worked until the papers were done. I texted Lottie, wishing her a good night, smiling at the slightly misspelled reply she eventually sent. I had a feeling she'd been into the wine with Brianna. She said something about a hot outfit and being a groupie. If that meant she was dressing up to see me tomorrow, I was good with that, but I decided not to question it too much tonight. I wanted her to have fun with her friend. From what I had gathered, Lottie didn't have enough fun in her life.

I glanced at my phone, thinking about another conversation from earlier. Carmen Runnalls had reached out. I had been surprised when Lottie asked me for my permission to give him my number, and even more shocked when he followed through. He had been straight to the point with me.

"I have seen you perform a few times, Logan. I liked what I heard."

"Thanks," I replied, unsure about where this was going.

"We're always looking for talent."

For a moment, I was stunned. I cleared my throat. "I'm honored, but I don't really have any interest in being a recording artist, Carmen. The limelight isn't for me."

He chuckled. "I figured that. I recalled how quickly you left the stage and how you disappeared. I wasn't able to find out much about you, and your gigs were never regular."

"I enjoy a small setting, but that is about where I draw the line."

"What about something else?"

"Such as?"

"Being in the background. Having your music recorded by someone else."

Now, my interest perked up. That was my dream—the one I had confided to Lottie.

"I would be open to a discussion," I said calmly, not giving away my emotions.

"Great. Let's set up a meeting."

We agreed to talk the following week. I hadn't said anything to Lottie tonight as I didn't want her to get her hopes up. I hadn't said anything to Trevor, because the bottom line was—I didn't want to get *my* hopes up. I might not like what Carmen had to say. He might not like my conditions.

Or, a voice in my head whispered, like with Lottie, another dream of mine might possibly be about to come true.

♫

"Who the hell is that?" Trevor demanded, looking over my shoulder.

I glanced around, my gaze immediately focusing on Lottie.

She was wearing a navy-blue swing coat, snow dusting on her shoulders and hair. She was talking with Brianna, who had already pulled off her coat, her revealing black dress clinging to all her curves. Brianna's hair was slicked away from her face, and she wore knee-high red boots. She was obviously the one who had Trev's attention, but it was Lottie that my gaze followed.

"That's Brianna, Lottie's friend I told you about," I mumbled as I stood, waiting for Lottie to come closer.

"You better introduce me. Talk me up."

I couldn't take my eyes off Lottie. She slipped her coat from her shoulders, showing the red dress underneath. Cut lower in the front than I was used to seeing on her, it hugged her curves and flared to her knees. It was sexy and pretty, but not over the top. She had her hair piled on top of her head in a messy bun, with tendrils dancing around her face and touching her shoulders. Her eyes looked huge in her face due to the makeup she was wearing, and again, the red lipstick on her full mouth made me want to kiss her. Hard. Our eyes had locked when she came in, and our gazes never wavered until she was in front of me. I slid my hand around her neck, pulling her close.

"You are stunning," I breathed into her ear, then kissed the sensitive spot on her neck. I smiled at the shiver that went through her. "Thank you."

I drew back and met her eyes again, taking her coat and kissing Brianna's cheek. "Brianna, nice to see you again. This is my roommate, Trevor." I winked. "He thinks you're hot."

"Asshole," he muttered.

Brianna laughed, the sound making Trevor smile. "Then I think we'll get along just fine, Muscles. How often do you work out?" she asked, her eyes roving over his torso.

He flexed and stood straighter, his shirt pulling taut across his chest. "I own my own gym, so every day."

She moved past me, standing in front of him. "It shows."

They sat down and started to talk. It was as if Lottie and I had ceased to exist. I met her amused eyes and pulled out a chair. As she sat, I moved beside her, my hand brushing her back. Her bare back. I leaned over, almost groaning at the expanse of skin left by the geometrical cut of the dress.

"Jesus," I whispered to her. "You are going to kill me tonight."

"Brianna said I needed to look good for you."

I slid my hand under her chin. "You always look good to me. Beautiful, in fact. But I love this look. It's sexy and fun." I shifted closer. "Too sexy."

She slid her hand up my leg, cupping me. "Problem, Logan?"

"Always, with you." I bit down on her ear. "I'm always hard for you, but looking like that? *Jesus.*"

She gazed up at me, her eyes dancing. "I'll make it up to you later." She squeezed lightly. "I'll be your groupie for the night."

I shook my head. "You'll never be a groupie to me."

Lottie rolled her eyes. "Tonight, I am, Logan," she insisted. "Tonight is all about fun." She paused. "Fantasy."

I slipped my hand under the table, holding hers tight to me. "Well then, Charlotte, whom I just met, brace yourself. Tonight is gonna be the best night of your life."

She moved closer, brushing her mouth with mine. "My rock-star fantasy."

"I'll do my best." I gripped her neck and kissed her. I kissed her hard enough to make that non-smudgeable red lipstick fade a little. I kissed her with so much ardent possession there was no doubt who she belonged to.

When I heard the sound of my name being called, I pulled away and stood, gazing down at her. Her lips were swollen and wet, her eyes glazed, and she was breathing heavily.

"That," I promised, "is just a sample for later."

Color infused her cheeks, and she shook her head. "I look forward to it, Logan."

I winked. "So do I."

♫

LOTTIE

I thought Logan was talented in the subway. But on that little stage in front of me, his voice amplified, he was larger than life. His voice filled the bar, echoing in the smaller space. His words dripped with emotion, his fingers flying over his guitar as he sang. Some moments, he was still, lost in the cadence of the music. Other times, his foot tapped, or he strolled the stage. Dressed in tight jeans, a simple white shirt with the sleeves rolled up, and a heavy brocade vest, he was sex on legs. His hair brushed the collar of his shirt, and he often pushed it away from his face, the light glinting off the heavy silver jewelry he wore. And his eyes—those sexy, whiskey-colored eyes—were at times intense and dark, emotional and captivating. And a great deal of time, focused on me. He rarely spoke between songs, other than a quiet thank-you or the inclination of his head. When his set ended, he sat with his head lowered, his hands clasped on the guitar as the notes faded away and the room filled with applause.

He was, indeed, my rock-star fantasy come to life.

He lifted his hand as he stepped off the stage and came to the table, sitting down and immediately lifting a tall glass of ice water and downing it. He wiped off his face and grinned. "How was that, my Snow Queen? Fantasy enough for you?"

It was my turn to grasp the back of his neck and kiss him. His lips were soft, salty from sweat, and his breath hot, mingling with mine. I could feel his carefully controlled passion simmering below his skin as he jerked me close. I eased back, smiling. "Quite enough."

"Good. I'm starving." He winked. "Not only for food, but I need to eat."

"Logan," a voice behind me spoke. I turned as Logan stood, looking surprised.

"Carmen, I didn't expect to see you tonight."

"I heard a rumor. I dropped by to see if it was true." He shook Logan's hand. "That was truly amazing."

Logan smiled, his hand gripping my shoulder. "Thanks."

Carmen greeted me. "Hello, Charlotte. I should have known his number one fan would be front and center."

"Hello, Carmen. You're right, it was amazing."

I noticed another man with him. He looked familiar, but it wasn't until he introduced him that I realized why.

"Logan, Charlotte, this is Bobby Hayes. He's one of our artists."

Bobby grinned. "You hope I'm one of your artists," he teased good-naturedly.

Carmen laughed with him, not looking worried.

Bobby Hayes was an up-and-coming star. His music was all over YouTube. He was one of the stars Roadside Records was chasing. So were other labels, from what Carmen had told me. He was determined to sign him.

Bobby stepped forward and shook Logan's hand. "That was fucking inspiring, man. Those songs, I mean...wow. I don't have words."

Logan looked shocked, but he acknowledged Bobby's praise with a tilt of his head and returned his handshake. "Thanks. I appreciate it."

Carmen clapped Logan on the shoulder. "Next week for sure, right?"

"It'll have to be the evening or early morning. I'm teaching all week."

Carmen nodded in agreement. "You name the time and place, we'll be there."

Logan frowned. "We?"

"I asked to be part of your meeting, Logan." Bobby spoke up. "If that's okay with you. I'm very interested in what Carmen has to offer you, and I'd like to get my two cents in."

"It's fine with me," Logan agreed. "I'll call you on Monday, Carmen."

They shook hands again and moved back to their table. I watched them go as Logan sat down. I met his gaze with a grin. "I think they'd like to have that meeting right now," I told him. "Bobby looked as if he was going to jump out of his skin."

He hummed. "I know. Odd."

I disagreed. "No. Inspired."

He moved closer. "The only one I want to inspire is you. You ready to leave?"

I glanced over at Brianna. She was so deep in conversation with Trevor, she hadn't even noticed Bobby and Carmen. He was so focused on her, he was oblivious as well. They had enjoyed Logan's set, but once it was over, they only had eyes for each other. I knew she wouldn't care if I left, but I felt bad since I came with her.

"You don't have another set?"

"No, I only agreed to one. My voice won't take two, and I need it to teach next week."

"Okay."

He sensed my reticence and caught Trevor's attention. "We're going to get something to eat. You good here, or you want to come with?"

"I'm good here," Trevor replied.

Brianna winked at me. "I'll call you tomorrow."

"I'll make sure she gets home safely," Trevor assured me.

Logan stood and pulled me to my feet. "Great." He grabbed his guitar case with a grin. "Behave, you two."

They laughed and waved us off.

We headed to the diner, Logan's arm wound tight around my waist. I could feel the tension in his body. The controlled power of his muscles. It was evident in his grip, his long strides, and the way he held himself. We sat down in the diner, Macy bringing over coffee without being asked. She smiled at Logan.

"The usual, hon?"

He nodded and looked at me. I ordered the same, knowing whatever I didn't eat, he would. He sipped his coffee and sat back with a sigh, his eyes shut.

I observed him for a moment, then rested my elbows on the table, tracing the back of his hand with my finger. "You don't enjoy that?" I asked quietly. "Being up onstage, the attention?"

His lips quirked, but his eyes remained closed. "That obvious?"

"You were amazing. You are so talented."

He hunched forward, opening his eyes and meeting my questioning gaze. "I love writing songs. I enjoy singing to a few people. I find larger groups overwhelming, if I'm being honest."

"Do you always sing and leave right away?" I had noticed he only spoke with a few people, didn't do an encore, and we had left out the back, avoiding most of the crowd.

"Usually." He paused. "I can't do two sets. Or, let me clarify. I can, but I would suffer the next day. I had throat trouble when I was younger and had surgery. There were some complications, and I've had to learn to live within the boundaries they recommended."

I clasped his hand. "I'm sorry."

He lifted my hand to his mouth and kissed it. "It happens. I've gotten past it. It left me with this rougher edge to my voice, which is great when I sing, but I can't do it for prolonged periods or I risk losing it."

I was horrified. "But you sing to me every night! You need——"

He cut me off with his finger on my mouth. "I croon, Lottie. It's different from belting out song after song to a large room. I don't overstretch my voice when I sing to you. That's why I stand where I do. I use the natural acoustics in the station to let my voice carry. And that's a short period. Not two-hour concerts."

"So, that is what stops you from pursuing a career in music?"

"Not just that. I love seeing people's reactions to my music, but I enjoy the process and the arrangement more than singing it myself—unless it's for you. I don't crave the spotlight or the attention."

Our food arrived, and he dove in, picking up his burger and taking a huge bite, chewing it slowly. "God, that's good."

I chuckled and added some ketchup to my plate. I loved watching him eat. I loved watching him sing. I pretty much loved watching him do anything.

I had to avert my eyes as I realized I probably loved it so much because Brianna was right. I was falling in love with him. It didn't matter if it had been a week, a month, or even a year. My feelings were real and solid. And I wasn't sure how to handle that.

"Hey, what's wrong?" Logan asked, his voice concerned. "Are you okay, Lottie?"

I was frozen, staring at him as the truth hit me. He leaned across, wiping a finger under my eye. "Why are you crying?"

I shook my head and reached for a napkin. "The onions are strong," I fibbed.

"They're fried. Try again. What is it, sweetheart?"

His endearment rocked me. The soft caress of his voice, the way he was watching me with concern. He made me feel as if I mattered.

I swiped at my cheek. "Nothing. Just so damn proud of you." I picked up my burger, changing the subject. I wasn't revealing my feelings over burgers at a diner. "And Carmen? What was he talking about?"

He told me about their phone call. He frowned as he dragged his fries through the ketchup and chewed them. "Did you tell him about the gig?"

"No. I haven't spoken to him since our meeting."

"Huh," was his reply.

I couldn't help but tease him. "He sought you out all on his own, Logan. No help from me."

He rolled his eyes and pushed my plate closer. "Whatever, woman. Eat. I need you strong. I've got plans for you, and you're going to have to keep up."

"That sounds promising."

He winked. "It will be."

CHAPTER 16

LOTTIE

After we ate, we walked. Logan seemed restless and edgy—unable to settle. There was a light snowfall, and the streets were deserted. We strolled, not talking, simply enjoying the time. I felt him relax, his grip loosening, his footsteps not as rushed. We finally ended up back outside my building, and I hurried up the steps, anxious for warmth. I hadn't wanted to admit to Logan the boots I was wearing weren't meant for long walks, nor was my coat as warm as what I would choose for an extended stroll. He followed, quiet and seemingly reflective, his mood confusing me.

I had stopped at one point, staring at a small Tudor-style house. They were well ahead of the game, their Christmas lights bright in the darkness. "What a pretty place," I murmured, admiring the lines of the house and the leaded windows that twinkled with the lights.

Logan stared at it. "You like that? It's not fancy or new."

"I don't want fancy or new. It looks homey. I bet the rooms are filled with all sorts of hidden alcoves and weird angles." I glanced around. "The neighborhood is quiet as well."

"It is. I walk here a lot."

We kept going, but I glanced over my shoulder, something about the house beckoning to me. I planned to walk past it again another time.

In my condo, I shrugged off my coat and ran my hands up and down my arms to warm them. Logan watched me, then cursed, yanking off his coat and boots and lifting me into his arms. I gasped at the unexpected move.

"What are you doing?"

He strode down the hall and into the bathroom, setting me on the counter. Wordlessly, he pulled off my boots, lifted me to my feet, and yanked my dress over my head, making short work of my lacy undergarments.

He turned on the shower, checking the temperature, and indicated the steaming water. "Get in."

I shuddered as the heat hit my skin, gasping when Logan stepped in, crowding me with his body. He rubbed at my arms briskly, muttering.

"I forgot you weren't dressed for a walk, Lottie. You should have reminded me."

"I was enjoying it."

He dropped to his knees, stroking my legs. "And now you're frozen."

"You're doing a good job of warming me up," I murmured.

He glanced up, his eyes dark. He stood, crowding me against the wall, his body teeming with tension, his skin hot against my cold.

"Do you know why I needed to go for a walk, Lottie? Stop and eat before coming here?"

"You were hungry?" I guessed. "Restless from performing?"

He inched closer, his chest melding to mine. He slid his hands down my arms, entwining our fingers and lifting my hands over my head, imprisoning them there. He stroked my neck with one finger, making me shiver, this time with desire and not cold.

"I was out of control. If we'd come right here, I would have fucked you. Hard. I would have taken my pleasure, and I'm not sure I would have cared about yours." He lowered his head to my neck, licking up the skin, biting at the juncture, his teeth teasing just short of pain, making me squirm against him. "I can't do that to you."

"I don't believe that. You always give me pleasure," I objected, then whimpered as he began to trail his tongue along my collarbone and cupped my breast with his large hand, strumming the nipple.

"I was wound too tight," he said. "It was too much. The crowd. You. Carmen. The reaction to my music. I needed an outlet. I still do."

"Use me," I begged, feeling desire sweep through me. I undulated against him, his cock hard and trapped between us.

"I don't want to use you," he protested. "You mean too much."

I knew one thing he wouldn't be able to resist. No matter what else he was feeling, his protectiveness for me was always paramount. He needed to care for me. I knew this with a certainty beyond belief. I slid my leg up to his hip, opening myself to him. He groaned as he curved his hand around my thigh.

"Warm me up, Logan. Fuck me. Please," I added breathlessly. "I need you."

I cried out as he lifted me, grasping my legs, and with one snap of his hips, slammed into me. I felt full, the angle intense, and his cock stretching me in the most delicious, aching way. He began to move—fierce, short thrusts. He covered my mouth, his lips hard and demanding. His tongue mimicked his hips, his body trapping me against the tile, his hands holding my hips tight. My nipples brushed against his rough chest hair, chafed and sensitive, his nipple ring heating in the warmth of the water. He hit my clit with every thrust, driving me wild with pleasure. He made low, guttural sounds in his throat, his chest vibrating as he took me.

The steam swirled around us, the heat building. I was on fire, the cold of a short while ago long forgotten. Everything narrowed down to our bodies, moving as one, the ecstasy building between us so intense it edged on pain. I whimpered as I surrendered, my body locking down, clenching around him. I screamed into his mouth as my release rushed over me, burning and strong. I gripped his shoulders, my fingernails digging into his skin as my orgasm kept going, one sliding into another as he broke from my mouth, cursing and chanting my name. The grip he had on my hips tightened, and he dropped his head back, a long, satisfied groan escaping from his chest. I went limp in his arms, unable to form words, thoughts, or even hold on. He thrust twice more, then stilled, but he continued to hold me. His heartbeat was a rapid staccato in his chest, his breathing fast and harsh. Both matched mine.

For a moment, there was only the sound of the rushing water and our heavy breathing. He lifted his head and kissed me, his mouth now gentle.

"Tell me you're all right."

I opened one eye and peered at him. "I'm better than all right, Logan."

He pulled from me, and I grimaced as he left my body, feeling empty. He set me on my feet and washed me, his touch tender, his voice low as he whispered unneeded apologies, mingled with kisses, words of adoration, and gentle ministrations. He cleaned himself quickly, then turned off the shower and wrapped a towel around me. He snagged another one and tucked it around his waist.

"You, ah, might want to wash your face," he chuckled, touching my cheek. "It's a bit…" He trailed off.

I looked in the mirror and had to giggle. My mascara was smudged under my eyes and my kiss-proof lipstick smeared on my cheek.

"I guess kiss-proof and fuck-proof are two different things," I chuckled and reached for the makeup remover, making fast work of the mess. I rinsed the cloth and turned to Logan. "Better now that I don't look like a drunken goth?"

He cupped my cheek and brushed his lips over my face, kissing my nose, cheeks, forehead, then pressing his lips to mine.

"I would fuck you no matter what, Lottie. You are beautiful to me every single moment of the day." Then his voice deepened. "And it was more than just fucking."

I opened my eyes, meeting his intense gaze. "Logan, it's okay to let yourself go with me. I know I'm, ah, more to you. I like making love, making out, dancing, touching, and yes, *fucking* you. All of it because it's you. Because it's us."

He cupped my face and kissed me, his lips gentle, his voice reverent.

"I don't know how I got so lucky to have you, Lottie. But know I will never take that gift for granted."

"Me either," I whispered. "You are the best thing that has ever happened to me. Ever."

He enveloped me in his arms, holding me tight. I nestled close, hoping this never changed.

I knew right then, I was in love with Montgomery Logan. Every single side of him, I adored.

And I wanted to keep him.

Logan and I spent Saturday together. We lazed around the bedroom in the morning, went ice-skating in the afternoon, and I made dinner. It was simple—spaghetti with a marinara sauce, but it was delicious, and it was nice to have dinner with him in the condo. We watched a movie, then I read for a bit while Logan strummed on his guitar, furiously writing in a notebook as he created a lovely melody that made me hum. I fell asleep listening to him play, and he carried me to bed, only waking when he crawled in beside me hours later. He pulled me back to his chest, kissing my shoulder, and I fell back asleep in the cradle of his arms.

Sunday morning, his phone rang early, and he walked down the hall, talking low and fast. When he came back to the bedroom, he pulled on his jeans, frowning. "Sorry, Lottie, I gotta go."

I leaned back against the headboard, admiring how his muscles flexed and moved as he dressed. "Other girlfriend demanding your time?" I asked lightly.

He bent over me with a hard kiss. "Yep. The teacher I was supposed to cover for next term had her baby about an hour ago. I'm meeting the principal to go over things." He chuckled. "And then apparently, going to the hospital to meet with Cindy. She insists she has to talk to me about her class."

"Wow, that's dedication."

He tugged his shirt over his head and sat on the edge of the bed. He rested on his arms, caging me between them. "I'm sorry I have to go—I wanted to spend another day with you." He tucked a strand of hair behind my ear. "Yesterday was one of the nicest days I've had in a long time, just being with you."

"Me too. But I understand."

"The next little while might be sort of crazy." He frowned. "Especially this week." He glanced down at his hands. "I hate the thought of not seeing you every day."

I cupped his cheek, running my fingers over his beard. "We can text and call."

He met my eyes, looking upset. "I might not be there at night, playing for you."

"Logan," I breathed. "I am not your responsibility. It's not your job to make sure my day is okay."

He held my hand against his skin, the heat burning into my palm. "Yes, it is," he insisted. "Everything about you is my business now, Lottie." He paused, searching my eyes. "I love you."

His words exploded in my brain. They settled into my fractured heart, mending and stitching it together. Such simple words —small and overused by many—but directed toward me, by this man, they were significant.

Life-changing.

He smiled at my silence. "I know it's early, and I don't expect you to feel the same, Lottie. I just… I just wanted you to know. Maybe it will help some days knowing, no matter what else, I'm close and I'm always thinking about you." He studied me. "Maybe if you knew someone wanted to be your happiness, it might make the day easier."

He started to get up, but I stopped him. I couldn't let him leave not knowing. Thinking he'd given his heart to me and I'd rejected him. Tears pooled in my eyes at the enormity of this moment.

He looked at me, concerned. "What? What is it?"

I sniffed. "Aside from Brianna, no one has said that to me since Josh died."

He grimaced, but I silenced him with a finger pressed to his lips. "You have no idea what it does to me to hear you say those words, Logan." I swallowed. "Because I love you too."

His expression morphed from worried to disbelief, then to happiness. "Say it again."

"I love you, Montgomery Logan. It's fast, it's crazy, but it's true. I love you."

He pulled me to him, surrounding me with his warmth. He held me, whispering quiet words of love and adoration. Assuring me we would work it all out. That time didn't matter—what did was the rightness of us.

It was only his phone going off again that pulled us apart.

"You have to go."

"I don't want to. I want to stay and bask in this."

I gently shoved at him. "We have lots of time to bask. Go do what you have to."

He backed toward the door, his whiskey eyes focused on me. "I love you."

I smiled. "I love you, Logan."

He smiled back, his dimple popping. He laid his hand over his heart, the gesture reminding me of the first night we actually spoke. Even then, I was half in love with him. "Those are the sweetest words I have ever heard. Thank you."

Then he was gone.

CHAPTER 17
LOTTIE

The next couple of weeks were busy for us both. Logan was teaching every day, preparing lesson plans and grading papers. Despite the projects I was working on being simpler than usual, I was still busy with investors, meetings, and making sure everyone was happy. My team was smaller, so we all had to work extra hard. Most nights, it was past eight when I left the building. Logan was rarely at the platform, although a few times, he met me there. But I gave him a key to my place, so often when I walked in, he was sitting at the table, working away. He always stopped to kiss me hello, make sure I ate, and at some point, sang to me. The nights he was absent, my place felt empty. My bed seemed too big, and I didn't sleep as well.

I wrapped up the deal with Ravaged Records and Roadside quickly. The investors I had in mind were enthusiastic and generous. The final papers were being drafted for signatures and a press conference being planned. I was both pleased and sad. It had been a fun project, unlike most of them. I liked the people I was working with and was passionate about their ideas.

It took everything in me not to question Carmen about his

meetings with Logan. They were both tight-lipped on what they were discussing, and I had to keep a professional distance. I knew when Logan was ready, he would tell me. He was juggling a lot right now, and I didn't want to waste the time we did have together trying to pull something out of him he wasn't ready to share.

I finally gave in and called my mother. There was no point in prolonging the inevitable. I was going to have to apologize in order for us to move forward. My father was distant and chillier than usual. When I closed the Ravaged deal, there were no pats on the back or words of appreciation for a job well done. Another project appeared on my desk, and that was all. It was his way of letting me know I had performed satisfactorily and he would trust me with another venture. Part of me hoped for something personal from him. That he would walk into my office and say something positive—anything—to open the door between us, but it didn't happen. I wasn't sure why I still wanted and hoped, but my silly heart did. I wondered if I made up with my mother if he would soften, so I reached out.

She was cool on the phone but agreed to meet me for lunch. I studied her as I sat across from her at her favorite place. I only ever went there with her, neither the food nor the stuffy décor my style.

She sipped her mineral water in silence. She had accepted my kiss on the cheek but hadn't offered anything aside from a stiff greeting. I withheld my impatience and smiled at her.

"You look lovely today, Mom."

She patted her hair. "I have a new stylist."

"Very flattering." Sadly, I recalled the days when she would jokingly complain about barely getting a shower in. When her idea of being fancy was blow-drying her hair and having a fresh blouse on when my father came home. My father calling out for his "Jo-Jo" when he walked through the doorway. The days when the evenings were spent laughing around the dinner table, making plans for the weekends as a family, and my world consisted of the love of the people at the table with me. Those times were long gone. My mom, Jo-Jo, slowly disappeared, and the distant woman, Josephine Prescott, firmly took hold.

"You look well," she stated. "Is the office better?"

"I've been very productive."

She raised her eyebrows slightly. I was sure my father described my job status somewhat differently.

We made small talk, the words stilted and uncomfortable.

"I heard from Brianna's mother that she is seeing someone. A business owner, I believe?"

My lips quirked. I doubted my mother would be so interested if she knew Trevor owned a gym and he was friends with Logan. So I made a humming sound of agreement.

I set down my glass and straightened my shoulders. "Mom, I'm sorry I upset you. Can we please make up and move past it?" I offered her a shaky smile, finding this harder than I expected. "I miss you."

Sadness filled her expression for a moment, then she frowned. "You were ungrateful and disrespectful to your father. More than once."

I swallowed down my retort. "I'm sorry you feel that way, but he overstepped."

"Are you still seeing that boy? Your father says he is a delinquent."

I bit back my anger. She made it sound as if I were dating a kid from the hood. "Logan is not a boy, nor is he a delinquent. He is an adult with a full-time job and very respectful. Dad didn't even give him a chance to introduce himself. He wrote him off because he had longer hair. Dad judged him on his own personal bias, not his character."

"He says he is distracting you from your work."

I disagreed. "You know I was struggling before I even met

Logan. If anything, he has helped me focus on what is really important."

It was true. I simply didn't tell her what I was focusing on mattered more than mergers and the boardroom deals that my father obsessed about.

"He's after your money."

I gaped at her. "What money?"

"The money you will get when your father and I pass."

I had to roll my eyes. "Since neither you nor Dad is ill, are both relatively young and healthy, I guess he has a very long wait. I highly doubt he targeted me on the off chance I'd come into money one day." I was quiet as the waiter slipped our organic salads in front of us, then departed. "I'm a little insulted you would think that is the only reason any man would be interested in me."

She pursed her lips. "Now you're putting words in my mouth."

I sighed. "He cares about me, Mom. He really cares. He treats me so well…" I trailed off as I realized how close to tears I was. Surprised, I cleared my throat. I rarely got emotional. "He is wonderful," I finished.

"He's a teacher."

"An honest job."

"Can he support you?"

"I support myself," I reminded her softly. "He makes me so happy. Shouldn't that be more important than his bank account?"

I thought of the few men I had dated. One guy at university. He was my first crush, and it ran its course. We parted friends and moved on. I had gone on a few dates, even suffered through some dinners with my parents and men I knew they were trying to push because they were acceptable—to them. They all bored me. I was already surrounded by suits and business talk all day. I had no desire for that to carry over into my personal life. My father had even tried pushing a couple of his higher-up staff my way. They were only too happy to make a run at the boss's daughter. I was horrified when I found out, and the one date I had agreed to go on before I found out why was a disaster. He was a younger version of my father, and I saw my life mapped out with him. Dull, predictable, and mind-numbing. I couldn't imagine a future with him. With any of them. But I could with Logan.

She was silent, stabbing her salad as if it had somehow offended her. I ate mine, wishing for some creamy ranch instead of the kiss of oil and vinegar on top of it. I wondered about asking for some bread, then decided against it.

"We need to meet him," my mother announced.

My fork froze partway to my mouth. I blinked and ate the bite of salad, chewing carefully.

"Will you be polite?"

She glared.

"I mean it. Will you give him a chance?" I reached out my hand. "Please, Mom. He is important to me."

Again, I was sure I saw a softening in her eyes. Thought she was about to say something significant. But she only cleared her throat. "How important?"

"Extremely."

"Brunch. Sunday. You will bring him."

"I will ask. I'll call you later and let you know."

She seemed to relax, and the rest of the lunch went fine. My mom told me all the gossip and news in her world. None of it had anything to do with me and she asked me very few questions, but at least she was talking to me. I was surprised when she kissed my cheek before getting into her town car. "Call me this evening, Lottie. Let me know about Sunday." She paused. "Is the boy allergic to anything?"

"No. *The boy* is a very good eater," I deadpanned.

She didn't get the joke, simply nodding and sliding into the car. "That makes it easier."

I watched her car leave, then turned and headed back to the office, wondering how Logan was going to take the invite.

Would he accept it or simply tell me no? He wasn't a big fan of my parents, so it wouldn't surprise me if he decided he didn't want to meet them at his point.

But he did surprise me.

"What time?" he asked, rubbing his chin, gazing at me across the table. He'd had grilled cheese sandwiches and tomato soup waiting when I got home, welcoming me with a kiss and a warm hug.

"Usually eleven."

"Do I have to be in a suit?"

I shook my head. "A nice shirt and pants would be appreciated."

He tilted his head. "By your mother or you?"

I grinned. He wore business casual clothes every day to teach in, and he often had his hair pulled back. He was still sexy, although his rough edge was softened. "Those black pants hug your ass pretty nice." I winked.

He chuckled and polished off yet another sandwich. "Okay. I can do civilized another day."

"Really?"

He smiled and took our empty plates to the kitchen. He came back and slid into the seat beside me. "They're your parents, Lottie. I want to meet them. I will show them respect as long as they do the same in return." He ran his finger over my cheek. "My father instilled manners into me. I can behave."

"I have no objections to your manners. "

He leaned forward, kissing me. "Outside the bedroom, anyway."

I giggled as he waggled his eyebrows. When it came to sex, he was extremely bossy and dominating in the bedroom. The bathroom. Against the wall or in the kitchen. Aggressive and dirty-talking. Yet there was an underlying gentleness with me I wasn't sure even he was aware of.

"I like those manners too, but maybe curb those instincts while we're eating with my parents."

"I can do that. I'll use a fork, not pick my teeth, and I won't talk about how sexy you are and how much I like to fuck you."

I threw him a look which made him smirk.

"I'll try not to steal anything either. I'll wait the thirty or forty years for your inheritance. I'm patient."

I groaned. I shouldn't have been so honest with him about what my mother said. He'd found it vastly amusing and had laughed hard.

"Please, Logan." I took his hand. "I've never brought anyone to meet them before who meant so much to me. I just want you to get along. For my sake."

He became serious. "I wouldn't do anything to hurt you, Lottie. I'll be on my best behavior. Do you think they'll offer me the same respect?"

"I don't know," I admitted. "I'd like to think so."

He shrugged. "It will all be fine. It's brunch. What can possibly happen over coffee and breakfast foods served late? They'll ask questions, I'll respond. I'll eat whatever they put in front of me and be polite. It'll be great."

He stood. "I have to get going. I have an early morning meeting, and I still have papers to grade." He bent and kissed me. "I just wanted a little time with you. I'll call you tomorrow."

He paused at the door. "Don't worry about Sunday, Lottie. It's all good."

He left, and I stared at the door, wondering if either of us really believed that.

♫

Sunday morning, I was tired and listless. Logan had spent the night on Friday, but we'd both had commitments on Saturday, and by the time he called later that evening, I was in bed with a headache and feeling exhausted. I didn't sleep well, my dreams filled with odd images that kept disturbing me. When I got up on Sunday, I wondered how much of it had to do with my nerves about brunch and the dread I could feel in my stomach at the thought of how my parents would treat Logan. Part of me wanted to cancel, but I knew that was a bad idea.

Logan arrived before nine, knocking when he arrived. I bit back my amusement—he only used his key when I wasn't home. Otherwise, he knocked and waited. I opened the door, not prepared for what I found. He stood tall and sexy in the doorway, wearing a navy overcoat. His hair was shorter, brushed back from his face, the bleached ends gone, leaving it dark and gleaming. His beard had disappeared, just a light dusting of scruff left along his jaw and chin. He smiled at me, his eyes warm. He bent low and kissed me, moving into the condo and lifting one eyebrow at my startled expression.

He slipped off his coat and laid it over the sofa, lifting his arms. "Will I pass?"

His subtle patterned button-down was tucked into my favorite black dress pants. He had the sleeves rolled up, exposing his forearms. There wasn't a single leather cuff on his wrist. Only one silver ring was on his hand.

I didn't know how to take it. He looked like Logan, but a sleeker, more professional version. Polished and shiny. Staged to make an impression.

For me.

It hit me he had done this for me. To make the brunch easier. My parents couldn't glare at his long hair or rocker-style look if it wasn't there. He wasn't in a suit and tie and oozing money, but he was every inch a confident, vital man. Still a little dangerous and sexy, but it was more subtle. A glossy veneer meant to defuse my parents' ire.

Tears threatened, the way they seemed to do these days, always close to the surface. Once again, he had shown how much he cared by trying to make things easier for me.

Logan frowned, stepping forward. "Lottie, sweetheart, what is it? You hate the shirt?" He looked down. "Trev said the white one looked too formal. I can go change it."

I wiped my eyes. "You look great. Amazing." I paused. "Respectable." My voice broke a little. "You-you cut your hair."

He wrapped his hands around my arms, pulling me close. "Is that what's upsetting you? My hair?"

"I don't expect you to change for me—to impress my parents."

He kissed my forehead. "I didn't do it for them, Lottie. Honest," he assured me. "It was time for a trim. Gretch did it last night and trimmed my beard. I needed to do it for school." He smiled down at me, teasing my chin with his long fingers. "Think about it. When I first started playing for you, my hair was shorter —not this short, but close. I let it grow over the fall. I got lazy and didn't cut it."

"Okay," I sniffled. "But your cuffs…and stuff?"

He held me tighter. "I love that you notice everything about me. I never wear them at work either. Just my dad's ring. I never take that off. Really, Lottie, this is just another side of me. I promise not to turn preppy or, what did you call me earlier? Respectable. I'm still me. Just cleaned up a little. I promise to ravish you thoroughly later and prove it."

I sighed and let his scent wash over me, calming me. He was warm and solid, his embrace comforting. My nerves eased, and the leaden feeling in my stomach loosened.

"Look at me," he ordered softly.

I peered up, meeting his whiskey-colored gaze. "Are you all right, Lottie? You seem off today. Are you that nervous?"

"Yes, I'm fine. Sorry. I was just..." I trailed off, unable to explain. "I never want you to think you have to change for me. I love you exactly the way you are."

"I know. I adore the way you look at me. I admit, last night, it was Gretch's suggestion to cut my hair, but she has been bugging me about it for a while. It'll make my boss happier too. Although she has been great, I'm sure it will go over big with her as well. Parents do like the people who teach their kids to be presentable." He kissed the end of my nose, his voice becoming playful. "Aren't I sexy anymore, Lottie?"

"Of course you are."

"Then it's all good. Some days I'll be your rockerish bad boy, and others I'll be the respectable teacher." He slid his hands down, cupping my ass. "Both sides love you."

I had to chuckle. He lowered his head and kissed me. It was long, deep, and soul-shattering. It set my heart soaring, elated and calmed me, all at once.

He eased back, dropping three gentle pecks to my lips. "Okay, baby. We need to go, or we'll be late. I don't want any more strikes against me."

He shrugged on his overcoat, and I slipped the top button closed. "I like this."

He winked. "It's Trev's. I borrowed it to keep with the image, but if you like it, I'll buy one. I have to admit, it's warmer than my leather jacket."

"I do like it. It shows off your broad shoulders. It's sexy on you."

He flexed and rolled his head. "Then we'll go shopping this week." He helped me on with my coat. "And you look lovely, by the way. Very pretty today. I love you in blue—it brings out your eyes."

His words warmed me. I was wearing one of my favorite weekend outfits. A bright blue tunic with a deep cowl neck and gray leggings I tucked into boots. I wore my hair up, and I had a heavy silver chain Brianna had given me cinched around my waist. "Thank you."

He looked pleased as he brushed his knuckles over my cheek. "You always blush when I compliment you."

"I'm not used to it," I admitted.

He pressed his lips to my cheek. "Then I'll keep doing it until you are."

He opened the door. "Let's do this, Lottie."

CHAPTER 18
LOTTIE

At Logan's insistence, we stopped and he purchased flowers for my mother. It was a small bouquet, but the flowers were lovely. I knew he was determined to make the best impression possible, and I hoped my parents appreciated the efforts.

The only clue that he wasn't as calm as he pretended to be was his stillness. I was used to his foot tapping, his fingers drumming to music only he could hear. He was always composing in his head, a sound or a beat he would hear often setting him off. He carried a small notebook that he frequently jotted lyrics and musical notes into when inspiration struck.

But today, there was no music in him. I slid my hand into his and squeezed. He smiled at me, kissing my lips with a wink, but even his fire was dimmed. He was focused on a goal. One I hated, because I was fearful of the repercussions if it failed.

We arrived at my parents' condo building, Logan whistling softly under his breath as we got into the elevator. "Impressive."

I shrugged. "Ostentatious. But they love it." They liked the doorman, the huge lobby with its imported marble and dark wood, the concierge, and the valet parking that all came with the hefty price tag of living here. They could well afford it, and it seemed to make them happy. Or at least as happy as anything made them anymore. I still fondly recalled the house I grew up in. It was large and spacious but homey. The condo we moved in to after Josh died was cold and impersonal, and this one was even more so. Decorated beautifully, without a single trace of the parents I remembered and missed.

Logan bent close to my ear. "They're spending the inheritance I'm after. You need to speak to them about that." Then he nipped my lobe with a low growl, making me chuckle. I was grateful he had seen the humor in my mother's warning and was trying to keep our spirits up.

We were still laughing when the elevator opened, and we approached my parents' door. My mother was waiting, the concierge having announced our arrival. She watched us approach, the way Logan had me tucked tightly to his side and our shared amusement. I wondered if she could see how we felt. If the love inside spilled over and radiated around us. It felt as if it did to me.

I smiled as we got close. "Hello, Mom."

She nodded, loosening her arms she had crossed over her chest. "Lottie." She tilted her head. "This must be Logan."

"It's a pleasure, Mrs. Prescott." He held out the bouquet. "Thank you for the invitation."

She stared, surprised at the flowers. A memory came to mind of me bringing another man to my parents. One of the approved, suit-wearing businessmen they wanted so desperately for me to have in my life. I hadn't wanted to bring him, but they insisted, excited that I was seeing someone they would approve of. He had walked in, acting as if he owned the place, ignored my mother, kissed my father's ass the entire time, and had angered me to the point I refused to see him again. It was obvious my father was the draw, not me. He hadn't thought to bring a bottle of wine, flowers, or anything.

But Logan had. Silently, I scored one for him in the win column.

A smile crossed her face. "How lovely," she murmured, lifting the bouquet and inhaling the scent. "Please come in."

We followed her in, and I took Logan's coat and mine, hanging them in the closet. We removed our wet boots, and I tried not to giggle at Logan's socks.

"Argyle?" I whispered.

"Seemed appropriate," he replied with a swift kiss. "Should I have brought shoes?"

"No, it's fine. I never do."

I introduced Logan to June, who beamed and welcomed him warmly, then offered us a drink. She returned a few moments later with coffee for us and the flowers in a vase which she handed my mother. I was shocked when Mom placed them on the table beside her, touching the petals of the freesias gently. There was something different in her gaze today. It looked softer. Accepting. I dared to hope maybe she was really going to try.

"Did Lottie tell you these were my favorite?" she queried.

"No," he replied honestly. "I chose them because they were so lovely. I'm glad they please you."

My mother hummed and turned to us. "Lottie tells me you are a teacher."

He nodded in agreement. "I am."

"What grade do you teach?"

He answered her, adding a couple of amusing stories. She didn't laugh, but I was thrilled she was being polite and hospitable. When Logan stopped talking and took a sip of his coffee, I spoke.

"Where's Dad?"

"Oh." She waved her hand. "Some to-do with business. He'll be along shortly."

As if summoned, my father appeared, striding into the room, a frown on his face. He didn't acknowledge Logan, or even greet me.

"It appears someone jumped the gun on your merger, Lottie, and leaked it before the press release happened." He sat down, crossing his legs. "Most inconvenient."

I was shocked at his rudeness, although I supposed I shouldn't have been. Logan took it in stride, standing, and extending his hand.

"Mr. Prescott. Montgomery Logan. I'm pleased to meet you, sir."

For one awful moment, I thought my father would refuse to shake his hand. But he slowly got to his feet and did so, examining Logan with barely concealed disdain.

"Lottie said your name was Logan. You go by your last name?" he asked as if it were a sin to do so.

Logan smiled and lifted one shoulder. "Montgomery is a mouthful, and I dislike Monty. Logan is easier to handle."

"Hmph." My father sat back down, turning to me. "So, the leak."

I tamped down my frustration. "Which merger? I have more than one."

"The record company deal."

I shrugged my shoulders. "It's not the first time, and it won't be the last. Especially given that industry. We almost anticipated a leak."

"I don't like it. Anyone you can think of who would have something to gain by leaking it?"

I didn't miss his sidelong glance at Logan. I braced myself for the onslaught that was about to happen. But my mother stood. "Charles, enough. It's Sunday. Lottie is here. Leave the office until Monday."

He opened his mouth, shutting it quickly when she glared at him. "Sunday, Charles. It's Sunday."

As a child, Sunday had always been enforced as the "no work" day. My mother insisted with the busy life they led, one day a week was not too much to ask. My father set aside the office, she didn't worry about housework, and we spent the day as a family. These brunches were all that was left of that dead tradition, so for her to bring up the past surprised me. That my father bowed to her wishes astonished me even more.

"Then let's eat, shall we?" he said and crooked his elbow for my mother to take.

Logan followed suit, winking at me and dropping a fast kiss to my head. "Survived so far," he whispered.

I nodded, hoping it continued.

♪

LOGAN

"You met in the subway?" Lottie's father, or *Mr. Prescott*, since he didn't offer to let me call him Charles, asked, his appalled tone letting me know what he thought of my statement. His wife hadn't corrected my use of Mrs. Prescott either, but somehow it didn't feel as insulting.

It had been the same the entire brunch. I had to admit his tone varied. Disgusted, dismissive, patronizing, contemptuous, and often bordering rude was the range. At each new tone, Lottie seemed to shrink a little more before my eyes. She picked at her food, admonished her father on occasion—not that it did any good. Every question he shot my way was designed to embarrass and belittle. Every response to my replies ensured everyone at the table knew he thought I was an idiot and didn't belong there.

I tried to direct my comments to Lottie's mother. She, at least, seemed to be trying. She had been unfailingly polite, gracious, and a good hostess. She attempted on occasion to stop Lottie's father, but he was determined to hate me, usually speaking over her and interrupting often. I thought him rude, overbearing, and an utter asshole.

I was certain he had similar thoughts about me.

"Yes," I replied smoothly. "I needed to sit down and get some notes out on a song in my head, and Lottie sat across from me. I was captivated." I glossed over the true story, knowing what a response that would get me.

"Oh, a wannabe singer, are you?"

"No, sir. I simply enjoy writing music. It's an outlet for me."

"Right," he snorted. "Because your life of *teaching* is so stressful."

I fought down a wave of anger. He was beginning to piss me off, but I refused to rise to the bait. He wanted me angry. He hoped I would show what he felt were my true colors and embarrass myself in front of Lottie.

"You don't know anything about my life, sir," I stated. "Or the stress and worries it contains."

For a moment, the table was silent until Lottie spoke. "And you never will if you don't begin to listen, Dad."

He glared at her, then looked at me. "Did you know about the record label merger?"

I sighed, knowing that somehow, he was going to try to blame the leak on me. "I did," I acknowledged. "But I assure you, the kids in my class promised not to say a word. I thought I could trust their discretion."

Lottie laughed at my joke, and even her mother's mouth quirked. Her father didn't see the humor. If anything, it made him angrier.

"Sabotaging a business deal is nothing to laugh at."

"Enough," Lottie's mom said. "No more business talk. You are being obstinate today, Charles. Behave."

Lottie looked at her father. "This merger is not going to suffer because of a leak. You know that. Logan had nothing to do with it. It was probably one of the companies themselves. We've seen it before." She paused. "Stop it, Dad. Please."

I knew her plea wasn't simply for the merger talk. She was asking him to lay off me. He stood, setting down his napkin. "Excuse me." He strode from the room.

"My husband has a lot on his mind," Mrs. Prescott said in the way of an excuse.

I wanted to tell her that was no excuse for his behavior, but I only nodded and finished my breakfast. My appetite was gone, but I refused to let them see how upset I was. I had been wrong when I assured Lottie nothing bad could happen over breakfast foods and coffee. My battle for acceptance by her parents was not going to be an easy one.

"I think we need to go," Lottie stated, standing. "I guess I had better make some calls."

Her mother nodded, looking disappointed. I excused myself to use the washroom, staring at my reflection in the mirror. Maybe I should have cut my hair even shorter. Worn a damn suit. I shook my head, knowing it wouldn't have helped. The only thing that would have aided my case was an Ivy League education, a large bank account, and a career her father found acceptable. Teaching wasn't one of them. Neither was music. I had a feeling the news I hoped to share with Lottie soon wasn't going to be celebrated by her father.

I stepped out of the room, somehow not shocked to find her father waiting, his arms crossed.

"Mr. Prescott."

He narrowed his eyes. "If you thought cutting your hair and putting on a clean shirt would help, you're wrong. I know your sort. A lazy drifter. Coasting through life on nothing. Latching on to my daughter, hoping for an easy ride."

"Wow…impressive," I shot back. "You got all that from breakfast and a one-sided judgmental conversation?"

He straightened, his arms dropping to his side. His hands were clenched in tight fists, much the same, I was certain, as his asshole. His sphincter must be in spasms by now, this guy was so tightly wound. His eyes were so much like Lottie's, yet different. Her soft blue radiated warmth. His were ice-cold and angry.

"You are not good enough for my daughter."

"I entirely agree with you."

My statement caught him off guard. I held up my hand.

"Yet, we're together. Your daughter is bright, beautiful, and makes me happy. Even though you want to throw something sinister and ugly into it, that's it in a nutshell. I had no idea who she was when we met, and it didn't matter then or now. I like Lottie for Lottie. For her warmth and her soul. Regardless of the pain she has suffered, she's such a giving person, and she brings so much to my life." I paused. "I am not giving her up."

"We'll see about that."

"The last time I checked, your daughter and I were both mature, capable adults. Completely able to choose who we spend time with. And Lottie has chosen me." I narrowed my eyes, suddenly tired of his attitude. "You really want to push this and see who wins?" I asked quietly. "The man who makes her feel guilty for being alive, or the man who adores her beyond all reason? Who would do anything, be anything, she needed to make her happy?"

His face paled.

"Do you really not care? Or are you trying to make her pay for something that wasn't her fault for the rest of her life? She doesn't deserve that."

"I *beg* your pardon?"

"You heard me. Don't push it, *Charles*. You won't like the result."

Before he could respond, Lottie came around the corner. She stopped when she saw us.

"What's going on?"

"Nothing," I assured her. "I was thanking your father for a delicious meal. We both agreed the company could have been better." I smiled at her. "I'll go say my goodbyes to your mother."

I turned and left them alone.

I'd face the fallout later.

CHAPTER 19
LOTTIE

W e were silent on the ride home. Logan had laced our fingers together, his thumb stroking my skin, but he remained quiet, staring out the window into the darkness of the subway tunnels. I watched his reflection in the glass, wondering what he was thinking. Brunch had been awful—my father acting worse than I had feared. My mother had been more receptive, but it wasn't enough. I had to avert my eyes, blinking away the sudden tears that were forming.

What the hell was wrong with me? I rarely ever cried, yet the last week I'd felt as if I were constantly on the verge of tears. And I was tired. I needed a break, I decided. A vacation. Tomorrow, I would check my schedule, figure out when I could clear some time, and submit a vacation request.

Logan tugged on my hand, and I realized he was standing, waiting for me as the stop approached. I offered him a rueful smile and stood with him, approaching the doors. My steps faltered as we passed the spot I usually sat to listen to him play, and I looked at the wall he always stood by, waiting for me.

"I remember the first time I saw you," Logan murmured,

following my gaze. "So beautiful, so troubled. You looked as if you carried too many burdens on your tiny shoulders. The second I saw your lovely eyes, it was as if my world changed. Remolded itself. I knew I had to help you."

"You did," I confirmed, squeezing his hand. "More than you know. That night and every night since."

"Do you miss me being here when you get off the train?"

I knew if I said yes, he would somehow figure out how to be there. Right there, leaning against the wall, playing for me. Ignoring the people who stood to listen, because all that mattered would be that I was listening. I smiled and shook my head. "I like walking into my place and you being there. Sharing a meal with you. Having a private concert." I met his concerned gaze. "Feeling your skin on mine as we make love."

His eyes darkened and he stepped closer. "I believe I promised you some ravishing when we got home."

Home.

Hearing him say that word made my heart beat faster. Because where Logan was now was home to me.

"Yes, I think you did."

He lowered his head and kissed me. He wrapped his arms around my waist, pulling me tight to his chest, and kissed me until I was breathless. The air around us pulsated with the heat building between us. In the background, I heard catcalls and whistles, but I didn't care. I wanted more. More of his kisses, more of his essence, more of everything that was Logan.

He broke the kiss and gazed down at me, his expression intense.

"Let's take this somewhere more private."

I could only nod.

♫

I lay sprawled on Logan's chest, exhausted, and oh so deliciously sated. He had, indeed, ravished me thoroughly, bringing me to a shattering climax with his mouth, then his fingers, and finally, his thick cock.

He played with my hair, stroking it gently, caressing the ends between his fingers. I loved how he kept me close after we were done. He held me, touched me, hummed, whispered low words of endearment.

"Lottie," he said. "Can I ask you a question?"

I lifted my head, meeting his eyes. "You can ask me anything."

"Are you happy?"

I frowned. "Right now? Yes."

"No, in the bigger picture. Are you happy with your life?"

I pursed my lips. "I'm happier now than I was a few weeks ago. Before you came into my life."

He stroked my cheek with the back of his hand. "I make you happy."

"Yes."

"What would you change to be happier?"

I sat up, pulling the sheet around my torso. "I know where you're going with this, Logan. I can't quit my job and bake cupcakes. It's not that simple."

He tucked an arm under his head. "I know that. But if you could do anything, if money weren't the constraint, what would you choose to do?"

I paused as I considered his words. "I would love to bake and create. I made a wedding cake once for a friend. It took me days of planning and baking, but I enjoyed every moment. I would love to be able to do that."

"Only one cake?"

I nodded. "I had some inquiries about doing more. But I had to take vacation to make that one. Work has been so busy, I haven't taken any time since, aside from one week with Brianna."

A thought occurred to me. "Oh—but I was thinking of taking a little time off. When is your Christmas break?"

"I'll have to check." He grinned. "Are you really going to take time off and spend it with me?"

"If you want that."

He slid his hand up my neck and brought me to his mouth. "Yes, I want. I'll get the dates and let you know." A strange look passed over his face. "I, ah, have a couple of commitments, but we'll figure it out."

"Okay."

He sat up, looking at me. "Lottie, I have to tell you something. Something important."

"All right," I said slowly, his serious tone startling me.

He slid from the bed, dragging on his pants. He paced the room, running his hands through his hair repeatedly, ramping up my anxiety. I grabbed my robe, slipping it on, no longer wanting to be naked for whatever he had to say. I had never seen Logan this serious, so I knew it had to be huge. A small nagging doubt hit me, and I spoke it out loud.

"Is this too much, Logan? Too fast? You want to stop seeing me?"

He stopped mid-stride and gaped at me. He crossed the room and gripped my arms. "Hell no. I never want to stop seeing you. Don't even think that way."

"What is it, then?"

He swallowed and sat beside me. "I'm not supposed to say anything. I signed a nondisclosure and I thought I could keep it to myself, but I can't."

I frowned. "A nondisclosure? With the school? Oh! Did they offer you full time?"

He shook his head with a smile. "Not even close, Lottie." He sucked in a long breath. "I signed a deal with Ravaged Roadside."

I blinked. Then again. "What?"

"I can't go into all the particulars, but I'm under contract with them now."

I flung my arms around his neck, holding him tight. "Logan —that is amazing! I'm so proud of you."

He returned my embrace. "It's been crazy, Lottie. Meetings and negotiations. More meetings. I had to get a lawyer." He snorted. "Me, get a lawyer. I never thought I'd see that day."

I laughed, knowing how much he would hate that. It smacked of the corporate world that Logan detested.

He cupped my face. "I've wanted to talk to you so often, but I can't. I shouldn't even be telling you this, but I can't keep it from you. I can't say much else, but I will tell you everything soon."

"I won't say anything. I promise."

"I know. I didn't want to put you in the position of lying to your father or causing you trouble."

"Can you tell me anything?"

He sighed, then his lips curled into a wicked smile. "I'll just say you weren't wrong when you thought the record label leaked the merger." He winked. "But you figured that out on your own."

I returned his smile. "They often do. It makes the press conference that much more exciting if they create a buzz."

"Yeah, they want a buzz."

I widened my eyes in understanding. "Are they announcing you at the press conference?"

"I'm not the star attraction, Lottie."

"What aren't you telling me?" I frowned. "What about your teaching? Are you giving that up?"

He stood. "I can't—I mean, I want to, but…" He trailed off, obviously frustrated. "I can't blow this."

I grabbed his hand in understanding. "It's okay. You can tell me soon?"

He held my hand to his heart. I could feel the rapid beat under my palm. "Yes, I promise. I will tell you everything."

"Then I'll wait."

He bent and kissed me. "Thank you." His lips pressed harder, and with a sigh, I opened to him.

His phone buzzed, and he groaned, touching his forehead to mine. "It never stops these days."

I had noticed it going off more than usual, but I had put it down to his new teaching gig. I had no idea his talk with Carmen had gone so far, so quickly.

He scanned the screen and heaved a sigh. "I have to go."

I tamped down my disappointment. "Okay."

"I'll try to come back later?"

I slid my hands up his chest, slipping them around his neck. "You have a key."

He beamed. "I do."

"I'll be here."

"That's all I need to know."

Hours later, I gave up. I hadn't heard from Logan and he hadn't replied to my text, so I assumed whatever took him away was keeping him occupied. I went for a long walk, the lure of the swirling snow in the dark too much to resist. I'd left a note in case he showed up, but it was still propped against the bowl on the hall table, so I knew he hadn't seen it.

Chilled and feeling a little sad, I poured a hot bath, throwing in some lavender salts. I brought a glass of wine and my wireless speaker into the bathroom and selected a soothing playlist. I slipped into the tub, shivering as the warm water lapped at my cold skin. I had walked longer than I realized. I wiggled my toes, took a sip of my wine, and laid my head back, letting the music relax me.

Or at least, that was my plan. The music didn't soothe. It reminded me I hadn't heard from Logan. What was he doing? What plans was he making? How would this affect him? Us?

I sat up in the water. If they signed him, he'd record an album. There was no doubt it would be a hit. That meant more time in the studio. Probably a tour. He'd be gone. Living a dream he never thought he would see come to fruition.

I was torn.

I was thrilled for him—he was so talented, he deserved to have his songs heard. Yet, I wondered what it meant for us. We were still new. He was going to be busy. Crazy busy. Writing, touring, press—all of it.

The one sip of wine I'd had turned sour in my stomach. He'd be gone, and I'd be here. Once again alone, stuck in a job I hated, and knowing the one bright spot in my life was somewhere else in the world. Traitorous tears streaked down my face.

What if I became a part of his past? The woman he serenaded and moved on from? Would I become a distant memory, someone he recalled in his thanks on the back of a CD cover? Would he remember me at all?

I wiped away my tears, impatient. I was being silly. Where were these thoughts coming from? This was Logan. *My* Logan. My protector and lover. Success wasn't going to change him. We could survive distance and periods of separation. I was certain of it.

Once he told me everything, we would discuss it—together. Logan was open and honest. We'd figure it out. I shook my head to clear my thoughts. I was being overdramatic and silly. One unanswered text was not the end of my relationship with Logan.

My head agreed. My heart, however, ached. I got out of the bath and dumped the glass of wine. What I needed to relax wasn't available.

And that, right there, was the problem.

I tossed and turned all night, my subconscious refusing to shut up. Logan was going to be too busy for me now. He was going to be traveling. The calls and texts that would start as soon as he left, telling me how much he missed me, would dwindle and become sporadic and less personal. Then they would stop.

I would become a memory to him.

He would be another person who left me.

I tried to shake off the moroseness that surrounded me, but I found it difficult. I had never been what I would consider an overly emotional person. I never showed my anger or irritation at work. I rarely lost patience with people. I didn't cry at pictures of puppies or shed many tears at the end of a romantic movie.

Yet lately, I'd had to bite my tongue several times. Count to ten before responding to a question. Tears came, unbidden and unwelcome, at the strangest times.

Logan sent a text around three saying he was sorry and had lost track of time. I didn't ask what he was doing at that ungodly hour of the morning. When I arrived at work, I sent him a response stating I hoped he would be able to make the press conference tonight at Ravaged Roadside. He had said he wasn't the star attraction, but I assumed he would want to be there, even if it was to hear the announcement of the merger anyway.

His reply was simple.

I'll meet you there.

My melancholy wrapped around me a little tighter as I realized he would not be going with me, but on his own.

Somehow, I hid my emotions all day, performing calmly under the scrutiny of my father. I briefed everyone at the meeting about the press conference and the leak.

"Carmen admits it came from someone at RR. He's handling it. The bottom line is that we go ahead as planned. Make the announcement, and the rest is up to them. They have an entire event scheduled this evening. Everyone is welcome."

Another staff member spoke up. "I heard a rumor they have another huge announcement they are making tonight."

I kept my face and voice neutral. "Nothing they have shared with me. I suppose we'll find out."

The rest of the meeting and the day were completed on autopilot. Logan clung to my every thought, no matter how many times I told myself I was being silly.

Brianna called, excited about coming to the press conference.

"I wasn't aware you were invited," I drawled.

"Trevor asked me to go with him."

"Trevor is going?" I said, surprised.

"Yes. Logan asked him, silly."

"Oh."

"Lottie, what is it?"

"Nothing."

She sighed. "You forget how well I know you. You sound off. What's wrong?"

"I didn't sleep well last night. I'm a little tired."

"Logan didn't fuck you until you were exhausted? The boy is falling down on the job."

"Logan wasn't there."

The words felt heavy between us. She knew how much time we had been spending together.

"Is, ah, everything okay between you?"

I had to clear my throat. "Yes. I mean, I think so. He's been really busy."

"What aren't you telling me?"

"Nothing," I lied. "Listen, I'll see you tonight, okay?"

"Lottie…" She trailed off.

"What?"

"Everything is going to be all right, okay? Blips happen. You guys are too good together for any other outcome."

"Thanks," I replied, my voice thick. "I hope so."

CHAPTER 20
LOTTIE

The place was packed. Even fuller than the other night when I'd been here with Logan. RR had insisted on holding the event in their building, and I was fine with that. It was their show —their announcement. They had been firm on that fact. Normally our company issued simple statements on our clients' behalf and let them follow up however they wanted, but this one was different.

The room was electric. I spied a few of the younger staff in the room as I walked around. I had dressed with care, knowing tonight I was representing Prescott Inc. I wore a simple black skirt and a brilliant blue silk blouse with ruffles around the neck and wrists. I topped it with a blue and black vest, pulling the outfit together. It was sleek and elegant. To tease Logan, though, I wore high-heeled black boots that made me feel sexy and powerful. I wore my hair up, and I kept my makeup simple. Looking around the room, I tried not to laugh. I was one of the most overdressed people there—but that was my role tonight.

I located Carmen and Alfred, shaking their hands. Roxanne hugged me, looking beautiful and sexy as always. I glanced around, hoping for a glimpse of Logan, but I didn't spot him anywhere. Disappointment hit me, and I wondered if he would come at all.

Carmen smiled widely at someone behind me, and I turned, hoping it was Logan. Instead, Bobby Hayes was approaching, a smirk on his face. He stopped, shook hands with Carmen and Alfred, kissed Roxanne, then grinned at me.

"Lottie, right? We met a while back."

"Yes." I extended my hand. He took it, then surprised me when he lifted it to his lips and kissed my knuckles.

"The beautiful muse."

"I'm sorry?"

He grinned again and took a swig of his drink. "I am honored to be the one who sings of your wonder."

I frowned. He had to be drunk since I didn't understand what he was rambling about. Before I could say anything, I saw him.

Logan.

Tall, broad, his hair brushed back and gleaming under the lights. Headed straight toward me, his whiskey eyes dark and intense. He was in full rocker gear tonight. He wore dark jeans, Doc Martens on his feet, a white shirt stretched across his chest and arms, rolled up his forearms, showing his taut muscles. He was wearing a vest, but his was leather, thick and manly. His cuffs, rings, and a heavy silver chain around his neck completed the look. He was sex incarnate as he made his way toward me, an intense need building as he came closer.

I felt three things all at once.

Relief at seeing him. Anger that he'd kept me waiting. Desire at the look in his eyes as he stared. He covered the ground between us quickly. Hunger for him built inside me as he drew closer, already holding out his hand. The longing to touch him, to be close, blossomed, and without a thought, I stepped toward him, extending my hand, all doubts and worries disappearing as our fingers entwined. He pulled me close, his kiss demanding, claiming, and possessive. My world, which had been gray all day, exploded into color. Yearning coursed through me. I needed more. More of his mouth. Of his touch. I needed all of him.

But he kept the hard kiss short. Eased back and dropped a kiss to my forehead. He cupped my face.

"I'm sorry I'm late." He brushed his lips to my forehead again. "I missed you."

My reply was breathless. "You're forgiven."

"Good." He tucked me into his side and turned to the small group watching us. "Hey."

They all laughed and greeted him, and I noticed the familiarity they seemed to have as a group.

"You ready?" he asked Bobby quietly.

"More than ready. I'm going to burst out of my own skin soon."

Carmen clapped him on the shoulder. "Can't have that. I'll go and start this off."

Bobby drained his glass. He glanced at me, then winked at Logan. "See ya on the flip side."

Logan only nodded, but his arm tightened on my waist.

I glanced around the room and saw my father on the edge, standing with a few people from the office. His arms were folded over his chest, his attitude closed off and annoyed. I knew I should go over and stand with him, but I didn't want to. He met my eyes, his gaze flickering over Logan and me, then he turned, facing the small stage that was set up, making my decision easier. I burrowed a little closer to Logan.

I spotted Brianna and Trev wrapped around each other, oblivious to anyone else, which made me chuckle, and I was surprised to see Rex and Gretch sipping drinks on the opposite side of the room. I was about to ask Logan about them being here, when Carmen stepped up to the microphone.

He kept it short and sweet, giving a quick history of the two companies, and formally announcing the merger of the two record labels. Amid the applause, he unveiled the new logo of Ravaged Roadside. It was simple—a torn-up road scattered with broken records, all black, with splashes of red.

After the applause died down, he made a point of thanking Prescott Inc., naming my father and pointing him out in the crowd. I was shocked when then he singled me out, describing my adept handling and enthusiasm for the merger as the reason it happened so quickly and easily.

"Charlotte's professionalism and dedication are a testament to the name Prescott Inc.," Carmen stated. "Thank you."

I nodded, embarrassed. Usually it was only my father and the company mentioned. I preferred to stay out of the spotlight.

Carmen had Alfred and Roxanne join him, and Alfred spoke for a few moments about the vision for RR.

"Discovering new talent, and providing it a place to grow and develop, is our mission. Giving them a voice. We want to offer the most diverse fusion of talent we can discover," he finished.

Roxanne joined the applause and stepped to the mic.

"The business side is now done. Any media questions can be directed to my office. But for now, we're going to move to our first order of business. A new signing with the label. You've all heard the rumors—" she paused as the clapping and hollers broke out "—and I am delighted to announce it is true. Please welcome Bobby Hayes to the stage."

I saw my father step back and melt into the crowd. His job was done—he'd made an appearance and represented his company. He'd have no interest in the talent or listening to the music. He would find Carmen and Alfred, shake their hands, and call it a night. I relaxed, knowing he wasn't going to approach me here and try to talk. I could relax and enjoy the music.

Bobby strode onstage, smiling and waving. His guitar was slung over his back, and he settled on a stool after shaking hands with everyone. He adjusted the microphone.

"Thrilled to be here tonight. And to be part of the launch of this new label. They have such vision and so many things in store for the world." His voice was low and smooth. "I've got a little glimpse of that for you tonight."

Then he began to play and sing. Alone, with the spotlight on his handsome face, he was mesmerizing. He was tall and wiry, with a head of curly blond hair that hung over his forehead, giving him a rakish look. His dark eyes were riveting and his voice magical. Growly, low, yet smooth. The song he played was intensely emotional, and his voice did it justice. The music was also familiar, yet I wasn't sure why. Bits of the bridge, some of the words, lingered on the edge of my memory, but I couldn't grasp how.

Beside me, Logan was tense, although his fingers tapped out the rhythm on my waist, and I could hear him hum at times.

When Bobby launched into his second song, I knew. I looked up at Logan. "That's your song." I recognized the melody, having heard him play it as he composed. I cupped his cheek and rolled up on my toes, my lips at his ear. "They bought a couple of your songs!"

He grinned down at me with a slight bob of his head, but he didn't say anything. As Bobby brought the next song to a close, Logan leaned down and kissed my forehead.

"Wait right here," he instructed. "This is for you."

He was gone before I could ask him anything. Bobby strummed his guitar, smiling into the crowd.

"Sometimes in life, you get to meet someone whose vibe speaks to yours. If you're lucky, you get to be friends with them. If you're extraordinarily lucky, you get to share their vibe and work with them. It is my great privilege to introduce the talent behind the last two songs, my new music partner, and the latest signing of Ravaged Roadside. Ladies and gents, I give you Logan."

I gaped as Logan strolled out onstage, his guitar ready. The lights glinted off the worn wood, the brass fittings gleaming. He looked calm and happy, smiling at the applause. He didn't say anything but stood close to Bobby with a nod, his fingers already strumming.

Bobby pressed close to the mic. "Lottie, this one is yours. Whatever you're doing to my friend here, keep it up."

Then Logan began to play. This one, I recognized, as he had played it often. But I had never heard the words he would scribble in the notebook that always accompanied him. Bobby's voice was drenched in longing and love. He sang words of adoration. Hope. Inspiration. He poured his heart and soul onto the stage, telling the story of a girl who changed the course and life of a lost soul, bringing him into focus. Of loving her beyond comprehension and needing her to live.

The entire time Bobby sang, my eyes were locked on Logan. His rich, intense gaze was pinned on me. It was as if only the three of us were in that room as Bobby crooned lyrics so deep and personal—so obviously Logan and me—I was moved to tears. They coursed down my cheeks unheeded. I wanted Logan to see them, to know I felt him and his love in that song. In all his songs.

As the final notes ended, Bobby's voice trailing off into a whisper of the last words, the room was silent. I felt my rapid breathing, the way my heart skipped and jumped in my chest. The room burst into loud applause, people stomping on the floor, yelling for more. I couldn't move, my hands pressed tight to my chest, overcome with emotion. The two men waved, Logan shook Bobby's hand, and disappeared. Bobby waited until the crowd quieted and spoke. "That was a rare appearance by my new partner. I promise you'll see him again. I have one more song for you."

I felt Logan before I saw him. He appeared by my side, his heat soaking into me. I turned and gazed into his eyes. He lifted his hand and wiped away my tears, then tugged me into a dark corner and cupped my face. "Hi," he murmured. "Good tears?"

I grabbed his wrists. "I am so proud of you."

He shook his head. "That—" he indicated the stage behind him "—was all because of you."

"No. That was because of your talent."

He bent and kissed me, the passion that shimmered between us all the time exploding with the energy we were both feeling. He dragged his tongue along my lip, and I opened for him, whimpering as he took control and kissed me with utter abandon. I shuddered at the long, sensuous passes of his tongue, nips of his teeth, and the way he held my head captive, controlling every aspect. Finally, he broke away, leaning his forehead to mine.

"I have so much to tell you."

"I want to hear it." I tilted back my head. "I guess they bought more than a couple of songs."

"You have no idea."

"When can we leave?"

"Not soon enough." He dragged me closer and ground his erection into me. "Talking is going to have to wait awhile, Lottie. This time, I want to take you along on this frenzy."

His eyes were so dark, the golden whiskey color was obscured. I felt the tension in his body—a coil wound so tight it was about to spring. His hands held me a little too firmly. He was desperate. Barely hanging on.

Recalling what happened last time he was this way, my own desire ramped up. "Let's go."

It took a while to leave the room. Trev and Brianna stopped us, congratulating Logan and wanting to talk. The same with Rex and Gretch. His friends were excited, shocked, and wanting to hear the whole story. He promised them time the next day, simply saying we had someplace to be. Brianna caught my eye, her eyebrows lifting at my expression. She stepped back, tugging on Trev's arm.

"We'll look forward to seeing you tomorrow."

We hurried away, stopping when Logan needed to shake

hands and accept a compliment. The last person who stopped our leaving was Bobby. He stepped in front of Logan, halting his forward progress.

"You are fucking awesome. Your talent." He clapped Logan's arms. "I can't get over your talent, man. Your words blow me away."

Logan smiled—a genuine one—and laughed. "You sang them. They loved you."

Bobby shook his head. "They loved *us*, man. Your music—my voice." He beamed. "Although when you join me, it's pure poetry."

Logan frowned. "You know my thoughts on that subject."

Bobby met my eyes, chuckling. "Talk to this stubborn fool, all right, Lottie?"

I had no idea what he was talking about, but I smiled. "Logan *is* rather stubborn. It's part of his charm."

Bobby smirked in agreement. "I know. And I'm grateful for him agreeing to be my partner in this. But—"

Logan interrupted him. "Listen, Bobby. We'll talk more tomorrow. I have someplace to be."

Bobby looked at us and the way Logan was holding my hand snug to his chest. A slow, knowing look spread over his face. He winked. "My car is at the back door. I'll get my driver to take you."

Logan nodded, his voice tight. "Perfect."

♫

In the darkness of the back seat, Logan was all over me. He touched me, his long fingers stroking along my skin, delving under my coat, and pulling my blouse from the waistband of my skirt. He drifted his hands up and down my spine, tracing the bones as he kissed my skin, licked his way up my neck, swirling his tongue on the sensitive area behind my ear.

"I am going to fucking take you tonight," he promised darkly, his voice a low hum in my ear. "Every inch of you, I'm claiming." He squeezed my ass, kneading it firmly. "Every inch."

I tried not to whimper, but I failed.

"If you don't want this, tell me now."

I remained silent.

At my building, he pulled me from the back seat, not even waiting for the driver to get out. In the elevator, his eyes burned with intensity, reminding me of that first night. Thank goodness it was only a short ride up, or I might have attacked him in the elevator. Logan was right behind me as I hurried down the hall. He already had his key out, sliding it into the lock. The door was barely shut before he was on me again. My coat was yanked from my shoulders and tossed away. I pulled his off, hearing the thump on the floor as the leather hit the wood. His mouth covered mine, his tongue deep and carnal as he kissed me. Cool air hit my back as my vest and blouse disappeared. I pushed his vest off his arms and tore at his buttons, ripping his shirt open, desperate to feel his skin. His nimble fingers made short work of my skirt. I started to pull back, and he shook his head with a low growl.

"The boots stay on."

Then I was pressed against the wall, trapped between his heat and the hard, smooth surface. He kissed me with everything in him. His chest rubbed my lace-covered breasts, abrading my sensitive nipples. I cried out as he yanked down the cups, making my breasts spill over. He teased them with his tongue and lips, pulling on the nipples until they were wet, red, and swollen. He pinned my hands over my head and slid one heavy thigh between my legs, grinding into me. He watched me the entire time, his gaze wild.

"I'm going to fuck you here, Lottie," he promised. "Then over the back of that sofa. You're going to come like you've never come before, you understand me?" He slipped his hand between my legs, finding me slick and ready for him.

"Yes," he groaned. "Look how sexy you are, wearing your boots and your racy thigh highs, your tits swollen from my mouth, and your pussy all wet and hot for me." He licked at the corner of my mouth. "You want this, don't you? You want me to fuck you hard."

His dirty words, his need, everything about this moment was so deliciously intense, so overwhelming and hot, I was certain I was going to combust. I undulated against his hand.

"Please, Logan."

"Please what?" he teased, sliding one finger inside me. "Tell me what you want, Lottie. I'll give it to you, baby. I'll give it all to you."

"Fuck me," I pleaded, breathless and needy.

I cried out when he removed his hand from me, then I began to shake as his pants hit the floor, the thunk of the metal belt loud as it dropped. He lifted me higher.

"Wrap those sexy boots around me, baby. I want to feel those heels dig into my skin as I take you."

I did as he asked, gripping his shoulders, crying his name as he wrapped his mouth around my nipple and sucked hard. He slid his fingers inside me again, steadily pumping, then with one snap, sank inside me. I let my head fall back to the wall as he curved his hands around my ass, sinking his thick thumb inside, the tight muscles closing around his digit and spasming. He slammed into me, the subtle gentleness I was used to, gone. He was like an animal, groaning and growling, using me. He pinned me to the wall, thrusting hard and intense, his thumb deep in my ass, the pressure turning into pleasure. I trembled as my orgasm raged through me, clutching at Logan and begging for more. He moved faster, sending me over the edge, and I gasped out his name. He rode out my orgasm, then grunted, held me close, and stepped back from the wall. In seconds, he had me flipped over the back of the sofa, pushing my legs apart.

"Look at that," he groaned. "Wet. Swollen. Dripping with

your need." He traced his finger around my ass. "You like me in here, don't you, Lottie?"

I spread my legs farther apart, lifting myself higher. I was so turned on and ready to come again, I'd give him anything. "Yes, Logan. Yours. All of it is yours."

"I don't want to hurt you."

A small flash of white caught my eye, and I reached over and grabbed the small bottle of lube left over from us fooling around earlier that week. It had been forgotten and stuck between the sofa cushions.

I held it up. "You won't."

He took the bottle, and I felt the cool liquid drip onto my skin and his fingers rub it in, sliding inside and stretching me. I knew he was adding some to his cock, and I whimpered in anticipation.

"Are you sure?" he asked again, sliding his hand down and teasing my clit. "You want to do this with me?"

"Yes," I groaned.

He slid his cock between my legs, spreading the lube more, then pressed the blunt, heavy head to my cheeks. "Show me."

I pushed back, feeling him entering. Stretching me. I closed my eyes at the burn, grasping the cushion under me. Logan eased back, then sank in a little more. He moved, his thrusts becoming deeper, sinking inside more with each pivot of his hips. I moaned and whimpered at his size, but I wanted this. I wanted all of him. When he was flush, he rested his head on my back, his breath hot on my neck.

"Your ass is strangling my cock, Lottie. You feel so good."

He slid his fingers to my clit, stroking and rubbing. Another wave of pleasure hit me, and I pushed back against his hand. He began to move, short, fast strokes inside me that made my legs shake and my entire body tremble. Soon, he had his thumb pressed to my clit, two fingers sunk inside me, and his cock up my ass. Touching, stroking, thrusting. Every movement brought its own pleasure. Every touch its own thrill. I was awash in sensation.

It was too much. It was dirty and lewd, wrong and yet so right because it was Logan. It was us. Every nerve in my body was on fire, and the orgasm building fast within me was going to tear me apart.

"I can't," I pleaded. "Logan, it's too much. I need—you need —oh god, please," I babbled.

"You can take it," he snarled. "Take me. All of me, Lottie. I want to hear you come again."

It happened. My orgasm hit me, strong and wicked. It tore through me, the pleasure like waves all over my body, small pinpricks of pain woven throughout an intense rush of pleasure I thought would make me pass out. I came, screaming and thrashing. Pushing back against his cock and his fingers. Wanting more, coming for what felt like hours as my body quaked with the intensity of his invasion and lost to the ecstasy of the act.

I came until I was limp and spent, unable to move or form a coherent thought. I knew he had orgasmed, the heat and wet filling me up, his low grunt and snarled growls in my ears telling me how much he had enjoyed it.

I drifted, trapped under his body, our slick skin melding together, our breathing rough and ragged. Slowly, he stood, dropping kisses on my back, rubbing my shoulders. He eased from me, and I grimaced as muscles never used protested and my body suddenly realized the awkward angle it was bent into.

Logan pulled me to standing, turning me in his arms. I was a mass of shaking limbs, sweating skin, and covered in him. I knew my hair was all over the place and, no doubt, my makeup smeared. My underwear was half hanging off my body, and without looking, I knew I had scruff burns everywhere. I was an utter and complete mess.

Yet looking at Logan's face, at the expression in his eyes, I knew, to him, I was beautiful. He stared back at me, the frenzy calmed, the storm passed, and he was there. My Logan.

I sighed as he set me on my feet and yanked up his pants, leaving them hanging low on his hips.

He cupped my face and kissed me, then lifted me in his arms, striding down the hall, his Doc Martens echoing on the wood.

I giggled, and he glanced down.

"You fucked me with your boots on. Mine too."

He smiled widely, setting me on the bathroom counter. He stroked my cheek. "I did. And now, I'm going to look after you."

I groaned in pleasure as he unzipped my boots, dropped them to the floor, and peeled off my thigh highs. He rubbed my calves and thighs, then turned around, starting the shower. I already anticipated the heat of the water pounding against my sore muscles. Logan kicked off his boots and pants, standing in front of me, naked and erect.

He wasn't done.

He loosened my hair, kissing me.

"I want to make love to you now. In the shower, Lottie. You, me, and my body loving you. Only giving this time. Slow and gentle. I need you one more time. Can you do that for me?"

I closed my eyes and nuzzled into his touch.

"Yes."

CHAPTER 21
LOTTIE

When I woke, Logan was beside me, his hand resting on my hip and his other arm tucked under his head. His beautiful eyes were focused solely on me as his fingers stroked my skin. It was still dark outside, snow swirling in the streetlight outside my window.

I blinked, the dim light burning in the corner casting shadows in the room. I recalled Logan carrying me to bed after our shower. He had tenderly washed me, taking great care, and had made love to me, so slowly and sweetly as I had clung to him, my orgasm a gentle swell of gratification in contrast to the tsunami of our earlier passion.

"Hi," he murmured, sliding his hand up my torso and cupping my cheek. He drew circles on my cheek with his thumb. "How are you?"

I stretched, testing my muscles, feeling the slight ache, but also feeling incredibly relaxed and satisfied. I smiled and leaned into his caress. "I'm good."

"I was too rough with you."

I shook my head. "No. I was right there with you, Logan. I'm a big girl, you know. If I want to say no, I can," I assured him. "Last night was just…wow."

His dimple appeared as he grinned. "Wow. I like that word."

"I like a lot of things about you."

"Good. I feel the same way."

I snuggled closer, enjoying his warmth. "You promised we'd talk."

He chuckled low in his chest. "I was too busy last night to talk."

"I'm free now."

He was quiet for a moment. "I met with Carmen, and he expressed interest in signing me to the label. He had seen me a few times but had never been able to pin me down or get a face-to-face with me."

"You never hang around after a gig," I recalled.

"No, I leave right away. I'm too full, too overcharged."

"Funny, that's how I felt last night. Overfull."

He laughed and kissed the end of my nose. "Anyway, we talked, and I explained my throat problem and the fact that I wasn't interested in an out-front sort of career." Logan chuckled. "Carmen seemed shocked and admitted not a lot of people say that to him."

"So…" I asked, trying to get him to open up.

"I thought that would be that. Bobby was at the meeting but didn't say much, except to tell me how much my music stuck with him. A few days later, he showed up at the school and was waiting when I came out. He wanted to talk to me directly."

"You must have been surprised."

"I was. I was already a fan of his—I like his style and his voice. He admitted to me he loved performing, but he was tired of doing covers. He also admitted to being a horrible songwriter. He had bits and pieces, but he could never put together a song that worked."

I lifted myself up on my elbow. "And you have that talent."

"He asked about buying a couple of my songs. I was open to that thinking. I figured that the sales plus the royalties would be a good source of revenue for me for the future." He paused. "I always wanted to hear my stuff in the hands of someone else. Hear how they interpreted my music. So we met again, and I gave him a couple of songs, and once I listened to him, heard how he *got them*, Lottie, I was hooked. It was as if he knew exactly how to sing the words, express them to make them come alive—the way I wanted to hear them."

"I think you do that as well."

He rolled closer. "I know, but I can't do it live. Not at the level Bobby can. We talked—we talked a lot. He went to Carmen and told him if they wanted him, they had to sign me as his partner. He didn't want a studio giving him songs, he wanted to sing what he wanted, which is something RR wanted to support. And he wanted my songs."

"And Carmen agreed, I take it."

Logan brushed a strand of hair away from my face. "It's a bit more complicated than that, but yes. I will work with Bobby. Write my songs. Do some studio work with him. I retain the rights to my work—that was the biggest sticking point. RR wanted to own them, but I refused. Bobby refused to sign until I was happy, and they wanted him desperately. He's huge—his EPs have been ripping up the charts and are being played everywhere. Ravaged wasn't the only label lusting after him. Some big ones in the States were after him too, but he wanted Canadian. He wanted a label that would respect him and his artistry. Much like I did. The only difference is he had the clout to demand it."

"Bobby became your clout."

"Yes. We finally reached a compromise, but there have been a lot of meetings and talking." He huffed a sigh. "I'm so sick and tired of talking and listening to lawyers."

He pulled me tight to him. "I wanted to tell you everything, Lottie, but I was under orders not to say a word until the deal was done. And frankly, I was certain something would happen and the deal would fall through, so I was too afraid to say much. Even now, I'm not supposed to talk about it. But I can't keep this from you."

"What about teaching? Are you giving that up?"

"I asked them to get another full-time person in to cover the mat leave. It's not fair when there are so many teachers looking for hours and I have another source of income. Plus, I don't want to do that to the kids. They need stability. I still want to sub if I can, but I have no idea what my days are going to look like. I've been burning the candle at both ends as it is, and I can't do that much longer."

I ran my hand through his hair. "You do look tired."

He frowned. "So do you. I thought so last night. Beautiful, sexy, but tired."

I dismissed his concern. "I guess we've both been working hard. Logan, I'm so proud of you. So excited for your future."

"Our future."

His words made my heart beat a little faster.

"Our future."

"This is going to change my life, Lottie. Our lives. I can offer you something. Financial stability—a future."

I frowned and sat up, pulling the blankets around me. "You already had something to offer me, Logan. Yourself. I don't need anything else."

He pulled himself up, facing me. "I know, my Snow Queen. But now I bring something to the table your father can't sniff at. What they paid me, what I can make with my words, my music, will set me up for life. I see a future with RR." He cupped my face, his long fingers warm on my skin. "All because of you."

"No. Because of your music."

He shook his head. "But without you, I never would have been heard. You, Lottie, are the key to everything good in my life."

"Then I guess we're a good team."

He kissed me. "The best." He hesitated then asked, "How much trouble is this going to cause between you and your father?"

I hadn't been thinking about my father. Or the office. All I had been thinking about was Logan and how proud I was of him.

I shrugged. "I'll deal with it. This had nothing to do with my father, the deal, or anything else, except your talent. The fact that it was Bobby who insisted on this deal says it all."

"Still, he won't be happy."

I pulled my knees to my chest and wrapped my arms around them. "I don't know. The more successful this merger is out of the gate, the better the reputation is. Which reflects on the company that helped bring the investors to the table. I think Prescott Inc. comes out looking even better."

"Let's hope your father sees it that way. I don't want him blaming you for this."

"There is no blame. Everyone wins here. If my father can't see that, then it is his problem. If he wants to punish me for it, then I'll take it and move on. Won't be the first time."

"I hate that," he growled.

"It's fine." I squeezed his hand. "Your life is going to change, Logan. You get to do something you love."

He studied me for a moment. "Our life," he said softly. "Are you really worried, Lottie? What do I have to do to convince you?"

Strangely enough, all my worries yesterday vanished last night when I heard the words he had written. His love for me poured out of each passage. Every note was infused with his feelings. The way he had looked at me from the stage had eased every worry and calmed every fear. But I was honest with him and told him how I had been feeling.

"Silly, I know." I shrugged when I finished explaining my feelings of inadequacy and worry.

He leaned forward and kissed me. "Not silly. I understand. But, Lottie, I love you. Nothing is going to change that. You matter more than all of it. Please remember that. Nothing is more important than you."

"I'll try. I've been a bit off the past little while. More emotional."

"You feel all right?"

"Yes, I'm fine. A bit tired from all the late nights, but good."

"I'll be around more now. Trying to do the music thing, the planning, the teaching, make sure I had time for the kids and everything else has been brutal." He pressed a kiss to my forehead. "I missed you. I'm sorry I wasn't there for you."

"No, you have been. I've just been stressed."

"Maybe we could move that time off up a little now that I don't have to wait until the holidays?"

"I'd like that." I cleared my throat. "You still okay for the party soon? Will you have time?"

"Absolutely. I'm looking forward to escorting the sexiest woman there."

"Oh?" I feigned shock. "Who are you taking?"

In a second, he had me on my back and was over me, a warm, heavy body pressing me into the mattress.

"You," he murmured low in my ear. "My beautiful, wonderful, *sexy* Snow Queen."

I wrapped my arms around his neck and pulled him down to my mouth. "Okay, then."

My father was waiting for me in the morning, sitting inside my office, behind my desk. It was a power move on his part, reminding me he owned the place and everything in it. I had seen him do it to other people—I'd just never expected it to happen to me.

I refused to let him see my inner turmoil, and I lifted one eyebrow in what I hoped was a condescending gaze, then set down my to-go coffee cup and took my time removing my coat, smoothing down my skirt, and sitting down in one of the visitor's chairs in my office after I shut my door. I wanted as few witnesses to this as possible.

He remained silent the entire time, not moving, never betraying his emotions. Unless you knew him. I saw the fury in his eyes, the one muscle that worked in his throat.

"Charles," I said simply, taking a sip of my coffee. "If I had known you were coming to see me, I would have picked you up your own coffee." My father always drank the coffee that was readily available to all the staff, but he did, on occasion, enjoy a cappuccino from the corner coffee shop where I picked up a cup most mornings.

His voice was icy when he spoke. "I am not interested in coffee. I am, however, interested to know how it is your *boyfriend* was signed to a record label you were involved in handling a merger for." The word boyfriend was spoken with such condescension, I could hear his hatred.

I took another sip. "Strangely enough, I asked that question myself."

That caught him by surprise.

"The boy used you to get ahead. Exactly the way I knew he would," he snarled. "I know his kind—useless, always riding others' coattails. You are better off without him." He launched into a rant about men like Logan, most of his words uncomplimentary and completely inaccurate.

I let him spout off, knowing I couldn't stop his hateful words. When he stopped to take a breath, I set down my cup. "Are you finished?"

"For now."

"No," I replied. "For good."

"I beg your pardon?"

Simply and without hesitation, I set the record straight. First, I addressed his lack of respect. "You don't know Logan, so stop casting aspersions on his character. And he is a full-grown man, not a boy. Stop referring to him as such." I didn't let him reply before I told him how Carmen asked me for Logan's number. That Logan refused his offer. His meeting with Bobby and their resulting partnership.

"It was Bobby who brought Logan to Ravaged, not me—not this deal." I tapped my finger on the desk for emphasis. "They sought him out, not the other way around. His talent sold them on him. Not me. Not any investor. I never once tried to sell Logan to Carmen. Logan would never—and I will repeat that—never have asked me for help. He is far too proud." I shook my head. "In many ways, he reminds me of you. The old you. His pride and the way he looks at the world. The way he puts others first." My voice dropped, filled with sadness. "The way you were before Josh died."

"Do not bring your brother into this conversation."

I laughed, the sound dry and brittle. "No, I'm never supposed to talk about him, am I? We all pretend we're great. That we've moved past losing him." I grimaced. "The truth is we're still stuck in that hospital, watching him die. He would hate that. He would hate what has happened to our family." I looked directly at my father. "He would hate you for allowing it."

The color drained from my father's face. "You will not see Montgomery Logan again. You will refrain from these hysterical outbursts."

"Or..." I let the word trail off.

"Or you will no longer be employed here. You insist you had nothing to do with that boy's sudden windfall. I disagree. I think he has you so confused, you have no idea what the truth is."

I stood. "I think you're wrong. I think you are the one blinded to the truth. Call Carmen. He will tell you exactly what happened. So would Alfred. Logan didn't use anyone. I did nothing wrong in my handling of the account."

"I intend to."

"Be my guest."

His eyes became frostier. "You forget, I don't need your permission. This is my company. You need to find your respect, Charlotte. I'm—"

"Disappointed. I'm aware. You've been disappointed in me since the day Josh died. You've made that very clear. It doesn't matter what I've done. Perfect grades. No trouble. Going to school and getting my degree, with honors, for a career I never wanted but hoped would finally win me your approval. But I'm never going to get it." I barked out another laugh. "I just got that —after all these years. I am *never* going to be the one you love, because that person died." I stared at him, realization sinking in. "All these years, you've wished it were me who got sick. That Josh lived."

My father stood so fast the chair hit the wall behind him. "Charlotte!" he roared, his voice bouncing off the walls. His face was ashen, his eyes wide with shock.

I held up my hand. "Get out of my office. My resignation will be on your desk by noon. I'm done."

"We are not finished with this conversation."

"Yes, we are. I can't keep trying to be something I'm not. I'm not Josh. I never will be, and I need to find my own life now."

He stared at me, his face now lax. "Charlotte," he began, his voice quieter.

I lowered my head, suddenly too tired to hold it up anymore. "Leave, please."

My father didn't say another word. I heard the door click shut behind him, and I sank into the chair, my legs trembling.

I had expected my father to be angry. What I hadn't expected was my reaction. The accusations. His face when I confirmed that he had wished it had been me who died, not Josh.

When I realized that no matter what I did, it would never be enough.

I wasn't enough for him. It didn't matter how many deals I put together. How many victories I won on his behalf. How much I lived my life in an effort to please him. Even if I married a man he chose and gave him grandkids—I would never be who he wanted.

Because I wasn't Josh.

A wave of dizziness hit me so hard, I had to put my head between my legs. I felt shame flood me, worry over what had just occurred filling my chest.

I had quit my job. Told off my father. Unraveled whatever fraying strands had been left of our relationship. I had no idea what my mother would do. Probably side with my father, so in effect, I had lost them both.

Not that I really had them, I had to remind myself.

My head began to pound, and my legs shook. My breathing became harsh, and I struggled to get in enough oxygen. The room pulsated around me. Somewhere in the background, I heard voices. Footsteps. I grabbed the edge of the desk, needing to stand, desperately trying to find my footing.

Why was the room spinning?

I heard noises, shouting, and suddenly, my door flew open, crashing against the wall. A voice, a voice I knew, a voice I loved, filled the room, and *he* was there.

Logan. His warmth was close, his hands on me, holding me upright.

"Lottie, baby, what is it?"

"H-help," was the only word that came out before the room went black.

CHAPTER 22
LOGAN

I paced the waiting room in the hospital, the last couple of hours a blur. I had gone home after Lottie left for work, but I was too restless to stay. Too worried about her father. I'd had a glimpse of him last night before he left the room. Lottie thought he had left, but he was at the back, and there was no doubt he heard the announcement. I didn't want her to suffer because of me, and I had a feeling she would.

When I got to the building, I made my way to her office. I had been there one other time with her when she had forgotten something, so I knew where to go. As I stepped from the elevator, her father was storming down the hall, his expression furious. When he spied me, pure unadulterated hatred crossed his face, and before I could move, he lunged, punching me with a strong left hook. I staggered backward, hitting the wall. He crowded my personal space, almost spitting in his rage, seemingly oblivious to the wide-eyed curiosity directed our way.

"Stay away from my daughter."

I held my aching jaw in my hand. The older man had a solid punch—I was impressed. "That's her decision."

"I'm making it mine. I will make your life a shambles. All the things you think are in your reach right now? Kiss them goodbye."

"As long as I have her, take them."

He looked so startled, I shoved past him, headed to her office, not caring he was yelling after me that he was getting security. I looked over my shoulder, expecting him to be following me, but another man was standing in his way, talking. Whatever he was saying that stopped her father, I was grateful. I planned on being out of there before they followed me or security arrived.

Nothing prepared me for what I found. A shaking, barely-able-to-speak Lottie. Her face was so pale, it was the color of the freshly fallen snow she loved so much, and her feeble grip on my hand was as cold as the flakes that fell outside the window.

I recognized the panic she was falling under. The anxiety. I grabbed her coat, sliding it over her shoulders and, without a thought, swept her into my arms and rushed for the elevator, stopping at the sight of her father walking toward us, his face like thunder. Behind him was a young girl hurrying in his wake, looking upset.

"Don't," I warned. "She needs help."

He narrowed his eyes, his hands curling into fists. I walked toward the elevator, on edge and worried.

"Hate me if you want," I told him. "Have me arrested later. I don't care. Don't risk losing another child because of your personal dislike of me."

I knew that was a low blow, but it stopped him. The girl hurried forward and pushed the button on the elevator. The doors slid open, and it was empty. I stepped inside, and she pressed the button for the main floor.

"Take care of her," she whispered.

I nodded. Outside, I grabbed a cab and instructed the driver to go as fast as possible to the closest hospital.

And since arriving, I had been pacing, waiting. Anxious and

tense. She had been almost catatonic in the cab, her gaze unfocused and her body shaking. It had been hard to release her into their care, even though I knew it was for the best. Luckily, I had remembered to grab her purse and was able to give them her medical number and insurance. When questioned about my relationship to her, the word fiancé fell from my lips without a thought. I knew it was the only way to get any information out of them, and I needed to understand what was wrong with Lottie.

Briefly, I wondered what occurred once we left the office. What her father was thinking as he saw me carry her away from him and out of the building. Others witnessed our fast exit but didn't try to stop us. I didn't care what they thought. My only focus was getting Lottie some help. I shut my eyes, knowing I would have to worry and deal with that situation later. I touched my jaw, the right side of my face aching from the vicious punch her father had landed. I was grateful I had been more concerned about getting to Lottie than retaliating. Part of me wished I had hauled off and punched him back, but I knew that would only have made matters worse.

My cell phone rang, and I lifted it to my ear. "Logan."

"It's Brianna. Logan, what the hell is going on? Lottie's dad called me, wanting to know where she is—he says you took her out of the building," she exclaimed.

I groaned. "I didn't kidnap her, for fuck's sake. She collapsed. I brought her to the hospital."

Brianna gasped. "What? Which one?"

"Victoria."

"I'm on my way."

"Tell him to stay away. He did this," I snarled.

I hung up, grateful Lottie's friend would be here soon. My phone chimed again, reminding me of a meeting, and I quickly texted Bobby, telling him I had an emergency and couldn't make it. Then I resumed pacing.

A nurse entered and called my name. I hurried forward, and

she asked if I had Lottie's purse. I handed it to her when she stated Lottie had requested it.

"How is she? May I see her?"

"Soon. They have a couple more tests, then you can see her."

"Is she all right?" I asked anxiously, laying my hand on her arm to stop her from walking away.

Her smile was kind. "She's awake and doing better."

I had to be satisfied with that answer. "Tell her I'm here."

"She knows."

Brianna arrived, looking worried. "What's going on?" She dragged me to the corner where there were a couple of empty chairs. "What happened?" Her eyes went wide, and she grabbed my chin. "What happened to your face?"

I grimaced and pulled away. "It met Lottie's father —officially."

"He *hit* you?"

I told her all I knew. "They must have had a huge disagreement. He met me in the hall, and we exchanged words. He hauled off and hit me," I finished.

"Did you hit him back?"

"I wanted to, but no."

"Good. Have they told you what is wrong with Lottie?"

"No. It's very frustrating."

"Stay here. I mean it. Don't move, Logan."

She stood and approached the busy nurses station. She spoke briefly to one woman, then disappeared around the corner. I narrowed my eyes, wondering where she was going. I began to tap my knee, the irregular beat keeping me occupied and stopping me from following her. After about fifteen minutes, she reappeared and sat down beside me. "You can see her in a couple of moments. They're keeping her in for observation. She's not too happy about that."

"You saw her?"

"For a few moments. I told them I was her sister and she'd called and asked me to bring her a few things she needed."

"Clever," I conceded. "How is she?"

She blew out a long breath. "Messed up."

I ran a hand through my hair. "This is my fault. I knew her father would go after her for this."

Brianna sighed and patted my knee. "This was a disaster on hold, Logan. Eventually, something had to break." She paused, a strange look crossing her face. "I admit, I didn't see it happening like this, but that's life." She met my eyes. "How much do you love her?"

"With my entire soul." I turned in my chair, fully meeting her serious gaze. "I know it's only been a few weeks, but she's everything I've spent my life looking for. She's my future." I had to swallow around the lump forming in my throat. "It kills me to know she's down the hall hurting, and I'm stuck out here, not able to comfort her."

"Would you change your life for her?"

It seemed like an odd question. "Change my life?"

"Give up your dreams if it was better for her?"

"In a heartbeat."

"Then you're going to be fine." She stood. "I know you thought your life changed last night, Logan, but hold on to your hat. It's only the beginning." She began to chuckle, enjoying some private joke. "I think right now, patience is in order." She bent down and brushed a kiss to my head. "I have a meeting I have to get to. They'll come get you in a minute." She began to walk away. "Oh, and call her mother. She deserves to know Lottie is doing okay."

She left me confused and dumbfounded. Brianna had a meeting? Brianna hated meetings and delegated the running of her little boutique to her manager. She admitted she liked her role as purchaser and left the rest to the people who knew what they were doing. And what was she talking about, when it came to changes? I hoped it meant Lottie was going to quit her job. With my new career, we'd be fine. She could find something she enjoyed or, even better, pursue the baking thing.

My name being called startled me, and I jumped to my feet. I followed the nurse to a small cubicle at the end of the hall where my "fiancée" was resting. I pushed open the door, stopping at the sight of Lottie. She was in the hospital bed, pale and worn-looking. Her eyes were shut, but it was obvious she wasn't asleep. She was too tense for that. Monitors beeped, and there was an IV in her arm, fluid dripping slowly from the bag hanging beside her. I could see she'd been crying, a tissue crushed in her hand and her cheeks still damp.

I hurried to the bed, leaning over and cupping her cheek. "Lottie, baby, I'm here."

Her eyes flew open, and she gasped, fresh tears pouring down her face. She gripped my wrist, the hold tight.

"Logan."

The one word was filled with pain, and without another thought, I sat beside her, pulling her into my arms. She wept, her head buried in my neck, her body shaking with the force of her sobs. I rocked her, desperate to soothe, unsure what to do.

I began to hum one of her favorite songs. Almost instantly, she began to relax, her sobs slowing, her body easing in my arms. I stroked her hair and down her back in gentle passes, humming until she was quiet.

"Better?" I murmured.

She relaxed back into the pillows, her blue eyes filled with sadness. She looked vulnerable and lost—more so than I had ever seen her. I stroked her cheek.

"Whatever it is, Lottie, I'm here. We'll face it together."

"I'm not so sure you'll feel the same once you hear what I have to say."

"I am. Nothing you can tell me will scare me away, Lottie. Nothing."

For a moment, there was silence, then she spoke.

"I'm pregnant, Logan."

♫

The words exploded in my head.

Pregnant.

I met her eyes. The worry and fear were blatant. Shock lingered in her expression—the same shock I knew she must be seeing in my gaze.

"Pregnant?" I repeated.

"It's early," she sniffled. "Really early, but the blood test came back positive."

"I-I thought you were on birth control?" I asked, unsure what to say or do. I felt as if I were having an out-of-body experience. Logically, I knew I was sitting beside Lottie in the hospital, but it felt as if I were running around the room, screaming. My breathing had picked up, and my chest felt tight.

Did she say *pregnant*?

She slipped her hand under the thin blanket and held out a small package of pills. "I forgot. One day." She shook her head. "I have never forgotten."

Numbly, I took the package, noting absently the days marked, and she was one pill behind.

"My period should have started. I was so caught up in everything, it slipped my mind."

I nodded, dumbfounded, still in shock. "It's been crazy," was all I could think to say. The past few weeks had slipped away in the blink of an eye.

The room was silent for a moment, my mind beginning to process again. To take in the words she was saying.

Lottie was pregnant. With my child. I was going to be a dad. That word echoed in my head.

"This is my fault, Logan. My responsibility. I don't expect anything from you."

Her words hit me like a sledgehammer.

She didn't expect anything from me. It was all her fault.

I cleared my throat, my brain finally kicking in and working again. I took her hand in mine.

I was going to be a dad.

"Pretty sure we were both there when this baby was created, Lottie."

"By accident."

"The day I met you was an accident too. That turned out pretty damn well."

"That was different."

I met her eyes. "Yes, but no less wondrous."

Her gaze widened. "You aren't angry?"

Slowly, I pulled the blanket away and slid my hand along her flat stomach. I spread my fingers wide, amazed that beneath them was a child. A tiny little being so small and yet already so precious.

My smile was wide. Brianna was right. Last night was nothing compared to this. Not a blip.

Because the little blip under my hand was real.

My child.

Our child.

I raised my eyes to hers. "Not angry, Lottie. Shocked, a little off-balance, but not angry. How could I be? We did this together. Maybe a little faster than I expected, but we created a child. How on earth am I supposed to be angry about that?"

Her hand rested on top of mine. "I was shocked and upset when they told me, and I had no idea how you were going to take it," she admitted. "But I was also…happy. All I could think about was holding your baby in my arms."

My baby.

The image of Lottie, rounded and glowing, came to the forefront of my mind. The thought of being there with her, watching over her, being part of this journey, filled me. A spark of happiness lit in my chest. Then I recalled why we were here.

I frowned in concern. "Are you all right, Lottie? What happened? Why are they keeping you?"

"My blood pressure is low. They want to keep an eye on it." She sighed heavily and rested back on the pillow. "It's been a bad day. An argument with my father, a panic attack, and then finding out I'd been careless and screwed things up and had to tell you I was pregnant." A tear rolled down her cheek. "I thought you would be so angry that I might lose you too. Even though I know how wonderful you are, I was so afraid…" She trailed off, her voice shaking.

I knew she was overwhelmed. Shocked by the news. Add in the fact that she heard it alone, and no wonder she was worried. I leaned close, brushing my fingers over her cheek. "Look at me, Lottie."

She opened her eyes, tears swimming in the lovely blue.

"It was a bad day until that moment you told me," I assured her. "Finding out we're having a child together is when the day went from bad to awesome. Understand me? I am thrilled, sweetheart." I lifted her hand and kissed it. "I don't ever want to hear you say that again." I paused as a thought occurred to me. "Unless…you don't want this baby?"

"No! I do. It's just so fast," she explained. "We've been so fast."

"Fast but right." I kissed her forehead. "Now, you rest so I can take you home." I laid my hand on her stomach. "My family." I couldn't help the grin that broke through. "Only one pill—my boys are a determined lot. We'll have to remember that in the future."

She returned my smile, although hers was still shaky.

I blanched a little. "I didn't—uh, last night. God, did I do this? Was I too rough?"

"No. I was fine until I had the fight with my dad. Last night was amazing, Logan." She paused. "Although we might want to refrain from, ah, the acrobatics for a bit."

"No acrobatics. Got it. But sex is okay, right?"

"Yes. The doctor recommended some books."

"I'll order them right away. I have a feeling I have a lot to learn." I winked at her, wanting her to relax.

"Me too. The news certainly explained why I've been so emotional and tired."

"One mystery solved."

"I'd like to know the mystery behind that bruise on your jaw. It wasn't there this morning when I left." She lifted one eyebrow in question.

"A story for another time."

"Did you punch him back?" She guessed correctly.

"Nope. I needed to get to you more than I needed to hit him."

"Thank you."

I smiled and kissed her again. She cupped my face in her hands, gently pressed a kiss to the sore spot. "I love you."

"And I love you. Both of you."

"Our little blip."

I shook my head. "Not a blip. That indicates a mistake." I ran my fingers over her skin. "A nugget. A tiny little nugget." I met her eyes. "Our nugget."

"Our nugget will be *so* loved," she whispered, a wide smile curling her lips.

"Yes. He or she will never doubt that. Ever," I promised. My mind was already racing, planning, and organizing what I needed to do. How I could look after Lottie and make sure she was all right. Take care of both of them.

She sat up, suddenly worried. "I quit my job today, Logan. What am I going to do?"

Hearing those words made me even happier than I had been a moment ago. "We'll figure it out."

"I have a mortgage and bills. Babies are expensive." She worried her lip. "Maybe I can convince my dad to forgive me and—"

I pressed a finger to her mouth. "No. We'll figure it out, Lottie. You aren't going back there. The stress isn't good for you —or the baby," I added, unable to keep from smiling at those words.

I bent and kissed her. "We'll figure it all out together."

She visibly relaxed. "I should call the office and tell HR I'm not coming in. I'll give my dad a few days to cool off then go talk to him. But I think I need to let my mother know I'm okay. She'll freak because of Josh. Hospitals upset her terribly."

"I'll make both calls," I assured her. I described the girl who stepped aside and pushed the elevator button for me, and Lottie confirmed it was Lorie.

"I'll call her and your mother. I'll take care of it. You rest— the sooner we stabilize your blood pressure, the sooner I can take you home."

Her eyes drifted shut, and I knew she was exhausted. I watched her float into sleep, her hand resting across her stomach in a protective gesture.

I slipped from the room and called Lorie, who told me Lottie's father was already at the hospital. I hung up, checking my texts and seeing there was one from Brianna saying Lottie's mother had contacted her, and she had told her Lottie was in the hospital but had assured her mother that Lottie would be fine. She'd obviously told her husband, who was now in the waiting room. I was shocked he hadn't demanded to be allowed to see Lottie or caused a scene about me being in with her.

I made sure Lottie was still sleeping, then walked to the waiting room. Charles Prescott was easy to spot, pacing the room, on his phone, his voice low and angry-sounding. When he saw me, he ended his call and waited for me to approach him. I inhaled and closed the distance between us, stopping in front of him. His eyes focused on the growing bruise on my jaw. I had a feeling he'd like to give my face a matched set.

"There are witnesses this time if you take a swing."

He ignored my remark. "Where is Lottie?"

"Resting."

"Why is she here? I don't understand what happened."

I crossed my arms. "Because of the argument you had. She had a massive panic attack. They're monitoring her blood pressure."

"I want to see her."

"Not a chance in hell of that happening."

He narrowed his eyes. "You have no say in the matter."

Anger made me stupid and my tongue reckless. "I have every say." I stepped closer. "You had your chance, Charles. You had her entire life to fuss and care about her. Instead, you ignored her. Treated her as if she were to blame for Josh's death."

"Don't be ridiculous. Josh died of leukemia—it had nothing to do with Lottie. She gave her stem cells, but it didn't work—the disease was too far advanced."

"Did you ever assure her of that? Tell her in no uncertain terms that his death wasn't because of her?"

He opened his mouth but faltered.

"From the day he died, she has spent her life thinking you blame her for Josh's death. Trying to atone for it—as if a child her age had anything to atone for. You left her alone in her grief and guilt, and it has stuck with her for her entire life. Are you aware of how much she hates her job? She only does it as penance. She does it to try to get you to love her."

His face paled at my words, but I kept going.

"You caused this. You and your wife have wasted all this time —why, I have no clue. You are missing knowing and loving the best, sweetest, most wonderful woman I have ever met." I shook my head, my voice dripping with fury. "If you had seen what I did when I walked into her office, even your black heart would have suffered. So if you think I am letting you even remotely close to my future wife and the mother of my child, you can think again, Charles. Because those two facts right there give me the right."

His face became ashen and he tried to talk, but I cut him off. "She is not coming back to work. I suggest you meet with your HR department and figure things out."

He sputtered, but I kept talking. "She is the most important thing in this world. I will protect her from you if it's the last thing I do. If I have to give up every other dream in the world to do so, then so be it." I stepped back, letting my loathing for him show. "I will love her so well, she will never doubt how important she is. And our child will know the same sort of love." I sucked in some much-needed air. "Now, excuse me. My fiancée needs me. Go back to the office, Mr. Prescott. It's where you hide the best. I'll be sure to let your wife know when Lottie can go home."

I turned and walked away. I knew I shouldn't have said anything about the baby. I also knew Lottie was my fiancée in name only, although I planned to change that very quickly. But my anger overtook my common sense, and there was nothing I could do to take it back. I paused as I left the waiting area, glancing over my shoulder.

He was sitting, his head in his hands, not moving. His shoulders were slumped, his entire frame defeated. I felt a small flicker of guilt, but I turned my head away. He deserved it.

Lottie needed me. And right now, that was all that mattered.

CHAPTER 23
LOTTIE

I sighed and burrowed farther under the blankets, grateful to be home. They released me from the hospital once my blood pressure leveled out, and Logan assured them he would be with me. When we got home after dinnertime, I had taken a quick shower, then Logan tucked me into bed. He got some noodles and dumplings delivered from The Koi House and insisted on sitting beside me in bed and feeding them to me.

I had to admit, it was nice to be spoiled. Trev and Brianna dropped by, bringing Logan some things. They said a quick hello to me, Brianna telling me she would come the next day and sit with me so Logan could go and see Bobby. I protested.

"I am fine. I'll be perfectly able to take care of myself tomorrow while Logan is out."

"No," they both stated in unison, making me roll my eyes.

"Logan is right," Brianna insisted. "I have something I want to talk to you about anyway."

"Fine." I conceded easily, seeing the determined look on Logan's face.

After they left, Logan pulled open the curtains and turned

down the lights so I could watch the snow falling. There was a strong wind, so the snow hit the glass on occasion and swirled madly in the air. I rubbed my stomach, whispering to the tiny little dot inside.

"You'll love snow, baby. We'll go for walks and make angels and have so much fun."

Logan walked in and sat in the chair he had dragged beside the bed. "Daddy will help you make snowmen too. Afterward, we can have hot chocolate with lots of marshmallows and whipped cream." He winked and lowered his head to my stomach. "That's the only way to have it, Nugget. Trust me."

I smiled. "Daddy's right."

His grin was wide. "I can't even begin to tell you how much I like that name." He paused. "Daddy."

"You'll be a great one."

"I'm going to give it my best."

He linked our fingers. "Your mother called. Twice."

"I had better call her."

"Not tonight. I told her you're resting. She plans to come over tomorrow." He cleared his throat. "She, ah, is bringing dinner?" He lifted his eyebrows, looking askance.

"Dinner?"

"That's what she said."

That seemed odd for my mother. She didn't bring dinner. She brought wine. Extravagant hostess gifts. Dinner was a *mom* thing to do. "Okay, then."

We were quiet, watching the snow. Logan sipped a cup of coffee and crossed his legs at his ankles. "So, how attached are you to your office in the spare room?"

I turned my head, already knowing where this was going. "It can go."

"Good size for a nursery."

"I was thinking the same thing."

He scratched his chin thoughtfully. "I don't have a lot of my own stuff, but I have a couple pieces I'd like to bring with me."

"Bring with you?"

He met my gaze. "You think we're going to maintain two households for our child, Lottie?"

"I hadn't really thought that far ahead."

"Wherever my child is, is where I'll be." He paused. "Wherever you are is my home, so I'll be right here—with both of you."

I felt a thrill at his words.

"They kept referring to you as my fiancé at the hospital."

His hand tightened on mine. "I told them that so I had access."

"I see."

"As soon as possible, it will be a fact."

Another thrill went through me.

When the doctor had examined me, taken some blood, and asked the routine question if I could be pregnant, something made me pause.

"I don't think so."

He had regarded me for a moment, and I asked the nurse about my purse. I always kept my pills there and took them at lunch. She had gotten it from Logan, and I pulled out the package, staring at it. I was a day behind and had never even noticed. I looked up at the doctor, who nodded. "We'll do a pregnancy test right away."

When he confirmed I was pregnant, I was terrified. As deeply as I felt for Logan and he for me, it was so soon. We were still getting to know each other. He was just starting on a new career. How was he going to take the news? The thought of him angry and walking out crossed my mind. I had no idea what to expect, and I was afraid to hope that once the shock passed, he would, like me, be excited.

At first, I had been unsure. He looked so stunned, and I had waited for his anger. Then, as if a light switch had been flipped, his expression changed, and the delight I had hoped for burst through. In one instant, he confirmed what I had secretly yearned for. He wanted this child too. From that moment on, his complete support only proved to me what I was already convinced of. We were meant for each other.

He had fussed and cared for me all day. The fact that he was planning on making it official really wasn't a huge surprise. Nor was the fact that he intended to move in and us being a real family. It was something we both had missed out on, and neither of us wanted to waste this unexpected opportunity.

"I see."

"Just saying what I'm thinking." He lifted my hand to his mouth, kissing it. "You aren't alone, Lottie. You won't be alone. We're in this together, and I'm not going anywhere. We're going to have a great life together."

"How did I get so lucky?"

He shook his head. "I'm the lucky one. Since the day we finally met, my life has gotten better." He stood. "Now, you need to sleep."

"Would you lie with me?"

He bent and brushed his lips over my head. "Yeah, sweetheart. I'll lie with you. We can look at the snow and plan the future. Our future."

♫

I stared at Brianna. "Excuse me?"

She calmly sipped her coffee, looking casual. Her words had been anything but.

"I said I bought a small coffee shop." She held up her cup. "This one, actually. I love their coffee and their philosophy. All organic, fair trade. And a simple menu. You don't need a different language to order a cup of coffee."

I sipped the small cup I was allowed. It was delicious. I knew Brianna could afford to buy anything she wanted, but she already had a small business she loved.

"What about the boutique?"

She looked over my shoulder. "My manager wants to buy it, so I'm going to sell it to her—she deserves it. It's her hard work that keeps the place going. Her daughter wants to do the purchasing, and frankly, I'm tired of traveling. I feel as if all I do is search for stuff for the store, for something solid in my life. I feel lost, Lottie. I want roots. I want to do something in my life I enjoy. Be more than just my money. I go to this place every day. When I found out she was planning on selling, I looked into it." Brianna was curled up on the sofa with me, and she sat up, looking excited. "I could see some areas for improvement. Like her baked goods. She brought them in from outside, but if they were done in-house, it would make them unique and better." She grinned. "That's where you come in."

"Me?"

She nodded. "There is a whole kitchen in the back. You could be my baker."

"Me?" I gaped, repeating myself.

"Yes. Your cookies and bars. People love those to go with coffee. Maybe some scones or something else. Nothing elaborate. I think I want to keep it all simple—people are craving that these days. A great cup of coffee, an awesome snack. Sit in and read, or take it to go."

"Wow."

"I know." She leaned forward. "I know you think it sounds odd, Lottie, but I'm so excited. I've done up business plans and ideas. I've talked to my finance guy, looked into some renovations to make the place mine, and the more involved I get, the more it feels right. I need to do this." She smiled. "Trev's been amazing with his ideas and sharing insights about running a business."

"You like him."

She flushed slightly, shocking me. Brianna never blushed. "He's awesome. He doesn't care about my money. He cares about me."

I squeezed her hand. "Logan says he's a good guy. Genuine."

She nodded. "He is. And he's been really supportive." She paused. "I want you with me on this, Lottie."

"But I'm pregnant."

She waved her hand. "So, you come in, be the baker, oversee the menu, train someone with your recipes. When it's time to pop out the kid, you're gone. When you're ready to come back, the shop will be there."

I burst out laughing. Not only at her description of giving birth, but her firm belief that her business would thrive and be there when I was ready to come back.

She grinned at my amusement. "I mean it."

"I know." I drew in a deep breath. "I told my dad I quit yesterday."

"Perfect. You're an unemployed bum. You need a job. You're lucky I have one for you."

"Brianna—"

She cut me off with a wave of her hand. "Lottie. Stop it. Stop living your life for your parents. You have a chance here. A new job. A man who loves you. A baby. Do you really want to stay working somewhere you hate? Why let that taint your life?" She pursed her lips. "Do you honestly think your father's business will suffer? How many other employees have left and Prescott Inc. is still standing? You always say you are just an employee there. If that is true, then your father carries on. If there was more to it, maybe your father would stop being such an asshole and your relationship would have a chance to develop."

Her words hit me, and I paused. She was right.

"When did you get so smart?"

She sniffed. "I always have been. I was waiting for the right moment to spring it on you." She eyed me warily. "Say you'll at least think about it."

"I will. I promise."

"Okay."

♫

LOGAN

Bobby stared at me, then picked up his bottle of water and took a swig. "Wow. Pregnant."

I strummed my guitar, grinning. "Yep."

"No need to ask how you feel about it. You look as if you're going to explode with happiness."

I rested my hand on the neck of my guitar. "I feel like it. I never expected Lottie. Or how she would affect me. Yesterday, when she told me, I was shocked—so was she—but after the surprise settled, all I felt was how right this was. Fast as hell, but right."

"You're not worried?"

"I'm scared as fuck. I have no idea about pregnant women or babies, but it's with Lottie, so I'll learn." I paused. "This is the start of our future together."

Another piece of music drifted through my head, and I shut my eyes as I fingered the notes, quickly scribbling them down. It had been happening more since yesterday. A song was building, something tender yet intense. Bobby listened as I played through the notes, nodding as his foot tapped the beat.

"She inspire that one too?"

"She inspires them all."

He clapped my shoulder. "I have a feeling the next while is going to be very productive for us."

"I think so as well."

"Carmen wants me in to record the song I sang the other night with you. He wants it out as a single right away. You'll back me up?"

"Yep."

"He wants us to be working on the album immediately."

"Makes sense."

"He's already counting on platinum. He'll settle for gold."

I smirked, hardly surprised. Carmen had deep pockets, a ton of contacts from his career, many of them based in the States. I knew he would rely heavily on their influence to make sure the record was a success not only in Canada, but in our far more lucrative neighbor to the south. He was honest with his plans, thorough in the details, and eager to set it all in motion.

I had received a great advance, plus a decent contract, and I knew Bobby's success would influence mine. I was hungry for it. What it meant for my future—for my family. I could write and play, enjoy hearing my work, and support the people I loved. I didn't want the fame that went with it. Bobby or any other artist I worked with could have that.

Another set of notes flowed in my head, and I worked them through as Bobby listened and hummed. He was a great partner, and we worked together well. He could find words or ideas that spurred my creativity, and I helped him focus. We were a good team, and I knew with time, we'd be even better.

I wrote down the notes and the words and pushed the book toward him. "Sing the chorus."

He studied the page then shut his eyes and sang as I played. When the notes drifted off, he clapped my shoulder.

"You and I are going to make history together, Logan. The Canadian version of Elton and Bernie. Mark my words."

"I'm all for that."

His amusement rang out. "Me too, my brother. Me too."

I stopped at the apartment to grab a few more things, accepting hugs and congratulations from Rex and Gretch, who were, as usual, playing video games since they both had the day off. Trev was at the gym, but I would see him tomorrow. They were thrilled over the music deal, as well as the news I was going to be a dad. Brianna had told Trev, who'd shared the news with them. I thanked them, cautioning it was very early and we weren't telling many people yet. They understood, but Gretch still hugged me tight, telling me she knew Lottie and I were perfect for each other and she was excited about the baby.

"I'll give him his first haircut!"

I hugged her back. "Let's get him or her born and growing some hair first."

Still, her excitement stayed with me, and I hurried to get what I had come for and rush back to Lottie.

She was sitting at the table, her laptop in front of her, when I walked in. I had met Brianna out front of the building. She assured me Lottie was fine and looking forward to me coming home.

"Good luck with her mother tonight."

I had no idea what to expect, but I planned on staying close to Lottie. If her mother crossed the line, I had no problem asking her to leave. "Thanks."

I kissed Lottie, smoothing my hand down her thick hair. "Hey, Snow Queen. How are you feeling?"

"I'm fine. Much better."

I drifted my hand down to her stomach. "Nugget?"

She laughed. "He or she is fine too."

"Excellent." I leaned down and pressed a kiss to her tummy. "Hi, baby. Daddy's here."

Lottie made a strange little noise, and I looked up and grinned. Her eyes were bright with tears, but I knew they were good ones.

I kissed her and held her in my arms, giving her a moment to gather herself. I liked seeing this softer, emotional side of her.

She eased back with a frown. "That is going to take some getting used to."

"Not an issue. I'm here for the whole ride."

That made her laugh. She asked about Bobby, and I filled her in on what we had discussed. She asked a lot of questions about my schedule for the next while, which I admitted would be crazy. Recording a record wasn't a nine-to-five job, and although I was excited, it worried me that I would be gone at unpredictable times. Lottie assured me she understood and would be fine.

"I'm already feeling better. Another few days of rest, I'll be back to my old self." She grinned. "With a tiny sidekick and a few more emotional outbursts."

I laughed and listened as she told me Brianna's news and offer.

"As much as you'd enjoy it, I'm not sure I want you on your feet all day," I admitted.

Lottie hummed in agreement. "I wouldn't be. She wants me to create the menu and teach it to someone else. I would oversee. She also wants me to help her run the place. She doesn't know much about the day-to-day running of a business. I took all those courses, so I can at least guide her."

"It interests you?"

"Yes." She was quiet for a moment, tracing her finger along the edge of the table. "I don't want to go back to Prescott Inc."

I lifted her hand and kissed it. "Then I guess you have a new career."

"I guess we both do."

Our gaze met and held. Her lovely blue eyes were peaceful today, soft and warm. I was pleased to see she had some color in her cheeks and she looked better. Rested and not so worn-looking.

Cupping her face, I kissed her. Her lips were full underneath mine, parting with a soft sigh as I traced my tongue over her bottom lip. Our tongues touched and stroked, languid and gentle, a kiss filled with love and promise.

I drew back, still holding her face. "Lottie, I whispered. "I want to ask you something."

She nestled into my touch. "Anything."

"I said something yesterday, and I want to clarify it today."

She furrowed her brow. "Okay?"

I shifted closer, dropping to one knee. "I called you my fiancée. I want to make that official." I swallowed as I held up the ring I'd pulled from the back of my drawer. "This was my grand-mother's ring. I want you to wear it as a symbol."

She looked down at my simple offering. My dad had shown it to me when I was younger, and when he died, it was one of the few things I was able to keep. I'd protected it vigilantly while I was on the streets. It had meant a lot to him; therefore, it was special to me. The same went for his guitar. I recalled him playing it when I was young. Although in my later years, he'd never had time. Still, it meant a lot to me, and I kept it safe. I never bought a new one since playing this one made me feel closer to him somehow.

The band of the ring was filigree, delicate and pretty. Flecks of diamonds were scattered on the sides, and the top was an octagon with seven small diamonds set in the platinum. It was neither showy nor extravagant, but the sentiment it held for me was great. Sentiment I hoped Lottie would share.

"I'll buy you something bigger one day. When I'm worthy of you," I murmured.

Her voice caught. "You're *already* worthy. And I don't want anything bigger." She exhaled, the sound shaky as I slid the ring onto her finger, marveling at the fit and how it looked on her hand—as if it were meant to be there.

"I love it. I love you."

I looked up, meeting her eyes. Her gaze was saturated with love. I felt it encompass me, soaking into my skin, nestling itself deep within my heart.

"Marry me."

"Because of the baby?" she whispered.

"Because I love you and I don't want to waste a moment of what we have. Our baby is simply the icing on the cake. I get both of you to love." I lifted her hand to my mouth and kissed it. "Let me tell the world that. Be mine."

A tear shimmered and slid down her cheek.

"Yes," was her simple answer.

And with that one word, my world was complete.

CHAPTER 24
LOTTIE

I wasn't sure what was more amusing. The nervous look on Logan's face before he opened the door and greeted my mother, accepting a casserole dish from her, or the uncomfortable look on my mother's face as she handed it to him. Both were floundering, Logan torn between his anger with my parents in general and his innate kindness toward people. My mother was clearly uneasy at being here—and especially greeting Logan. Her hands fluttered, and she hesitated, unsure whether to shake his hand, cross her arms, or walk past him. Logan stared at the covered dish, then glanced up at my mother. He cleared his throat.

"Thank you. For, ah, whatever this is."

"Mac and cheese. Lottie's favorite."

I stepped forward and took the casserole. "June made it?"

Her words stopped me. "I made it. You always said I made the best. You especially liked it when you weren't feeling well. You always asked for it."

I froze. She did—when I was a child. She hadn't made me

mac and cheese since Josh died. The one time I'd asked, she said no. I never asked again.

I met her eyes. Her dark gaze was hesitant—almost fearful. She lifted her elegant shoulders. "I had to start somewhere, Lottie."

My voice caught, realizing how hard she was trying. "This is a good place."

Logan took the casserole from my hands and pressed a kiss to my head. "Go sit with your mom. I'll take care of this." He sent a smile in Mom's direction. "I'll bring tea, Mrs. Prescott."

She offered him a nod. "Thank you."

My mom followed me to the sofa and sat across from me. She hunched forward, anxious. "How are you feeling?"

"I'm fine," I assured her.

"You were in the hospital." A strange tremor crept into her voice, and without thinking, I grasped her hand. Part of me was shocked that she gripped mine back.

"I had a panic attack. A bad one. But I'm fine."

Her gaze fell to my hand and the ring that now rested on my finger. She lifted her eyes to mine.

"So, it is true."

"Which part?" I asked, worried we were about to start fighting. I was too tired to deal with that right now, and I was feeling optimistic and happy about my future for the first time in a long while. But her voice was mild when she replied.

"You're engaged."

"And pregnant," I responded.

There was a beat of silence. Her next words shocked me. "And happy?"

My gaze flew to hers. There was no judgment. No anger. No disconnect. My mom was there—the woman I remembered from all those years ago.

"So happy," I whispered. "And scared."

She laughed quietly. "We're all scared when we find out we're going to be a parent. I remember when I found out I was pregnant—" she swallowed and paused "—with Josh. I was more scared than excited for the first while. I had no idea how to look after a baby. But I figured it out." She was quiet for a moment. "When I found out I was pregnant with you, happiness was the first emotion." She patted my hand. "It's quite normal."

I gaped at her. She'd mentioned Josh.

"I've made a lot of mistakes, Lottie," she said, her lips pursed into a frown. "So many." She sat up a little straighter. "I've been going to therapy for the past few weeks."

I was speechless. I recalled the instances I thought she looked as if she were about to confide something to me. The way her gaze seemed different. The few times she'd brought up Josh's name. I stuttered, finding my words. "Mom, that…that's great."

"I have a lot to atone for."

Logan came in, carrying a tray. I bit back my laughter as he set it down in front of us. Two mugs of tea, neither in her preferred china, milk in both since he knew that was how I liked it, and a plate of store-bought cookies. Five of them arranged in a perfect circle on the small plate. "Ladies," he intoned. "I'll leave you to it."

I glanced at him, and he brushed my cheek with his fingers. "I'll be in the other room, writing. Right there, if you need me."

My mother watched him walk away and turned to me. "Very protective of you, isn't he?"

"Yes."

She glanced at the tray, and I was surprised to see a smile tug on her lips. Then she shocked me yet again by picking up the mug and taking a sip. She grimaced a little. "Other than the sugar, not a bad cup of tea." She tapped the tray. "Better effort than your father could manage."

Once again, her words caught me off guard.

"Dad used to bring you tea in bed."

"Dad used to do a lot of things. So did I." She took a sip of her tea, not mentioning the awkward mug it was in. "Then I lost myself. Allowed your father to drift away on his own island of guilt. We became two polite strangers dwelling under the same roof." She met my astonished gaze. "We became two grieving people locked in the past, unable to talk, move forward, or break the cycle. And the worst part of it is, we left you alone."

My voice cracked. "Mom."

She held up her hand. "I cannot go back. I cannot change things. But I can move forward. I can ask you to give me a chance. To let me be a small part of your life." Her gaze drifted lower. "To be part of your child's life in some way." She paused. "To be a real part of *your* life in some way."

My breath caught, and I stared at her. My heart sped up, my breathing becoming faster. They were words I had longed to hear and given up on doing so. I had to blink away the moisture building in my eyes. She kept talking.

"I know I can't ask for your forgiveness until I deserve it. I also know you may never grant it. But I am asking for that chance to earn it."

"I want that." I managed to choke out. "But Dad—"

She held up her hand. "No, this is you and me. I'm not going to ask on his behalf. He has to do that."

"I can't work for him anymore."

"I know. He told me you quit." She picked up a cookie, studying it as if it were a science experiment, then took a bite, chewing it slowly. "That was a job Josh would have loved. From the time he was a toddler, he sat on your father's lap, absorbing everything. He was destined to work with your father, not you, Lottie." She put the cookie back on the plate and set down her mug. "Logan said some things to your father." She clasped my hands between hers, her touch evoking memories from my childhood. Ones I had missed so much. "You were not responsible for his death. You did nothing wrong. Nothing. You didn't fail, Lottie. The illness was too aggressive. On top of everything else I have to atone for, allowing you to think that I thought you were anything but brave and wonderful to try to help your brother is my biggest sin. That, I will *never* atone for." A tear slipped down her cheek. "Never."

I watched the tear flow over her skin, quiver on her jaw, and drop to her knee. Her lips trembled, and I saw how she was struggling to hold in her emotions. I flipped over my hands and held hers tight.

"I want my child to know his or her grandmother," I stated simply. "I would like to get to know my mother."

"I want that as well."

I held up one hand. "There are rules. I am going to live my life for me now. You have to accept my decisions."

"Of course."

"You need to let Dad and me work things out—or not."

She pursed her lips but tilted her head in agreement.

"Logan asked me to marry him. I said yes. He is a huge part of my life now, and I demand he be given the respect he deserves as our child's father and my husband. He might not be what you envisioned for me, but he is everything I wanted and then some. I consider myself the luckiest woman in the world."

Mom was silent, then she bent closer, her voice low. "He is rather dreamy."

I gaped at her, and a shout of laughter escaped my mouth. She lifted her shoulders. "I am your mother, Lottie, but I have eyes—and a pulse." She began to laugh with me. It was a sound I hadn't heard in years. It stirred memories, brought up the love I always carried for my mom, and lightened the intensity around us.

"I'm going to try very hard," she assured me. "My therapist tells me she has every confidence I can do this."

"Me too."

Logan appeared, looking confused. "Everything all right?"

"Yes," I assured him.

"More tea?"

My mom held up her mug. "I would love some. You make a lovely cup of tea, Logan."

"Thank you, Mrs. Prescott."

She waved her hand. "Please, call me Josephine."

His grin was wide. "All right then, Josephine. I'll get you that tea."

♫

I was still reeling hours after my mother left. We had talked more, her insisting Logan stay with us. She apologized to him, and he was gracious when he accepted her obviously sincere words. After she left, Logan had played some new music he was working on for me and sang. Nothing relaxed me as much as his voice. It was going to take a long time before my mom and I had what might be considered a normal relationship—if, in fact, we ever reached that place. But she was trying, and I wanted her in my life. Perhaps we could be friends since the whole mother/daughter thing seemed too unattainable. Too much time and pain had passed for me to imagine that ever happening. But I was determined something positive would come from all of this. Logan had listened to me talk after she left, agreeing with me that we had to go slow and find our way. He carefully reminded me that she was my mother, and given that he had lost his own father, giving her a chance seemed to be the right thing to do.

"She reached out to you," he reminded me.

"Because of the baby." I absently rubbed my stomach.

He lifted his shoulders. "All the better. If our child can heal that sort of rift, then I'd say we're on the right track." He winked and kissed me. "Our kid is magic."

I smiled as I thought about his words. Logan saw things in a unique way, but he was right. I studied him, sitting across from me. He was busy jotting a few notes when I spoke up. "My mom thinks you're 'dreamy.'"

He chuckled, not looking up. "Does she now?"

"Uh-huh."

He set aside his guitar and leaned forward, crossing his arms over his knees. "And what does her daughter think?"

"Oh—double dreamy."

He ran a finger over his mouth, his gaze darkening. "I see. Nice to know. Anything else?"

I pretended to think. "Sweet and wonderful."

He eased back, extending his arms across the back of the sofa. His chest was bare, the light playing off his muscles, highlighting his form. His nipple ring glinted in the light. He was relaxed and teasing, his gaze filled with adoration—and longing.

"Oh," I added, suddenly breathless. "Sexy too."

He met my eyes, the golden, rich whiskey of his boring into mine. I felt my body react to him. I felt so much better today. Lighter, easier. I knew he'd spoken to the doctor more in depth about sex. It had amused me watching the tips of his ears go red as he tried to be nonchalant in his queries. This bold, confident man embarrassed about wanting to have sex with me and worried about hurting me at the same time. It only made me love him more.

"Lottie," he murmured. "You need to rest."

"Logan," I replied. "I need you more." I batted my eyelashes. "I can rest after."

His eyes began to darken even more. "No more sofa antics."

I could work with that—at least the sofa antics that involved anal sex. For now. But I wanted him.

"Our bed is pretty comfy." I pulled on the loose neck of the T-shirt I was wearing.

That did it. He stood and scooped me into his arms, carrying me down the hall. "*Our* bed. You had to say that, didn't you?"

I gripped his shoulders and kissed his neck, breathing him in. "Worked, didn't it?"

He settled me on the mattress, hovering over me.

"Yeah, baby, it worked. Now, lose the shirt."

♫

I lasted three days before I was bored out of my mind. Logan was busy, yet stayed close, checking in on me often if he was out. I slept the entire first day, and by the afternoon of the second day, I felt perfectly fine—my energy level high, my mind clear, and the constant disconnect I had been experiencing gone. I felt like Lottie—but better. The last time I had felt this good was when I was off for a week of holidays with Brianna three years ago. It boggled my mind that was the last time I had taken time off. Before that, it was the few days I needed to make the wedding cake. Otherwise, I was at the office every day.

Logan left that morning after a long, lingering kiss. His fear had dissipated quickly, and the last couple of days he had been the usual dirty-talking, sexy man I had fallen for. He was intense, yet gentle—walking the fine line between the two perfectly. I was looking forward to the next nine months if that was the way he approached my pregnancy.

I stared out the window, looking at the sun glistening off the snow. I had been restless all morning, unable to settle. I was so used to being busy, productive. The truth was, there was nothing stopping me from doing so. I was healthy and the baby fine. What had occurred had been due to the enormous stress and pressure I was feeling. I blew out a long breath, knowing why I was restless. I had unfinished business to handle. I needed to talk to my father. And I needed to do it in order to move forward.

I dressed simply in warm slacks and a pretty sweater. I called Logan to tell him I was going out. He was silent for a moment.

"I don't suppose you'd wait and let me go with you to see him?"

"How did you know I was going to see my father?"

"Because I know you."

"I have to do this, Logan. And I need to do it on my own."

"Promise me if he upsets you, you'll leave."

"I promise."

"Don't let him guilt you into going back."

I laughed. "Pretty sure that ship has sailed. I am going to talk to him, get a few things I want from my office, and I'm done. I'll be home when you get here."

"I'll be waiting."

Those simple words made my heart soar. "I love you."

"Ah, Lottie. You have no idea how much I love you back."

I hung up, his words bolstering me. I called Lorie, who assured me my father was there and she would make sure I got in.

I pulled on my coat and mitts and headed out. It felt familiar, the walk and the subway ride, but this time, it was different. There was no pit of fear in my stomach, no worry or tension running down my spine. I was nervous about seeing my dad, but it was a personal kind of anxious. I didn't have to deal with clients or numbers. Present facts and figures to people and convince them to invest. Worry and fret about the details. Today would be the last day I walked through the doors of Prescott Inc. as an employee. I wondered as I headed toward the building if I would ever come back. Would I ever walk in as Charles Prescott's daughter for a visit? Bring my child to see his or her grandfather? Watch him bounce them on his knee the way he did me as a child?

I had to stop and wipe away a tear. There was only one way to find out. I squared my shoulders and walked into the building.

It felt odd to be back—as if it had been years, not a matter of days, since I had walked the halls. I went straight to my father's office. Lorie took me into his private area, assuring me he was almost done with his meeting in the boardroom and would be right in.

"I miss you around here," she whispered. "You're not coming back?"

"No."

"I'm sorry."

I shook my head. "Don't be. I'm happy. Relieved, if I'm being honest. Maybe we can do lunch sometime."

"Oh, I'd love that."

We exchanged numbers, and I sat and waited for a few moments, my nerves suddenly tight. I felt my anxiety creeping in, and I wondered if perhaps I should have waited for Logan. He would have held my hand and whispered silly things to distract me. Made rude comments about my father's swanky office. Lewd promises about what he'd do to me once we got home.

I concentrated on my breathing the way they taught me at the hospital, and I felt myself calm. My phone buzzed, and I peeked at the screen, smiling at the simple words that made me feel better instantly.

You got this, Snow Queen.

My father walked in, his footsteps measured and unhurried. I stood and turned, surprised to see him looking very un-Charles-Prescott-like. To the rest of the world, he probably looked normal, but I saw the pallor under his skin. The weary pull around his eyes. His tie was slightly askew.

He cleared his throat. "Charlotte."

"Charles."

He rounded his desk, sitting down heavily. "I was surprised when Lorie said you were coming in."

"I wanted to close this chapter before I moved on."

His gaze drifted over my shoulder. "So, you really aren't returning?"

I shook my head. "I think it's for the best, for both of us."

He ran a hand through his hair, leaving a small tuft sticking up. It seemed so out of place with the rest of his neat, orderly persona, and I had to ask.

"Dad, are you all right?"

He looked startled when I used the word dad. He stood and rounded the desk, sitting across from me in the other visitor's chair. He clasped his hands in front of him, hunching forward.

"My daughter had to be rushed to the hospital because of me. I hit a young man I barely know. I find out my daughter is pregnant and leaving the company." He drew in a shaky breath. "The worst part is the young man I hit told me some very hard truths about my life. About what I've done. Or, to be more accurate, what I haven't done."

Tentatively, he reached over and took my hand. I stared down, recalling how it had felt when he'd held my hand as a child. I'd always felt safe. Loved. Strangely, there were still echoes of that feeling in my heart now.

"Josh died because he was sick. Not because of you. I'm sorry I never told you that. I'm sorry I was never there for you, Lottie. I was so lost in grief, so angry because I was so helpless—unable to save my son, to stop the pain that ripped my wife apart, to ease the heartache in your eyes..." His voice trailed off. "I forgot to be the parent I needed to be, or the husband I should have been. This place—" he waved his hand "—was the one thing I could control, and I poured everything I had into it."

For a moment, the room was silent. He stared down at our hands. "I have been such a blind fool. I gave everything I had to this place instead of to your mother and you. Instead of cherishing the family I still had, I mourned what I lost. And now, it's all gone."

"No, Dad. Mom is still with you. She's trying." I swallowed. "I'm here."

He looked up, and I was shocked at the glimmer of tears in his eyes. "To say goodbye."

I shook my head. "To get my things, hand in my keys, and perhaps start a new path for us. Father and daughter. Not boss and employee."

"You've always been more than that, Lottie. I was always so damn proud of you."

"You never told me that."

"I know. Another mistake." He kept his eyes on the floor. "I thought at times, if I loved you too much—you, too, would be taken away from me." He laughed, the sound bitter. "Except I did that by myself. I drove you away."

"No," I whispered, repeating myself. "I'm here, Dad."

He tightened his grip on my hand. "I know your mother talked to you, and you offered her your forgiveness. I'm asking for the same, Lottie. Give me a chance and let me be part of your life. I'll do anything if you let me try."

I was reeling. What I thought was the end with my parents seemed to be the beginning. Could I forgive them and forge a relationship with them? The child in me wanted it—she wanted their love and approval still. The adult was a little leerier, but still hopeful.

"You need to apologize to Logan. You were horrid to him."

"I know. I will meet the boy and talk to him."

"He is *not a boy*."

My father chuckled. "He is to me. Just like you're still my little girl."

Those words made me gasp. I hadn't been his little girl since that awful day in the hospital. He lifted his shoulders in understanding. "You always will be," he added gently.

There was a knock on the door, and my father stood, going to the door and speaking quietly with someone on the other side. He returned and sat at his desk.

"I, ah, have some papers for you to sign."

"Of course," I replied, straightening my shoulders.

"Our talk isn't over, Lottie. I thought perhaps you would like to continue it someplace you're a little more comfortable." He glanced around. "Someplace you hate less."

"I don't hate the office, Dad. I hated my job," I replied.

"Yet you did it so well." He shook his head. "Would you have hated it less if I had told you that more?"

I thought about it. "It would have made the days less painful, thinking you noticed my work and appreciated it, but no, Mom was right. This place was Josh's dream, not mine." I huffed out a sigh. "I should have been honest and told you that."

"I didn't make that easy, though, did I?"

"No," I admitted.

"Then let's finish it here today. No more boss and Charlotte." He looked hopeful. "Maybe we can work on Lottie and Dad—when you're ready." He paused. "Maybe Grandpa—if you let me."

"I'd like that."

"All right. Let's get you out of here and home."

Half an hour later, I sat back down in the office, a small box beside me of the few items I had at my desk, including my little clock. I'd turned in my company cell phone and my keys, grateful that Logan had picked up a new cell phone for me to use. I signed the papers, accepting the check for my holiday time, unused sick days, bonuses, and a severance package my father insisted I take. It was a generous amount, even after taxes.

"I would do it for another employee, Lottie. You deserve all of it and more."

I told him about working with Brianna, and the plans Logan and I had. He listened, actually listened, even offering a few suggestions and saying he would call Brianna to set up a meeting with her.

"Would Logan be amenable to meeting with me?" he asked.

"You would have to ask him that."

He accepted my response. "If you ask him to call me, I would appreciate it."

I wrote down Logan's number. "Call him yourself."

He stared down at the piece of paper. "I will."

His phone buzzed, and he picked it up, listening, then spoke. "I'll be with them in a moment."

I stood. "You need to get back to work, Charles."

"Dad," he corrected, startling me. "No more Charles."

"Dad," I repeated.

"Let me get my car to take you home."

"No, I'm fine."

He sighed. "Still stubborn. Leave the box, and I'll drop it off. I don't want you carrying it on the subway."

I agreed to that and stood, slipping on my coat. My father walked me to the door, suddenly nervous again. He stood with his hand on the knob, not opening the door.

"I'll miss seeing you around the office, Lottie."

"Then we can look forward to seeing each other outside these walls."

"You'll still come to the party, won't you?" he asked. "You always enjoy it. You, ah, you can bring Logan."

"We'd love to."

He bent slowly, giving me time to back away, and kissed my cheek. "Let me know you got home safe, please."

"I will."

He opened the door, meeting my eyes. "Thank you."

I could only nod, my emotions too close to the surface to talk anymore. I waved to Lorie and headed to the subway. I felt tired again—drained, but more at peace.

I could hardly wait to tell Logan. I sent him a fast text telling him I was on the way home, then joined the lineup for the train. I had so much to tell him.

♫

I heard him before I saw him. The sounds of him strumming his guitar greeted me as I stepped off the train and headed to the stairs. I came around the corner and met his whiskey-colored eyes. He was propped against the wall, the way he always was, his guitar case open, smiling and tilting his chin in acknowledgment as people dropped in coins and bills. But when he saw me, his smile grew wider and he began to sing, his rich voice filling the station. It was one of his older songs, one I had always loved. It was melodic and beautiful, the lyrics poignant, and his voice was perfect for it.

Smiling, I sat on the bench I always used and listened. I shut my eyes, letting the music flow over me. Any residual stress from the day melted away, and my shoulders relaxed. As the notes faded, I opened my eyes and watched as Logan shut his case, slung it over his shoulder and walked my way.

Tall, sexy, he walked with confidence. He stopped by the bench and bent low, cupping my face and kissing me. "Hey, Snow Queen."

"Hi," I breathed out.

He sat, linking our fingers.

"You're here."

"Where else would I be? This is where we started. I thought you'd need me again."

"I'll always need you."

He grinned. "Good thing. I love being needed by you." He paused. "Things go okay?"

"Yes."

He studied me, brushing a stray lock of hair behind my ear. "You look tired, but not upset."

"My dad sort of surprised me today."

"Like your mom?"

"Yes."

He nodded. "Amazing how clear things become at times. As scary as it was, you collapsing might have woken them up."

"I think maybe the news about Nugget did as well."

He smiled wide. "Told you. Our kid is magic."

"I guess he is."

"He?"

"Or she."

He turned, shifting closer, dropping his voice as he placed his hand across my stomach. "How is my nugget?"

"Hungry."

"I think I can help there. How does Nugget feel about a burger?"

"Extra cheese?"

"You know it." He lifted my hand to his mouth and kissed it. "Diner?"

"Can I have cake?"

"You can have anything you want."

I squeezed his hand. "I have everything I want right here."

He kissed me. Long, slow, lingering, and sweet. "Me too, Snow Queen. Me too."

EPILOGUE
LOGAN

L ottie looked up as I strode into The Java Way, the bell above my head announcing my arrival. She smiled widely and waddled around the counter.

There was no other word to describe it. Lottie waddled like a duck these days. She was so tiny, she'd looked as if she were well into her second trimester before she'd even finished the first. Now, with only a few weeks to go, she looked as if she were ready to burst. It made me smile every time I saw her.

I bent down, kissing her upturned mouth. "Hey, ducky."

She laughed. Brianna had nicknamed her first, teasing her constantly as she filled out.

"You're pregnant from the nose down!"

Lottie had taken it all in stride, even chuckling at her nickname. She glowed these days, relaxed and peaceful, always smiling.

I loved her new curves. The subtle fullness of her cheeks. The way her breasts overfilled my hands and the softness of her rounded hips. I especially loved the swell of my son she carried so heavily in front. Safe, protected, and deeply loved.

The day we found out it was a boy was one of the happiest I had ever known. I had stared at the ultrasound, unable to talk.

A son. We were having a son. For days, I carried around the picture, showing it to everyone, whether they wanted to see it or not. Lottie had been amused and, I was certain, secretly enjoying my excitement.

Lottie rolled up on her toes, meeting my mouth. "Hi."

My hands went to her stomach. "How's Nuggetman?"

"Active. I think he's playing football."

Bobby strolled in behind me, laughing. "I keep telling you, Lottie. He's going to be a drummer. He's practicing."

"He needs to take a break," she replied.

I laughed and rubbed her tummy. "Settle down, little man. Give Mommy a break."

Lottie sighed and ran a hand over her neck. She looked tired today. I wanted her to give up coming in, but she loved the coffee shop. The atmosphere and the baking. Talking to people, trying new recipes. Brianna's vision for the place was working. Business was good—busier all the time as word of mouth spread. Lottie's cookies, slices, and mini pies were sold out every day. She had two bakers now just to keep up.

Jo-Jo came from the back, a smile breaking out on her face. "Logan, my boy!"

I laughed at her nickname, knowing it would forever stick. We had come a long way in the past months, growing closer as the time passed, and I had become incredibly fond of her. I was her boy, and she was simply Jo-Jo.

When I had arrived with Lottie to the holiday party, I was unsure if I should even be there with her. I was still concerned about her father's reaction. He had been polite, shook my hand as we walked in, but otherwise was silent. It was her mother who took me by the arm, introducing me as Lottie's fiancé. She made sure I was comfortable. Sat beside me at dinner, a pleasant distraction from the quiet demeanor of Charles. When I asked her to dance, she had been light on her feet, obviously enjoying the music, and we had taken to the dance floor more than once. She quietly told me that Lottie's father was more embarrassed at himself than he would admit, and she appreciated the patience I was showing. Her words bolstered me, and I assured her I would continue to try to get along with him.

For the next few months, Lottie's father and I were polite with each other, but there was no doubt bad feelings still lingered on both our sides and it would take a while for them to be resolved. We had met a couple of times, the conversation stilted. He offered an awkward apology, and for Lottie's sake, I accepted it. We were more comfortable when Lottie and Jo-Jo were with us, and slowly, we'd been building a rapport. I often sought out his opinion, which seemed to help him open up more. The last month had been a turning point with us spending a lot of time together, and I hoped we continued in that forward direction. I knew how much it meant to both Lottie and Jo-Jo.

No one was more shocked than Lottie when her mom asked Brianna if she could help out in the shop. Jo-Jo was a proficient baker and enjoyed coming in and working with Lottie. They had grown closer as the months progressed, and I loved seeing the happiness it brought Lottie. She had attended a few of her mother's therapy sessions, which seemed to benefit both of them. Lottie had gone to some therapy on her own, and it helped bring her closure to losing Josh. She was far more at ease with the past now and able to move forward without guilt. Jo-Jo tried so hard to be a part of our lives. Exclaiming over ultrasound pictures, dropping by for visits, and bringing Lottie's favorite meals from when she was a child. Insisting on Thursday night dinners and making plans for when the baby was born. She always requested I make her tea when she visited and never once made a comment over the mug or the sugar I added. She always patted my cheek and smiled, informing me it was the best cup she'd had all week. Her praise made me smile.

Lottie laughed when she told me how her mom boasted about her dreamy son-in-law to her friends who came into the shop. Went on about being a nana. The nursery was full of gifts from her already—onesies, outfits, tiny socks, coats, and jackets. Stuffed animals. She'd begged to be allowed to buy the furniture, insisting as grandparents, it was their right. I couldn't refuse since it made her happy, and Lottie was overjoyed. How Charles felt about it, I had no idea. He was happy about being a grandpa, an ultrasound picture proudly displayed on his desk. His face had been filled with wonder when Lottie grabbed his hand and he felt the baby kicking. A tender, wistful expression had crossed his face, and for a moment, I saw the pain he hid. It made it easier to reach out to him.

And now, it was time to see how Lottie felt about my inclusion of her father in my latest plan.

I bent, accepting a kiss from Jo-Jo. "Hey," I greeted her. She was excited, knowing full well what I had up my sleeve.

Her smile became wider as she spotted Bobby. He grinned and held out his arms.

"Come to me, Momma J."

I had to chuckle, watching her hug him. She fussed over him constantly. Lottie thought it was because he reminded her of Josh. Whatever it was, it was good to see her maternal side out in full force these days with all of us. She'd even warmed up to Brianna, and she adored Trevor. Rex and Gretchen were both welcome additions to her growing circle.

I smiled at Lottie. "You have time to come with me?"

"Where are we going?"

"You'll see."

She shook her head. "So mysterious."

"You love my surprises."

My last one had been our wedding. We'd applied for the license, and once we had it, I couldn't wait. With Brianna's and Roxanne's help, I borrowed the top floor of Ravaged Roadside and threw a party. A wedding party. Our friends, family, my Ravaged family, some other guests, and us. We exchanged vows in the flower-filled room, I had The Koi House supply us with dumplings and all Lottie's favorite dishes, and after we had our fill, we danced as Bobby sang. I took to the stage and performed a few songs for my bride, then we danced the night away with a great DJ provided by RR. We left the next morning and enjoyed each other for a few private days at a spa up North.

All Lottie had had to do was pick a dress and show up. When I confessed to what I had done, her eyes had grown round.

"I don't want to wait to marry you," I explained.

"But all the details…" She trailed off.

"Handled. Brianna and your mother are picking you up in the morning to get a dress. That's all you have to do."

"My parents…"

"I spoke to them. It's our wedding. Not theirs. I told them to invite whoever they wanted, but I did give them a limit. Thirty people."

"I bet that went over well."

I shrugged, unconcerned. "Jo-Jo was good with it. Your father can figure it out. I refused his offer to pay for it, although your mother insisted on paying for the flowers and the dress. That's all I allowed them to do. The rest is my gift to you." I paused. "As long as you say yes."

She smiled, her eyes glowing. "Then, yes."

Carmen refused to accept anything for the room, Bobby's gift to us was himself, the photographer was supplied by RR. I paid The Koi House well for the catering, knowing that it was an unconventional choice, but not caring. Lottie constantly craved Chinese food, so the decision was easy for me and went along with our relaxed vibe. People raved about the food—I even saw Charles going back for more. It was simple and perfect—it was us.

Lottie had been gorgeous in a knee-length, lacy pink dress. I wore a suit, although I removed the jacket as soon as the vows were done and sported a vest. I didn't wear a tie, but Lottie was good with that.

Neither of us had stopped smiling that day. I'd barely stopped smiling since. I had no idea life could be this good.

I shook my head to clear my thoughts. I had another surprise for Lottie. One I hoped she would love.

"What are you up to?"

I held out my hand. "Come and find out."

Bobby threw me a wink. "Car's waiting. I'm gonna feast on cookies, drink my weight in coffee, and hang with my girls."

I laughed and helped Lottie slip on her coat. I glanced at her feet, noting the swelling in her ankles. She really needed to listen to me about not working anymore. The baby was due in a few weeks. It was time to relax a little.

In the car, she was curious. "Logan, where are we going?"

"To see something I want to buy."

"Oh."

We pulled up in front of a familiar Tudor-style house. Lottie stared at it in recognition, then got excited. "Oh my god, whatever they have for sale, we need to take a long time to decide. I've been wanting to see inside this place forever!"

I chuckled at her enthusiasm and helped her from the car. It took a lot of effort these days. We walked to the door, and I opened it, indicating she should go inside. She hesitated.

"Um, shouldn't we knock?"

"Nope, we're expected."

Inside, she was confused, glancing around. "Logan, there's no one here."

"The owners are here," I assured her.

She looked around again, and I could see the moment realization hit. Her eyes went wide, and she stared at me.

"What have you done?"

"Bought you a house."

"This house?"

"Well, if not, then technically, we're breaking and entering."

"Logan…" she breathed out.

"You love this house. Every time we walk past it, you stop. I see how you look at it."

"Logan," she repeated, her hand flying to her stomach and rubbing it in an unconscious gesture. "How? When? Can we…" She trailed off, the nervous edge to her voice bothering me.

I rested my hands on top of hers, stopping the constant rubbing. It was a huge tell for her now—when she was upset or worried, the baby got a massage.

"Hey, everything is good. Come explore with me, and I'll answer all your questions."

We toured the house, and I watched her fall in love. She exclaimed over the original details, the hardwood floors and cove moldings. The layout and size of the rooms. The large converted gas fireplace that would warm the room and look nice on a cold night. She loved the master bedroom that overlooked the back-yard with a window seat. The kitchen was a good size, recently updated, along with new appliances, and the bathrooms were fine for now. It gave us a few projects to work on. I planned on turning the basement into a small recording studio, but that was far into the future.

Lottie loved all the nooks and crannies she discovered—the ones she had imagined the house contained. Her enthusiasm grew, her longing evident, and judging from the belly rubs, her nerves. She paused by the large bay window in the living room, looking outside.

"A Christmas tree would look great right here," I murmured, standing behind her and wrapping my arms around her waist. "Imagine sitting here by the fire, looking outside as the snow falls."

She turned, tears in her eyes. "I love it, but I don't understand."

I smiled and wiped away the tears. "I saw it go up for sale a couple of months ago. I knew you loved it, so I made inquiries. I came to see it and knew you would love it too."

"I didn't know you were thinking about a house."

"I want you to have a home, Lottie. One we can watch our

kids grow up in. We've talked about a house instead of the condo."

"I-I thought in the future. When we're more financially, ah, steady."

There was one chair left in the house. A large wingback I had asked the owners if I could purchase. They had left it, and it sat to the left of the large window. I guided Lottie over and helped her sit.

"I *am* very financially stable, Lottie. We both are." I paused. "I sold some songs to Idleman. He paid me a huge amount of money, plus I get royalties. And he wants more."

My writing and songs had taken off in a bigger way than I had ever dreamed. I was sought after by other artists, although my main focus, as always, was Bobby. His career was flying high, and he was in huge demand. We both were. I knew in another couple of years, I would never have to worry about money again. Especially given the simpler way of life we preferred. Buying this house had been an easy decision. A smart one, her father had informed me, a small gleam of pride in his eyes.

"Instead of investing in stocks, I'm investing it in this house. In our future."

She blinked. "You didn't tell me."

"I was waiting to surprise you." I cupped her cheek. "I brought your dad to see the house. To get his advice."

Her eyes grew round. "Oh."

"He helped me with the offer. The man is a shark."

She chuckled. "Not a surprise."

I drew in a deep breath. "He wanted to buy the house for us in lieu of a wedding gift. I told him no." I knew neither Lottie nor I wanted that.

"Good."

"I did, however, accept his offer to hold the mortgage." I winked. "I'm not stupid enough to turn down a half-percent mortgage. With the big down payment I made and his terms, we'll own this place in about ten years."

"We can do it faster with the proceeds if we sell the condo."

"We can. I wasn't sure if you wanted to sell or rent it out."

"I don't want to be a landlord."

"Okay, then, we'll figure that out. Rex wants the apartment, and Trev is looking to buy. Maybe he would be interested in your condo. I'll talk to him." I held her hands. "We have possession, Lottie. The house is ours. We can move in, or if you hate it, I'll resell it."

"I love it. I really do. I can see us here, raising our family." Her eyes glowed. "I want it, Logan."

I smiled. "Good. Since I rejected the house offer, your dad insists on paying for the move. I don't want you touching a thing, so I agreed. They'll come in, pack us up, and move us in, and do all the unpacking too."

"Wow."

"Trev, Rex, and I are gonna host a paint party this weekend. I'll supply the paint and equipment, the beer and pizza, and we'll have the place painted in a day. I got a dozen people coming."

"Really?"

I chuckled. "I've been a part of lots of them. It's my turn to collect. I just need you to pick some colors."

Excitement filled her eyes. "I can do that."

"If possible, I want to move us in in two weeks. We should be settled before Nuggetman shows up."

She flung her arms around my neck, holding me tight. "I love it. I love you."

I held her close. "I love you, Lottie."

She eased back and cupped my face. "Thank you."

I smiled. "Welcome home, baby."

♫

A week later, Lottie walked around the house, frowning. I followed her, unsure about her mood. Had we painted the rooms the wrong color? I had double-checked before we started, and I was certain we had done it right. I hadn't let her in the house until I was sure the fumes had faded. She'd been excited to come here today but had been withdrawn when she had woken up, rubbing her back and complaining about her sore feet. She seemed tense on the ride over, Brianna coming with us to see the house. Even she noticed Lottie's odd mood and was subdued herself.

"You don't like it, sweetheart?"

"It's perfect."

I exchanged a glance with Brianna, both of us confused. Lottie waddled slowly to the wingback, and I hurried behind her to help her get settled. She grimaced as she sat, and I kneeled beside her. "Nugget kicking hard?"

She nodded, looking distracted.

"Baby, what is it?"

"Nothing. I'm just tired. The house looks perfect." She smiled, but the effort didn't reach her eyes. They were still dim. She fidgeted a little, then settled, her hand resting on top of the rounded swell of her tummy. I noticed her grimace again and decided she needed to go home and rest.

"Is the idea of the move bothering you? I swear, you have to do nothing. You and Brianna are going for a spa day, and when you get here, everything will be done."

We'd already brought over the nursery items. I'd spent the last two days putting the crib and changing table together. Today, I'd carried in the rocking chair. We were well ahead of the game.

Suddenly, she gasped, and tears ran down her face. Shocked, I cupped her cheeks. "Lottie, baby, talk to me."

She grabbed her stomach, pain filling her eyes. "Nugget."

"What? What's wrong with Nugget?" I laid my hands over hers, gazing down in panic.

Brianna laughed. "Uh oh."

Then I saw it. Lottie's water had broken, seeping into the chair, the material becoming darker.

"He's coming?" I asked, standing. "He's early. Dr. Roberts said usually first babies are late!"

"Not this one," Brianna chortled. "I'll get the car."

I grabbed my phone.

"What are you doing?" Lottie asked, her eyes wide with fear.

"Calling your mother. She'll know what to do."

Lottie groaned. "Just get me to the hospital." She grabbed my arm. "Fast."

"Jo-Jo," I spoke into the phone fast when she answered. "It's time. Meet us at the hospital. I need Lottie's bag." I hung up, not giving her a chance to talk. Bending, I scooped Lottie into my arms.

"I'm getting you wet," she protested.

"I don't care, woman. My son is coming!"

She gripped my neck as another contraction hit her. "Oh god, he's coming soon."

I ran.

I stared down at my son's face, transfixed. I had barely put him down since they'd placed him in my arms. Red-faced and screaming, he had settled quickly, making little snuffling noises and burrowing close. He had a head full of dark hair and blue eyes like his mother. Lottie told me all babies had blue eyes when they were born and she hoped they'd change to look like mine, but I wanted them to stay the way they were right now. Other than the dark hair and eyes, he was me, right down to the little fold on top of his right ear—exactly like mine. His jaw was square, and when he opened his eyes, he had a stubborn, deter- mined set to his face.

I had a feeling I was going to be dealing with a mini me for the next thirty years or so. God help me.

"You need to put him down, Daddy."

I glanced up with a smile. "Soon."

Lottie tilted her head. "We have to name him."

We had talked names, chosen many, then discarded them. One combination had stuck with me, but I'd stayed silent until my son was born. But looking at him, he suited the name. I was certain Lottie would like it.

"I have the perfect name. I've been keeping it secret."

She held out her hand. "Tell me."

I stood and settled our son into her arms. She waited patiently as I gazed down at them. My family. I bent and kissed them both.

"Joshua," I said softly. "Joshua William Logan. In memory of the men we both loved and lost too soon."

Tears filled her eyes. "Perfect," she whispered.

I wiped under her eyes. "You're perfect. You amazed me today, Lottie. Completely amazed me."

"Sorry about the chair."

Bowing my head, I laughed. "The chair is fine. Nothing matters but you and Nugget J."

She giggled. "Nugget J?"

"Gives him some street cred. He sounds badass."

She laughed at my silliness, which was what I wanted. She'd been emotional for days and so strong while she gave birth. Intense and focused. Now, I wanted her to smile. Our son was here; he was fine. She was fine. It was time to celebrate.

"There is a whole bunch of people waiting to meet him."

I knew her parents were still there. So were Brianna, Trev, Rex, Gretch, and Bobby. An enormous arrangement had already arrived from the label, plus a personal bouquet from Carmen. There were flowers from the people at the shop whom Lottie worked with, and I had seen the huge yellow duck Brianna had with her the last time I went to give them an update. Lottie's labor only lasted a few hours before Josh screamed his way into the world, angry and filled with attitude. They all knew he was here and healthy but hoped to be able to meet him.

From the weary look on my wife's face, I decided maybe I should send them all away until tomorrow. Except I would allow her parents in for a moment. Charles had been great the past while, even showing up to the painting party. When he relaxed, he was a decent guy, and I knew he was anxious to meet his grandson. I wouldn't deny him that. I wanted my son to know his grandparents. I wanted them to be part of his life.

"I'll get your parents and send the rest of them home."

"No, let them come in. They've been waiting so long."

I sighed. "Okay—your parents first, then a couple at a time, and only five minutes. They can come back tomorrow. Your parents can come in and stay a bit." I bent and kissed her. "After that, you're going to sleep." I smirked as she yawned. "If you stay awake that long."

"You'll stay?"

"I'm not moving a muscle. I'll sing you to sleep," I promised. When she'd gotten upset during delivery, it was my humming that soothed her. I'd sung to her and Josh the whole pregnancy, making up silly songs at times to make her smile. I liked the fact that my voice seemed to soothe them both.

"Okay."

I walked to the waiting room. Several sets of anxious eyes met mine, and I smiled. "Jo-Jo, Charles, your grandson is waiting to meet you."

"Have you named him?" Brianna asked. "Or is he still Nugget?"

"We have. It's Nugget J."

Bobby snorted, but the others stared at me aghast, which made me laugh. "For short. His name is Joshua William. Joshua William Logan." I felt my throat thicken. "My son."

Jo-Jo covered her mouth, and even Charles's eyes glistened. I held out my hand.

"Come meet him. You're going to love him."

♫

I walked through the house, unable to stop the smile on my face. Charles Prescott was a formidable opponent, but when he was on your side, the man made things happen. I grudgingly had to admit I was beginning to like him. Watching Charles with Josh in the hospital had shown me the tender, loving side Lottie had often described. He stared down at my son, talking softly, almost cooing.

I swore my kid had magical powers to bring people together. Maybe his namesake had something to do with it. He had already earned the nickname Joshy, and everyone called him that. I had a feeling once he was old enough to object, he would. Until then, Joshy it was.

In the two days Lottie was in the hospital, the condo was packed up, moved, and unpacked. My few possessions had been transported, the extra bedroom now a makeshift office and music room. The furniture was placed in the rooms by her mother and Lottie's pictures hung up. Her mismatched china was in the cupboards. Jo-Jo had resisted and not bought a single new thing for the house with the exception of the gifts for Joshy, which were vast and many. And a full larder and refrigerator, which I was more than happy to accept. And Charles had overseen it all.

Lottie had been shocked when we came here after leaving the hospital and not the condo, but incredibly happy.

She looked around in wonder. "It already feels like home!"

We settled in fast, and the house had seen a steady stream of visitors. The freezer was filled with casseroles, the tables held many arrangements, and there were a lot of stuffed animals in the nursery—the duck taking the most prominent spot.

I paused at the doorway of the nursery. Lottie sat in the rocking chair, feeding Joshy, cooing at him as he stared up with his big blue eyes. He loved to eat, and his appetite was voracious. I set down a large glass of water beside her, stroked my son's head, bent to kiss my wife, then settled on the floor. I reached for my guitar and strummed my fingers across the strings. At the sound, Joshy's head turned.

"You know that sound, don't you, my boy?" I murmured. They said it was too soon, but I had been playing and singing to him Lottie's entire pregnancy. Like his mother, as soon as I sang, he relaxed. He knew music. He knew me. His eyes followed me in the nursery, and he reacted every time I picked up my guitar. I didn't care what they said. I knew it in my heart.

"What were you working on earlier?" Lottie asked, lifting Joshy to her shoulder to burp him. Her ring caught the light as she stroked his back, following it up with gentle taps. "It sounded pretty."

"A new one I wrote."

"What's it called?"

"Heart Strings."

"I like that. What's it about?"

I smiled and began to play. I sang softly about my family. Finding the music. The love they inspired. The way my heart had healed. The strings that stitched my heart back in place and held it firm. I wasn't surprised to see Lottie's tears. Mine were suspiciously close to the surface.

I finished, crossing my arms over my guitar and gazing at my wife. "That one is for you and Joshy. I'm not selling it."

"You should. The world needs to hear those words."

"They get enough. It's for you. Only you."

"Thank you."

"Bobby and I will record it, but it will be private."

She leaned forward, and our lips met over the guitar that brought her to me.

The one I played for her that helped heal her soul.
So she, in turn, could heal mine.
I sat back and gazed at the center of my world.
My wife, my son, my music.
My heart strings.
***

Thank you so much for reading **HEART STRINGS**. If you are so inclined, reviews are always welcome by me at your eretailer.

I want to thank the admins of The Korner|Romance Reader Group on Facebook. With encouragement of Bedtime Stories on Book+Main, Logan and Lottie got their happily ever after.

If you love a beta on the streets but alpha in the sheets, Reid Matthew's story, REID, is a standalone within the Vested Interest series. You meet a sweet, quiet hero in Reid, who shows his alpha side once he finds his other half.

If you enjoy standalone contemporary romance, Beneath The Scars, is a beloved story that I would recommended as a stand-alone to read next. It is a Beauty and the Beast themed story set in the beautiful Maine coastline.

If you'd like another glimpse into Logan and Lottie's future, click below to grab a little more time with them - Heart Strings Extended Epilogue available at Bookfunnel: https:// BookHip.com/GTRJDP

Enjoy reading! Melanie

ACKNOWLEDGMENTS

As always, I have some people to thank. The ones behind the words that encourage and support. The people who make my books possible for so many reasons.

Lisa, thank you for your edits, your laughter, and your long-lasting patience.
One day I will shock you. Maybe.

Beth, Trina, Melissa, Peggy, and Deb—thank you for your feedback and support.
Your comments make the story better—always.

Kim—welcome to the team.
Thank you for all you do and I hope we haven't scared you too badly.
It's coming. Brace yourself.

Karen—what can I say that hasn't already been said.
My world is brighter, my author life easier, and

my credit card well used. Teasing. Sort of.
Love your face.

To all the bloggers, readers, and especially my promo team.
Thank you for everything you do. Shouting your love of books—
of my work, posting, sharing—your recommendations keep my
TBR list full, and the support you have shown me is deeply
appreciated.

To my fellow authors who have shown me such kindness,
thank you.

I will follow your example and pay it forward.
My reader group, Melanie's Minions—love you all.

ABOUT THE AUTHOR

NYT/WSJ/USAT international bestselling author Melanie Moreland, lives a happy and content life in a quiet area of Ontario with her beloved husband of thirty-plus years and their rescue cat, Amber. Nothing means more to her than her friends and family, and she cherishes every moment spent with them.

While seriously addicted to coffee, and highly challenged with all things computer-related and technical, she relishes baking, cooking, and trying new recipes for people to sample. She loves to throw dinner parties, and enjoys traveling, here and abroad, but finds coming home is always the best part of any trip.

Melanie loves stories, especially paired with a good wine, and enjoys skydiving (free falling over a fleck of dust) extreme snowboarding (falling down stairs) and piloting her own helicopter (tripping over her own feet.) She's learned happily ever afters, even bumpy ones, are all in how you tell the story.

Melanie is represented by Flavia Viotti at Bookcase Literary Agency. For any questions regarding subsidiary or translation rights please contact her at flavia@bookcaseagency.com

Connect with Melanie

Like reader groups? Lots of fun and giveaways! Check it out Melanie Moreland's Minions on Facebook.

Join my newsletter for up-to-date news, sales, book announcements and excerpts (no spam). Click here to sign up Melanie Moreland's newsletter

or visit https://bit.ly/MMorelandNewsletter

Visit my website www.melaniemoreland.com

facebook.com/authormoreland

twitter.com/morelandmelanie

instagram.com/morelandmelanie